WAR, PEACE AND SOCIAL CHANGE:
EUROPE 1900–1955

DOCUMENTS 2: 1925–1959

This collection is one part of an Open University integrated teaching system and the selection is therefore related to other material available to students. It is designed to evoke the critical understanding of students.

A318 War, Peace and Social Change: Europe 1900–1955

Book I Europe on the Eve of War 1900–1914

Book II World War I and Its Consequences

Book III Between Two Wars

Book IV World War II and Its Consequences

Book V War and Change in Twentieth-Century Europe

Prepared by the course team and published by the Open University Press, 1990

Other material associated with the course

Documents 1: 1900–1929, eds Arthur Marwick and Wendy Simpson, Open University Press, 1990

Documents 2: 1925–1959, eds Arthur Marwick and Wendy Simpson, Open University Press, 1990

War, Peace and Social Change in Twentieth-Century Europe, eds Clive Emsley, Arthur Marwick and Wendy Simpson, Open University Press, 1990 (Course Reader)

Europe 1880–1945, J. M. Roberts, Longman, 1989 (second edition) (set book)

If you are interested in studying the course, contact the Student Enquiries Office, The Open University, PO Box 71, Milton Keynes MK7 6AG.

Cover illustration: 'Nyet!' (Sovietsky Khudozhnik Publishers)

WAR, PEACE AND SOCIAL CHANGE:
EUROPE 1900–1955

DOCUMENTS 2: 1925–1959

Edited by Arthur Marwick and Wendy Simpson

Open University Press
in association with
The Open University

Open University Press
Celtic Court
22 Ballmoor
Buckingham MK18 1XW

and
1900 Frost Road, Suite 101
Bristol, PA 19007, USA

First Published in 1990. Reprinted 1992, 1995 (twice)

British Library Cataloguing in Publication Data

Documents 2: 1925–1959. – (War, peace and social change
   series. : Europe 1900–1955).
   1. Europe, history
   I. Marwick, Arthur, *1933–*   .   II. Simpson, Wendy
   III. Series
   940

   ISBN 0-335-09303-5
   ISBN 0-335-09302-7 (pbk)

Library of Congress Cataloging number available

Typeset by Rowland Phototypesetting Ltd,
Bury St Edmunds, Suffolk
Printed in Great Britain by St Edmundsbury Press Ltd,
Bury St Edmunds, Suffolk

1.2

PREFACE

Primary sources – or documents as they were called before the great expansion from the traditional, purely written sources to all kinds of visual and non-traditional sources – are the raw material of history. The subject of war, peace and social change, an absolutely essential one in the study of twentieth-century European history, gives rise to many vigorous debates. Did the wars have significant social consequences? What is the relationship between the First World War and the Russian, Austrian and German revolutions? Do wars lower or improve the status of women? What is the relationship between war and the arts? Did total war produce mass society, or was mass society produced by total war?

These debates can be followed in the writings of historians, but they should also be studied from the primary sources. In all their variety – and in this book are reproduced extracts from diaries, social surveys, acts of parliament, international treaties, novels and poems, newspaper reports, and texts taken from many different countries – primary sources bring one directly into contact with the real texture of history.

This collection, together with its companion volume *Documents 1: 1900–1929*, is designed to accompany the Open University course A318 *War, Peace and Social Change: Europe 1900–1955*, but it will prove of immense value to anyone interested in twentieth-century European history, over which two cataclysmic wars have had a profound influence, and especially to anyone with a particular interest in social history.

The documents in this volume have been divided into two sections, which correspond to Books III and IV of the course. Section I covers the period up to 1939, while Section II covers the period of the Second World War and its aftermath. Although the documents are of many types and relate to many different topics – political, economic, diplomatic and cultural, as well as social – there is no sub-organization within these sections. Indeed, the documents have been arranged in the order in which they are used within the Open University course. This means that they can be approached without any deep preconceptions about which particular topic any of the texts relates to. In fact, depending on the questions asked, primary sources can suggest an amazing range of answers. This method of ordering the documents also results in some fascinating juxtapositions – poems with acts of parliament, personal reminiscences with international treaties.

The documents have been selected (and sometimes translated) by members of the course team responsible for *War, Peace and Social Change*.

ARTHUR MARWICK
WENDY SIMPSON

ACKNOWLEDGEMENTS

Grateful acknowledgement is made to the following sources for permission to reproduce material in this volume:

I.1: B. R. Mitchell, *European Historical Statistics 1750–1975*, Macmillan, London and Basingstoke, 1980; *I.3(b)*: B. Spuler, *Rulers and Governments of the World*, vols. 2 and 3, Bowker, 1977, © Martia Ross (whom we were unable to contact); *I.3(c)*: A. J. P. Taylor, *English History 1914–1945*, Oxford University Press, 1965; *I.6*: P. Fearon, *The Origins and Nature of the Great Slump, 1929–32*, Macmillan, London and Basingstoke, 1979; *I.8*: D. H. Aldcroft, *The Inter-War Economy: Britain 1919–1939*, Batsford, 1970; *I.9*: J. Stalin, *Problems of Leninism*, Foreign Languages Press, 1953; *I.13 and I.14*: J. Noakes and G. Pridham (eds) *Nazism 1919–1945*, vol. 2, *Nazism – State, Economy and Society 1933–39*, University of Exeter, 1984; *I.15 and I.16*: Richard Taylor (ed. and trans.) *The Film Factory: Russian and Soviet Cinema in Documents 1896–1939*, co-edited and intro. by Ian Christie, Routledge, 1988; *I.17*: translation of Adolf Hitler's speech from the 'Twilight Rally' sequence of *Triumph of the Will*, 1934 (*Triumph des Willen*, directed by Leni Riefenstahl), Imperial War Museum; *I.22*: W. K. Hancock and J. van der Poel (eds), *Selections from the Smuts Papers*, Cambridge University Press, 1966; *I.23*: Adolf Hitler, *Mein Kampf*, trans. J. Murphy, Hurst and Blackett, 1939, Century Hutchinson Publishing Group Ltd; *I.28*: Neville Chamberlain, *The Struggle for Peace*, Hutchinson, 1939; *II.4*: excerpts from *Wartime*, by Milovan Djilas, copyright © 1977 by Harcourt Brace Jovanovich, Inc., reprinted by permission of the publisher; *II.6*: Robert V. Daniels (ed.) *A Documentary History of Communism*, vol. 2, University of New England, copyright 1984 by the trustees of the University of Vermont; *II.5, II.33 –II.36*: originally reprinted in Joseph M. Siracusa (ed.) *The American Diplomatic Revolution*, Harcourt Brace Jovanovich, Australia; *II.7*: *Victory: War Speeches of Winston S. Churchill 1945*, compiled by Charles Eade, Curtis Brown Ltd. on behalf of the Estate of Sir Winston Churchill. Copyright Sir Winston Churchill; *II.8*: Sir Charles K. Webster and Noble Frankland, *The Strategic Air Offensive Against Germany, 1939–1945*, vol. 4, HMSO, 1961, reproduced with the permission of the Controller of Her Majesty's Stationery Office; *II.9*: Sybil Bannister, *I Lived Under Hitler: An English-woman's Story*, Rockliffe Books, 1957 (we were unable to trace the copyright holder); *II.10*: *Protocol of the Proceedings of the Berlin Conference*, HMSO, 1947, reproduced with the permission of the Controller of Her Majesty's Stationery Office; *II.11, II.12 and II.13*: © Oxford University Press 1978. Reprinted from *Resistance in Vichy France*, by H. R. Kedwood (1978) by permission of Oxford University Press; *II.19*: *Parliamentary Papers, 1942 –3*, vol. VI, Cmd 6404, HMSO, reproduced with the permission of the Controller of Her Majesty's Stationery Office; *II.23*: Günter Grass, *The Tin Drum*, trans. Ralph Manheim, Secker and Warburg, 1962; *II.24*: Jean Bruller ('Vercors'), *Le silence de la mer*, Editions de Minuit, 1942; *II.25*:

H. Josephson and M. Cowley (eds), *Aragon: Poet of Resurgent France*, 'I salute you, my France' and 'Tears are alike', trans. R. Humphries and M. Cowley, Pilot Press, 1947, reproduced by permission of Harper & Row Ltd.; *II.26*: Helen Zenna Smith (Evadne Price), *Not So Quiet . . . Stepdaughters of War*, copyright Helen Zenna Smith 1930, published by Virago Press Ltd, 1988; *II.27*: extract from the Federal Archive, Koblenz, 20 January and 12 May 1941, reprinted in Erwin Leiser, *Nazi Cinema*, trans. Gertrud Mander and David Wilson, Secker and Warburg, 1974; *II.28*: translation of commentary to *Der Ewige Jude*, 1940, Imperial War Museum; *II.29*: commentary from Ministry of Information film, *London Can Take It*, 1940, reproduced with permission from The Post Office; *II.30*: J. B. Priestley, *Postscripts*, Heinemann, 1940, © The Estate of J. B. Priestley; *II.31*: Desmond Hawkins (ed.), *War Report: D-Day to VE-Day*, Ariel Books, 1985, reproduced with the permission of BBC Enterprises Ltd.; *II.37*: reprinted from *A Documentary History of Communism*, vol. 2, 'Communism and the World', edited by Robert V. Daniels, reproduced by permission of University Press of New England. Copyright © 1984 by the trustees of the University of Vermont; *II.38–II.42*: reprinted in Beate Ruhm von Oppen (ed.), *Documents on Germany Under Occupation 1945–1954*. Published by Oxford University Press in association with the Royal Institute of International Affairs, 1955; *II.43*: C. Bettelheim and S. Frère, *Une ville française moyenne: Auxerre en 1950: Etude de structure sociale et urbaine*, Armand Colin, 1950; *II.44*: Simone de Beauvoir, *The Second Sex*, trans. H. M. Parshley, Jonathan Cape, 1968, reproduced by permission of the Estate of Simon de Beauvoir and H. M. Parshley; *II.46*: *A Defeated People*, 1946, Central Office of Information film script – Humphrey Jennings; *II.47(a)*: *Welt in Film Issue No. 7*, 29 June 1945, translation of German commentary by Roger B. N. Smither and Kay G. T. Gladstone, Imperial War Museum; *II.47(b)*: *Welt im Film – die Welt Blickt auf Berlin*, June 1948, transcript of English language version of film, *Berlin – World Focal Point*, Imperial War Museum.

CONTENTS

I Between Two Wars

II World War II and Its Consequences

I
BETWEEN TWO WARS

I.1 France, Germany and the UK, industrial disputes 1914–39

	France			Germany			United Kingdom		
	Number	Workers Involved (thou)	Days Lost (thou)	Number	Workers Involved (thou)	Days Lost (thou)	Number	Workers Involved (thou)	Days Lost (thou)
1914	672	162	2,187	1,223	238	2,844	972	447	9,878
1915	98	9	55	141	48	46	672	448	2,953
1916	314	41	236	240	423	245	532	276	2,446
1917	696	294	1,482	562	1,468	1,862	730	872	5,647
1918	499	176	980	532	716	1,453	1,165	1,116	5,875
1919	2,026	1,151	15,478	3,719	2,761	33,083	1,352	2,591	34,969
1920	1,832	1,317	23,112	3,807	2,009	16,755	1,607	1,932	26,568
1921	475	402	7,027	4,455	2,036	25,874	763	1,801	85,872
1922	665	290	3,935	4,785	2,566	27,734	576	552	19,850
1923	1,068	331	4,172	2,046	1,917	12,344	628	405	10,672
1924	1,083	275	3,863	1,973	2,066	36,198	710	613	8,424
1925	931	249	2,046	1,708	1,115	2,936	603	441	7,952
1926	1,660	349	4,072	351	131	1,222	323	2,734	162,233
1927	396	111	1,046	844	686	6,144	308	108	1,174
1928	816	204	6,377	739	986	20,339	302	124	1,388
1929	1,213	240	2,765	429	268	4,251	431	533	8,287
1930	1,093	582	7,209	353	302	4,029	422	307	4,399
1931	286	48	950	463	297	1,890	420	490	6,983
1932	362	72	1,244	648	172	1,130	389	379	6,488
1933	343	87	1,199	(69)[1]	(13)[1]	(96)[1]	357	136	1,072
1934	385	101	2,393	—	—	—	471	134	959
1935	376	109	1,182	—	—	—	553	271	1,955
1936	16,907	2,423	—	—	—	—	818	316	1,829
1937	2,616	1,133	—	—	—	—	1,129	597	3,413
1938	1,220	324	—	—	—	—	875	274	1,334
1939	—	—	—	—	—	—	940	337	1,356

[1] First quarter only.

(B. R. Mitchell, *European Historical Statistics 1750–1975*, London, Macmillan, 1980)

I.2 Number of seats won and percentage of votes in: (a) German *Reichstag*, 1918–33; (b) French *Chambre des Deputés*, 1902–36; (c) British House of Commons, 1918–45

(a) Germany

Number of seats won in the *Reichstag*, 1918–33

	1919	1920	1924 (May)	1924 (Dec.)	1928	1930	1932 (July)	1932 (Nov.)	1933
Centre Party	91	64	65	69	62	68	75	70	74
Social Democrats	163	102	100	131	153	143	133	121	120
German Democratic Party	75	39	28	32	25	20	4	2	5
German National People's Party	44	71	95	103	73	41	37	52	52
German People's Party	19	65	45	51	45	30	7	11	2
Hanoverian Party	1	5	5	4	3	3	0	1	0
Independent Social Democrats	22	84	0	0	0	0	—	—	—
Middle Class Party	4	4	10	17	23	23	2	1	—
Bavarian People's Party	—	21	16	19	16	19	22	20	18
Communist Party	—	4	62	45	54	77	89	100	81
Land League	—	—	10	8	3	3	2	2	1
National Socialists/Nazi Party	—	—	32	14	12	107	230	196	288
Farmers' Party	—	—	—	—	8	6	2	3	2
People's Land Party	—	—	—	—	10	19	1	0	—
People's Rights Party	—	—	—	—	2	0	1	0	—
Christian People's Service	—	—	—	—	—	14	3	5	4
Others	2	0	4	0	2	4	0	0	0
Total Seats	421	459	472	493	491	577	608	584	647

Percentage of votes (territory of the Federal Republic only) 1919–33

	1919	1920	1924 (May)	1924 (Dec.)	1928	1930	1932 (July)	1932 (Nov.)	1933
Centre Party	27.9	20.4	19.7	19.8	17.6	16.9	17.7	17.0	15.8
Social Democrats	35.4	21.1	18.7	23.5	26.9	21.9	19.1	18.0	16.5
German Democratic Party	16.2	8.2	5.5	6.2	4.8	3.9	1.0	1.0	0.8
German National People's Party	5.9	10.5	13.0	14.8	9.8	4.0	4.6	6.6	6.1
German People's Party	6.1	12.4	8.9	9.8	8.7	4.6	1.2	2.0	1.2
Hanoverian Party	1.8	2.1	1.9	1.6	1.1	0.9	0.2	0.3	0.2
Independent Social Democrats	4.3	13.8	0.8	0.4	0.0	0.0	—	—	—
Bavarian People's Party	—	7.6	5.9	6.8	5.6	5.4	5.7	5.5	4.8
Communist Party	—	1.8	12.1	7.9	8.6	11.2	13.0	15.3	10.8

	1919	1920	1924 (May)	1924 (Dec.)	1928	1930	1932 (July)	1932 (Nov.)	1933
National Socialists/Nazi Party	—	—	6.5	2.6	3.3	17.5	34.5	30.9	41.8
Christian People's Service	—	—	—	—	—	3.0	1.3	1.5	1.1
Others	2.4	2.1	6.9	6.6	13.6	10.7	1.7	1.9	0.9

(b) France

Number of seats won in the *Chambre des Deputés*, 1902–36[1]

	1902	1906	1910	1914	1919	1924	1928	1932	1936
Radical Socialist Party	75	241	121	140	106 ⎫	162	120	157	109
Socialist Republicans	—	—	—	27	17 ⎭		30	37	56
Socialist Party	—	53	78	103	67	104	99	129	149
Independent Socialists	—	18	24	—	5	—	—	—	—
Socialists	46	—	—	—	—	—	—	—	—
Communist Party	—	—	—	—	—	26	14	12	72
Conservatives I	147	109	112	73	88	25	26	33 ⎫	
Liberal Popular Action	18	69	11	—	—	—	—	—	
Left Republicans	180	52	71	57	79 ⎫	53	74	72	
Independent Radicals	120	39	67	96	51 ⎭		52	62	222
Republican Union	—	—	103	96	201	204	182	76	
Popular Democratic Party	—	—	—	—	—	—	—	16 ⎭	
Others	3	0	0	0	2	0	5	11	0
Total seats	589[2]	581	587	592	616	574	602	605	608

[1] Including Algerian deputies.
[2] Including deputies from Réunion and the French West Indies.

Percentage of votes, 1902–36

	1902	1906	1910	1914	1919	1924	1928	1932	1936
Valid votes	76.1	77.7	74.6	74.6	70.2	80.7	81.9	81.6	82.3
Party votes									
Radical Socialist Party	10.1	28.5	20.4	18.1	17.4 ⎫	38.0	17.8	19.2	14.4
Socialist Republicans	—	—	—	3.9	3.5 ⎬		4.6	5.4	7.6
Socialist Party	—	10.0	13.1	16.8	21.2 ⎭		18.0	20.5	19.9
Independent Socialists	—	2.3	4.1	—	1.8	—	—	—	—
Socialists	10.4	—	—	—	—	—	—	—	—
Communist Party	—	—	—	—	—	9.8	11.3	8.3	15.3
Conservatives I	28.3	29.2	19.0	15.4	14.0	4.2	2.3	6.1 ⎫	
Liberal Popular Action	4.6	14.0	1.8	—	—	—	—	—	
Left Republicans	29.7	8.0	12.1	9.7	10.9 ⎫	11.7	23.2	13.6	
Independent Radicals	16.8	7.9	11.4	16.6	6.2 ⎭			10.0	42.7
Republican Union	—	—	17.4	18.8	22.3	35.3	22.0	12.9	
Popular Democratic Party	—	—	—	—	—	—	—	3.2 ⎭	
Others	n.a.	0.1	0.6	0.7	2.7	1.0	0.9	0.9	0.2

(c) United Kingdom

Number of seats won in the House of Commons 1918–1945

	1918	1922	1923	1924	1929	1931	1935	1945
Conservative Party	382	344	258	415	260	473	388	199
National Liberal Party	—	—	—	—	—	35	33	11
National Labour	—	—	—	—	—	13	8	—
National Democratic Party	9	0	—	—	—	—	—	—
Lloyd George Liberals	127	53	—	—	—	4	—	—
Liberal Party	36	62	158	44	59	33	21	12
Labour Party	62	142	191	151	287	46	154	393
Irish Nationalist Party	7	—	—	—	—	—	—	—
Irish Republicans	73[1]	3	3	1	3	2	2	2
Communist Party	—	1	0	1	0	0	1	2
Scottish National Party	—	—	—	—	0	0	0	0
Welsh Nationalists	—	—	—	—	0	0	0	0
Independent Labour Party	—	—	—	—	—	6	4	3
Others	11	10	5	3	6	3	4	18
Total seats	707	615	615	615	615	615	615	640
Unopposed returns	107	57	50	32	7	67	40	3

[1] 73 Sinn Féin MPs refused to take their seats in the House of Commons.

Percentage of votes, 1918–45

	1918	1922	1923	1924	1929	1931	1935	1945
Valid votes	49.0	66.2	65.6	73.2	75.4	72.5	67.0	72.6
Party votes[1]								
Conservative Party	39.6	38.5	38.0	46.8	38.1	55.3	48.1	36.8
National Liberal Party	—	—	—	—	—	3.7	3.7	2.8
National Labour	—	—	—	—	—	1.5	1.5	—
National Democratic Party	1.7	0.4	—	—	—	—	—	—
Lloyd George Liberals	12.6	9.4	—	—	—	0.5	—	—
Liberal Party	13.0	18.9	29.7	18.4	23.6	6.7	6.8	9.0
Labour Party	21.4	29.7	30.7	33.3	37.1	29.3	38.1	48.0
Irish Nationalist Party	2.2	—	—	—	—	—	—	—
Irish Republicans	4.6	0.4	0.4	0.2	0.1	0.4	0.4	0.4
Communist Party	—	0.2	0.2	0.3	0.2	0.3	0.1	0.4
Scottish National Party	—	—	—	—	0.0	0.1	0.1	0.1
Welsh Nationalists	—	—	—	—	0.0	0.0	0.0	0.1
Independent Labour Party	—	—	—	—	—	1.5	0.6	0.2
Others	4.9	2.5	1.0	1.0	0.9	0.7	0.6	2.2

[1] Percentages have been adjusted to allow for two member seats which lasted until 1950. In calculating the percentage of votes, each vote in a two-member seat has been counted as half a vote.

(figures for (a) and (b) taken from various political reference publications; figures for (c) from F. W. S. Craig, *British Parliamentary Election Statistics 1918–1970*, Chichester, Political Reference Publications, 1971, pp. 1–13, 46–7)

I.3 Summary of governments of (a) Germany, 1919–32, (b) France, 1918–40, (c) Britain, 1919–39

(a) Germany: summary of Reich *governments, 1919–32*

	Chancellor	Period of office	Participating parties
1	Scheidemann (SPD)	13 February 1919–21 June 1919	SPD, Centre, DDP, np
2	Bauer (SPD)	to 27 March 1920	SPD, Centre, DDP
3	Müller (SPD)	to 21 June 1920 (1st cabinet)	SPD, Centre, DDP
4	Fehrenbach (Centre)	to 10 May 1921	Centre, DDP, DVP
5	Wirth (Centre)	to 26 October 1921 (1st cabinet)	Centre, SPD, DDP, np
6	Wirth (Centre)	to 22 November 1922 (2nd cabinet)	Centre, SPD, DDP, np
7	Cuno (np)	to 13 August 1923	Centre, DDP, DVP, BVP, np
8	Stresemann (DVP)	to 6 October 1923 (1st cabinet)	DVP, Centre, SPD, DDP, np
9	Stresemann (DVP)	to 30 November 1923 (2nd cabinet)	DVP, SPD, Centre, DDP, np
10	Marx (Centre)	to 3 June 1924 (1st cabinet)	Centre, DVP, DDP, np
11	Marx (Centre)	to 15 January 1925 (2nd cabinet)	Centre, DVP, DDP, np
12	Luther (np)	to 20 January 1926 (1st cabinet)	DNVP, DVP, Centre, BVP, DDP, np
13	Luther (np)	to 17 May 1926 (2nd cabinet)	Centre, DVP, DDP, BVP
14	Marx (Centre)	to 29 January 1927 (3rd cabinet)	Centre, DVP, DDP, BVP
15	Marx (Centre)	to 29 June 1928 (4th cabinet)	Centre, DNVP, DVP, BVP, np
16	Müller (SPD)	to 30 March 1930 (2nd cabinet)	SPD, DDP, DVP, Centre, BVP, np
17	Brüning (Centre)	to 30 May 1932	Centre, DVP, DDP, BVP, Economics Party, Conservatives, np

Notes

1 SPD = German Social Democratic Party; DDP = German Democratic Party; DVP = German People's Party; BVP = Bavarian People's Party; DNVP = German National People's Party; np = non-party expert(s).

2 The Bavarian People's Party always voted with the Centre Party.

(b) France: summary of governments, 1918–40

Chief minister	Period of office
Georges Clemenceau (second time)	17 November 1917 – 18 January 1920
Alexandre Millerand	19 January – 20 September 1920
Georges Leggues	24 September 1920 – 10 January 1921

Chief minister	Period of office
Aristide Briand (sixth time)	16 January 1921 – 12 January 1922
Raymond Poincaré (second time)	15 January 1922 – 26 March 1924
Raymond Poincaré (third time)	28 March – 1 June 1924
Frederic François-Marsal	8 June – 13 June 1924
Édouard Herriot	15 June 1924 – 10 April 1925
Paul Painlevé (second time)	17 April – 27 October 1925
Paul Painlevé (third time)	29 October – 22 November 1925
Aristide Briand (seventh time)	23 November 1925 – 6 March 1926
Aristide Briand (eighth time)	10 March – 15 June 1926
Aristide Briand (ninth time)	23 June – 17 July 1926
Édouard Herriot (second time)	19 July – 21 July 1926
Raymond Poincaré (fourth time)	23 July – 6 November 1928
Raymond Poincaré (fifth time)	11 November 1928 – 29 July 1929
Aristide Briand (tenth time)	29 July – 22 October 1929
André Tardieu	2 November 1929 – 17 February 1930
Camille Chautemps	21 February – 25 February 1930
André Tardieu (second time)	2 March – 5 December 1930
Théodore Steeg	13 December 1930 – 24 January 1931
Pierre Laval	27 January 1931 – 12 January 1932
Pierre Laval (second time)	13 January – 16 February 1932
André Tardieu (third time)	20 February – 10 May 1932
Édouard Herriot (third time)	4 June – 14 December 1932
Joseph Paul-Boncour	14 December 1932 – 29 January 1933
Édouard Deladier	31 January – 23 October 1933
Albert Sarraut	26 October – 24 November 1933
Camille Chautemps (second time)	27 November 1933 – 27 January 1934
Édouard Deladier (second time)	30 January – 7 February 1934
Gaston Doumergue	9 February – 8 November 1934
Pierre Étienne Flandin	9 November 1934 – 30 May 1935
Fernand Bouisson	1 June – 4 June 1935
Pierre Laval (third time)	7 June 1935 – 22 January 1936
Albert Sarraut (second time)	24 January – 4 June 1936
Léon Blum	4 June 1936 – 21 June 1937
Camille Chautemps (third time)	27 June 1937 – 14 January 1938
Camille Chautemps (fourth time)	18 January – 10 March 1938
Léon Blum (second time)	13 March – 8 April 1938
Édouard Deladier (third time)	10 April 1938 – 20 March 1940

(c) Britain: summary of governments, 1919–39

Prime Minister	Period of office	Party
David Lloyd George	January 1919 – October 1922	Coalition
A. Bonar Law	October 1922 – May 1923	Conservative
Stanley Baldwin	May 1923 – January 1924	Conservative
J. Ramsay MacDonald	January – November 1924	Labour
Stanley Baldwin	November 1924 – June 1929	Conservative
J. Ramsay MacDonald	June 1929 – August 1931	Labour
J. Ramsay MacDonald	August – November 1931	National
J. Ramsay MacDonald	November 1931 – June 1935	National
Stanley Baldwin	June 1935 – May 1937	National
Neville Chamberlain	May 1937 – September 1939	National

((a) compiled from tables in Erich Eyck, *A History of the Weimar Republic*, trans. Harlan P. Hanson and Robert G. L. Waite, Cambridge, Mass.,

Harvard University Press, 1963; (b) B. Spuler, *Rulers and Governments of the World*, vols 2 and 3, London, Bowker, 1977; (c) A. J. P. Taylor, *English History 1914–1945*, London, Oxford University Press, 1965)

I.4 (a) Mark/dollar exchange rate, 1914–23; (b) *Reich* cost of living index, Feb. 1920–Dec. 1923

(a) Mark/dollar exchange rate, 1914–23 (monthly averages)
(Note: The exchange rate in July 1914 was 4.20 Marks = 1 Dollar)

	1918	*1919*	*1920*	*1921*	*1922*	*1923*
January	5.21	8.20	64.80	64.91	191.81	17,972
February	5.27	9.15	99.11	61.81	207.82	27,918
March	5.21	10.39	83.89	62.45	284.19	21,190
April	5.11	12.61	59.64	63.53	291.00	24,457
May	5.14	12.85	46.48	62.30	290.11	47,670
June	5.36	14.01	39.13	69.36	317.44	109,996
July	5.79	15.08	39.48	76.67	493.22	353,412
August	6.10	18.83	47.74	84.31	1,134.56	4,620,455
September	6.59	24.05	57.98	104.91	1,465,87	98,860[1]
October	6.61	26.83	68.17	150.20	3,180.96	25,260[2]
November	7.43	38.31	77.24	262.96	7,183.10	2,193,600[2]
December	8.28	46.77	73.00	191.93	7,589.27	4,200,000[2]
Year average	6.01	19.76	63.06	104.57	1,885.78	584,914[2]

[1] thousands
[2] millions

(b) Reich cost of living index, Feb. 1920–Dec. 1923 (1913–14 = 1)

1920	*Total Cost of Living*	*1921*	*Total Cost of Living*	*1922*	*Total Cost of Living*	*1923*	*Total Cost of Living*
		January	11.79	January	20.41	January	1,120
February	8.47	February	11.47	February	24.49	February	2,643
March	9.56	March	11.38	March	28.97	March	2,854
April	10.42	April	11.27	April	34.36	April	2,954
May	11.02	May	11.20	May	38.03	May	3,816
June	10.83	June	11.67	June	41.47	June	7,650
July	10.65	July	12.50	July	53.92	July	37,651
August	10.23	August	13.33	August	77.65	August	584,045
September	10.15	September	13.74	September	133.19	September	15.0[1]
October	10.71	October	15.04	October	220.66	October	3,657[1]
November	11.18	November	17.75	November	446.10	November	657[2]
December	11.58	December	19.28	December	685.06	December	1,247[2]

[1] millions
[2] billions

(Statistisches Reichsamt (ed.) *Zahlen zur Geldentwertung in Deutschland 1914 bis 1923*, Berlin, 1925, p. 33)

I.5 Unemployment in Germany, Britain and France, 1919–1939

Year	Germany No. (000s)	% of working population	Great Britain No. (000s)	% of working population	France No. (000s)
1919	—	—	—	2.4	—
1920	—	—	—	2.4	13
1921	346	1.8	—	14.8	28
1922	215	1.1	1,543	15.2	13
1923	818	4.1	1,275	11.3	10
1924	927	4.9	1,130	10.9	10
1925	628	3.4	1,226	11.2	12
1926	2,025	10.0	1,385	12.7	11
1927	1,312	6.2	1,088	10.6	47
1928	1,391	6.3	1,217	11.2	16
1929	1,899	8.5	1,216	11.0	10
1930	3,076	14.0	1,917	14.6	13
1931	4,520	21.9	2,630	21.5	64
1932	5,603	29.9	2,745	22.5	301
1933	4,804	25.9	2,521	21.3	305
1934	—	—	2,159	17.7	368
1935	—	—	2,036	16.4	464
1936	—	—	1,755	14.3	470
1937	—	—	1,484	11.3	380
1938	—	—	1,791	13.3	402
1939	—	—	1,514	11.7	418

Notes: Great Britain figures for 1919–23 are unemployed in trade unions; 1923 on are averages of monthly numbers of registered wholly unemployed, though the percentages only relate to insured workers who were unemployed. Figures for France, % of working population, not available.

(figures for Germany from V. R. Berghahn, *Modern Germany*, Cambridge University Press, 1987, p. 284; figures for France and Britain from B. R. Mitchell, *European Historical Statistics 1750–1975*, London, Macmillan, 1980)

I.6 Indices of industrial production for major industrialized countries, 1927–1935

(1929 = 100)

	1927	1928	1929	1930	1931	1932	1933	1934	1935
Austria	90	99	100	81	69	60	62	68	77
Belgium	93	99	100	89	81	69	71	72	83
Canada	83	93	100	85	72	58	60	74	81
Chile	74	81	100	101	78	87	96	105	120
France	79	91	100	100	89	69	77	71	67
Germany	102	99	100	86	68	53	61	80	94

	1927	1928	1929	1930	1931	1932	1933	1934	1935
Hungary	96	98	100	94	87	77	84	98	111
Italy	—	92	100	92	78	67	74	81	92
Japan	83	90	100	95	92	98	113	129	142
Norway	81	90	100	101	78	93	94	98	108
Netherlands	86	98	100	91	79	62	69	70	66
Poland	87	100	100	82	70	54	56	63	66
Sweden	84	89	100	99	95	90	96	116	127
UK	96	94	100	92	84	84	88	99	106
USA	89	93	100	81	68	54	64	66	76
USSR	64	80	100	131	161	183	198	238	293

(P. Fearon, *The Origins and Nature of the Great Slump, 1929–32*, London, Macmillan, 1979, p. 11)

I.7 'The Matignon Agreement' (1936)

Meeting under the chairmanship of the Prime Minister (Léon Blum), the delegates of the General Confederation of French Industry (CGPF) and the Confédération Générale du Travail (CGT), after arbitration by the Prime Minister, have reached the following agreement:

Article One – the employers agree to the establishment of collective agreements.

Article Two – these agreements, in particular, must embody Articles Three and Five below.

Article Three – within the requirements of all citizens to obey the law, the employers recognize the freedom of opinion of the workers and their right freely to join and to belong to trade unions established in conformity with Book III of the Labour Code.

In all questions of the hiring and organizing of labour, of dismissals and disciplinary measures, the employers agree that the fact of membership or non-membership of a union shall not be taken into consideration.

If it is alleged that a worker has been dismissed through asserting his right to organize and belong to a union set out above, the two parties agree to seek out the facts and arrive at a just adjudication. This in no way prejudices the rights of the parties to obtain legal reparation for any damage caused. The exercise of trade-union rights must not give rise to acts which infringe the law.

Article Four – with effect from 25 May, 1936, and upon the resumption of work, the wages of all workers will be raised by a scale ranging from 15 per cent for the lowest paid to 7 per cent for the highest paid. In no case will the total increase in any establishment be greater than 12 per cent. Increases already conceded since 25 May, 1936 will be counted towards these increases. But higher increases already awarded will continue to operate.

The negotiations for the collective settlement of minimum wages by regions and by occupations, which the parties agreed to initiate at once, must, in particular, take up essential revision of abnormally low wage rates.

The employers agree to carry out all necessary adjustments to retain normal differentials between the salaries of white-collar workers and hourly wages.

Article Five – with the exception of special cases already determined by law, each establishment containing more than ten workers shall, upon the conclusion of an agreement between the organizations of management and labour, or, in the absence of such organizations, between the two interested parties, have at least two shop stewards, depending upon the size of the establishment. These shop stewards shall have the right to raise with management any outstanding individual agreements relating to laws, decrees, labour-code regulations, wage scales, and health and safety provisions.

All workers, male or female, aged eighteen and over shall be eligible to vote for the shop stewards, provided that at the time of the election they have been employed in the establishment for at least three months and have not been deprived of their civil rights.

Those eligible to vote will also be eligible for election as shop stewards, provided that they are French citizens of at least twenty-five years of age, and have been in continuous employment at the establishment for at least one year. However, this last requirement shall be waived if it results in fewer than five workers being eligible for election.

Workers involved in any kind of retail business, whether themselves directly or through their spouses, are ineligible to stand as candidates.

Article Six – the employers promise that no reprisals will be taken against strikers.

Article Seven – the CGT delegation undertakes to request all workers on strike to return to work as soon as their managements have accepted this agreement and as soon as negotiations to bring it into being have begun.

(G. Lefranc, *Histoire du Front Populaire*, 2nd edn, Paris, Payot, 1974, annex no. 15, pp. 488–9; trans. Arthur Marwick)

I.8 Wages, prices and real earnings, Great Britain, 1913–38

	Weekly wage rates	Retail prices	Average annual real wage earnings
	(1930 = 100)		
1913	52.4	63.3	82.8
1919	—	136.1	—
1920	143.7	157.6	92.2
1921	134.6	143.0	94.1

	Weekly wage rates	Retail prices	Average annual real wage earnings
	(1930 = 100)		
1922	107.9	115.8	93.2
1923	100.0	110.1	90.8
1924	101.5	110.8	91.6
1925	102.2	111.4	91.7
1926	99.3	108.9	91.2
1927	101.5	106.0	95.8
1928	100.1	105.1	95.2
1929	100.4	103.8	96.7
1930	100.0	100.0	100.0
1931	98.2	93.4	105.1
1932	96.3	91.1	105.7
1933	95.3	88.6	107.6
1934	96.4	89.2	108.1
1935	98.0	90.5	108.3
1936	100.2	93.0	107.7
1937	102.8	97.5	105.4
1938	106.3	98.7	107.7

(D. H. Aldcroft, *The Inter-War Economy: Britain 1919–1939*, London, Batsford, 1970, pp. 352, 364)

I.9 Josef Stalin, 'The tasks of business executives', speech delivered to the First All-Union Conference of Managers of Socialist Industry (4 Feb. 1931)

Comrades! The deliberations of your conference are drawing to a close. You are now about to adopt resolutions. I have no doubt that they will be adopted unanimously. In these resolutions – I am somewhat familiar with them – you approve the control figures of industry for 1931 and pledge yourselves to fulfil them.

A Bolshevik's word is his bond. Bolsheviks are in the habit of fulfilling their pledges. But what does the pledge to fulfil the control figures for 1931 mean? It means ensuring a total increase of industrial output by 45 per cent. And this is a very big task. More than that. Such a pledge means that you not only promise to fulfil our five-year plan in four years – that is a settled matter, and no more resolutions are needed on that score – *it means that you promise to fulfil it in three years in all the basic, decisive branches of industry.* . . .

It must be admitted to our shame that even among us Bolsheviks there are not a few who exercise their managing functions by signing papers. But as for going into the details of the business, learning technique, becoming master of the business – why, that is out of the question.

How is it that we Bolsheviks, who have made three revolutions, who emerged victorious from the bitter Civil War, who have solved the vast problem of building up a modern industry, who have swung the peasantry to the path of socialism – how is it that in the matter of industrial management we bow to a slip of paper?

The reason is that it is easier to sign papers than to manage production. And so, many business executives chose this line of least resistance. We, too, in the centre, bear a share of the blame. About ten years ago a slogan was issued: 'Since Communists do not yet properly understand the technique of production, since they have yet to learn the art of management, let the old technicians and engineers – the experts – carry on production, and you, Communists, do not interfere with the technique of the business; but while not interfering, study technique, study the art of management tirelessly, in order, later on, to become, together with the experts who are loyal to us, true leaders of industry, true masters of the business.' Such was the slogan. But how did it work out? The second part of this formula was cast aside, for it is harder to study than to sign papers; and the first part of the formula was vulgarized: non-interference was interpreted to mean refraining from studying the technique of production. The result has been nonsense, harmful and dangerous nonsense, which the sooner we discard the better.

Life itself has more than once warned us that all was not well in this field. The Shakhty case was the first grave warning. The Shakhty case showed that the Party organizations and the trade unions lacked revolutionary vigilance. It showed that our business executives were disgracefully backward in regard to the knowledge of technology; that some of the old engineers and technicians, working without supervision, were more prone to engage in wrecking activities, especially as they were constantly being besieged by 'offers' from our enemies abroad.

The second warning was the 'Industrial Party' trial.

Of course, the underlying cause of wrecking activities is the class struggle. Of course, the class enemy is furiously resisting the socialist offensive. This alone, however, is not an adequate explanation for the luxuriant growth of wrecking activities.

How is it that sabotage has assumed such wide dimensions? Who is to blame for this? We are to blame. Had we handled the business of industrial management differently, had we started much earlier to learn the technique of the business, to master technique, had we more frequently and efficiently intervened in the management of production, the wreckers could not have done so much damage.

We must ourselves become experts, masters of the business we must turn to technical science – such was the lesson life itself was teaching us. But neither the first warning nor even the second brought about the necessary change. It is time, it is high time that we turned towards technique. It is time we cast aside the old slogan, the obsolete slogan of non-interference in technique, and ourselves become specialists, experts, complete masters of our economy.

It is frequently asked: Why have we not one-man management? We do not have it and will not have it until we have mastered technique. Until there are among us Bolsheviks a sufficient number of people thoroughly familiar with technique, economics and finance, we will not have real one-man management. You can write as many resolutions as you please, take as many vows as you please, but, unless you master the technique, economics and finance of the mill, factory or mine, nothing will come of it, there will be no one-man management.

Hence, the task is for us to master technique ourselves, to become the masters of the business ourselves. This is the sole guarantee that our plans will be carried out in full, and that one-man management will be established.

This, of course, is no easy matter; but it can certainly be accomplished. Science, technical experience, knowledge, are all things that can be acquired. We may not have them today, but tomorrow we will. The main thing is to have the passionate Bolshevik desire to master technique, to master the science of production. Everything can be achieved, everything can be overcome, if there is a passionate desire to do so.

It is sometimes asked whether it is not possible to slow down the tempo somewhat, to put a check on the movement. No, comrades, it is not possible! The tempo must not be reduced! On the contrary, we must increase it as much as is within our powers and possibilities. This is dictated to us by our obligations to the workers and peasants of the USSR. This is dictated to us by our obligations to the working class of the whole world.

To slacken the tempo would mean falling behind. And those who fall behind get beaten. But we do not want to be beaten. No, we refuse to be beaten! One feature of the history of old Russia was the continual beatings she suffered because of her backwardness. She was beaten by the Mongol khans. She was beaten by the Turkish beys. She was beaten by the Swedish feudal lords. She was beaten by the Polish and Lithuanian gentry. She was beaten by the British and French capitalists. She was beaten by the Japanese barons. All beat her – because of her backwardness, military backwardness, cultural backwardness, political backwardness, industrial backwardness, agricultural backwardness. They beat her because to do so was profitable and could be done with impunity. Do you remember the words of the pre-revolutionary poet: 'You are poor and abundant, mighty and impotent, Mother Russia'? Those gentlemen were quite familiar with the verses of the old poet. They beat her, saying: 'You are abundant', so one can enrich oneself at your expense. They beat her, saying: 'You are poor and impotent', so you can be beaten and plundered with impunity. Such is the law of the exploiters – to beat the backward and the weak. It is the jungle law of capitalism. You are backward, you are weak – therefore you are wrong; hence, you can be beaten and enslaved. You are mighty – therefore you are right; hence, we must be wary of you.

That is why we must no longer lag behind.

In the past we had no fatherland, nor could we have one. But now that we have overthrown capitalism and power is in our hands, in the hands of the people, we have a fatherland, and we will defend its independence. Do you want our socialist fatherland to be beaten and to lose its independence? If you do not want this you must put an end to its backwardness in the shortest possible time and develop genuine bolshevik tempo in building up its socialist system of economy. There is no other way. That is why Lenin said on the eve of the October Revolution: 'Either perish, or overtake and outstrip the advanced capitalist countries.'

We are fifty or a hundred years behind the advanced countries. We must make good this distance in ten years. Either we do it, or we shall be crushed.

This is what our obligations to the workers and peasants of the USSR dictate to us.

But we have other, still more serious and more important obligations. They are our obligations to the world proletariat. They coincide with our obligations to the workers and peasants of the USSR. But we place them higher. The working class of the USSR is part of the world working class. We achieved victory not solely through the efforts of the working class of the USSR, but also thanks to the support of the working class of the world. Without this support we would have been torn to pieces long ago. It is said that our country is the shock brigade of the proletariat of all countries. This is a fitting definition. But this imposes very serious obligations upon us. Why does the international proletariat support us? How did we merit this support? By the fact that we were the first to hurl ourselves into the battle against capitalism, we were the first to establish a working-class state, we were the first to start building socialism. By the fact that we are doing work which, if successful, will change the whole world and free the entire working class. But what is needed for success? The elimination of our backwardness, the development of a high Bolshevik tempo of construction. We must march forward in such a way that the working class of the whole world, looking at us, may say: This is my vanguard, this is my shock brigade, this is my working-class state, this is my fatherland; they are promoting their cause, which is *our* cause, and they are doing this well; let us support them against the capitalists and promote the cause of the world revolution. Must we not live up to the hopes of the world's working class, must we not fulfil our obligations to them? Yes, we must if we do not want utterly to disgrace ourselves.

Such are our obligations, internal and international.

As you see, they dictate to us a Bolshevik tempo of development.

I will not say that we have accomplished nothing in regard to economic management during these years. In fact, we have accomplished a good deal. We have doubled our industrial output as compared with the prewar level. We have created the largest-scale agricultural production in the world. But we could have accomplished more had we tried hard during this period really to master production, the technique of production, the financial and economic side of it.

In ten years at most we must make good the distance which separates us from the advanced capitalist countries. We have all the 'objective' possibilities for this. The only thing lacking is the ability to take proper advantage of these possibilities. And that depends on us. *Only* on us! It is time we learned to take advantage of these possibilities. It is time to put an end to the rotten policy of non-interference in production. It is time to adopt a new policy, a policy adapted to the present times – the policy of *interfering in everything*. If you are a factory manager, then interfere in all the affairs of the factory, look into everything, let nothing escape you, learn and learn again. Bolsheviks must master technique. It is time Bolsheviks themselves became experts. In the period of reconstruction technique decides everything. And a business executive who does not want to study technique, who does not want to master technique, is a joke and not an executive.

It is said that it is hard to master technique. That is not true! There are no fortresses which Bolsheviks cannot capture. We have solved a number of most difficult problems. We have overthrown capitalism. We have assumed power. We have built up a huge socialist industry. We have swung the middle peasants to the path of socialism. We have already accomplished what is most important from the point of view of construction. What remains to be done is not so much: to study technique, to master science. And when we have done that we will develop a tempo of which we dare not even dream at present.

And we will do that if we really want to.

(J. Stalin, *Problems of Leninism*, Moscow, Foreign Languages Press, 1953)

I.10 Extracts from Royal Decree concerning Fascist youth organizations (9 Jan. 1927)

Art. I: The Militia of *Avanguardisti* and *Balilla* is intended to give moral and physical training to the young, in order to make them worthy of the new standard of Italian life. . . .

Art. III: The recruiting of *Avanguardisti* and *Balilla*, within the age limits specified by the law, is voluntary.

In order to be allowed to join the organization, children require the consent of their parents or guardians. After their sixteenth year of age they shall also provide a certificate of good conduct. Admission is not limited in number.

Art. IV: The corps of *Avanguardisti* and *Balilla* are organized on military lines. They shall march by three.

Bodies are formed as follows: *Squadron*, eleven boys and a leader; *Manipulum*, three *squadrons*; *Centurium*, three *manipula*; *Cohort*, three *centuria*; *Legion*, three *cohorts*.

In places where the number of *cohorts* is over three but under six a single *legion* is formed. . . .

Art. X: In order to achieve the ends specified in the law, and in Art. I of the present regulations, the *Balilla* institution shall:
1. teach the young the spirit of discipline and of military training, and give them:
2. premilitary training;
3. physical training through gymnastics and sports;
4. spiritual and cultural training;
5. professional and vocational training;
6. religious teaching.

Art. XI: Discipline means respect and obedience to military commanders and to persons who are entrusted with the civil and military training of the *Avanguardisti*. . . .

Art. XXVII: Physical training through gymnastics and sport is given according to the official programme for the secondary schools of the Kingdom. It is supplemented by excursions, camping, games, etc. Those who attend to the planning of these schemes should bear in mind that physical training also influences the spiritual education of the young.

Therefore the *Avanguardisti* and Militia are intended to train the young to appreciate beauty and strength, since intellectual life can only develop fully in a healthy and vigorous body. . . .

Art. XXX: The National Balilla Institution shall also train the conscience and minds of these boys, since they are destined to become the Fascist men of the future, from whose ranks national leaders will be selected.

The National Balilla Institution is highly qualified to carry out this task, since it has control over large groups of the young, whose minds are readily formed by proper care and education.

Art. XXXI: In order to achieve this end the National Institution may found schools for cultural training and centres of study and propaganda.

The doctrine of Fascism, its logical development and its historical significance, shall be taught in these schools. . . .

Art. XXXVIII: Religious instruction shall consist in the teaching of Catholic ethics, Christian doctrine, the Old Testament and the Gospels, and shall be imparted in such hours as specified in Article XL. The form of worship is that practised by the Roman Catholic Church.

(Charles F. Delzell (ed.) *Mediterranean Fascism 1919–1945*, London, Macmillan, 1971)

I.11 Benito Mussolini, extracts from 'The doctrine of Fascism' (1932)

(i) FUNDAMENTAL IDEAS

[. . .]

7. Against individualism, the Fascist conception is for the State; and it is for the individual in so far as he coincides with the State, which is the

conscience and universal will of man in his historical existence. It is opposed to classical Liberalism, which arose from the necessity of reacting against absolutism, and which brought its historical purpose to an end when the State was transformed into the conscience and will of the people. Liberalism denied the State in the interests of the particular individual; Fascism reaffirms the State as the true reality of the individual. And if liberty is to be the attribute of the real man, and not of that abstract puppet envisaged by individualistic Liberalism, Fascism is for liberty. And for the only liberty which can be a real thing, the liberty of the State and of the individual within the State. Therefore, for the Fascist, everything is in the State, and nothing human or spiritual exists, much less has value, outside the State. In this sense Fascism is totalitarian, and the Fascist State, the synthesis and unity of all values, interprets, develops and gives strength to the whole life of the people.

8. Outside the State there can be neither individuals nor groups (political parties, associations, syndicates, classes). Therefore Fascism is opposed to Socialism, which confines the movement of history within the class struggle and ignores the unity of classes established in one economic and moral reality in the State; and analogously it is opposed to class syndicalism. Fascism recognizes the real exigencies for which the socialist and syndicalist movement arose, but while recognizing them wishes to bring them under the control of the State and give them a purpose within the corporative system of interests reconciled within the unity of the State.

9. Individuals form classes according to the similarity of their interests, they form syndicates according to differentiated economic activities within these interests; but they form first, and above all, the State, which is not to be thought of numerically as the sum-total of individuals forming the majority of a nation. And consequently Fascism is opposed to democracy, which equates the nation to the majority, lowering it to the level of that majority; nevertheless it is the purest form of democracy if the nation is conceived, as it should be, qualitatively and not quantitatively, as the most powerful idea (most powerful because most moral, most coherent, most true) which acts within the nation as the conscience and the will of a few, even of One, which ideal tends to become active within the conscience and the will of all – that is to say, of all those who rightly constitute a nation by reason of nature, history or race, and have set out upon the same line of development and spiritual formation as one conscience and one sole will. Not a race,[1] nor a geographically determined region, but as a community historically perpetuating itself, a multitude unified by a single idea, which is the will to existence and to power: consciousness of itself, personality.

10. This higher personality is truly the nation in so far as it is the State.

[1] 'Race; it is an emotion, not a reality; ninety-five per cent of it is emotion' (Mussolini).

It is not the nation that generates the State, as according to the old naturalistic concept which served as the basis of the political theories of the national States of the nineteenth century. Rather the nation is created by the State, which gives to the people, conscious of its own moral unity, a will and therefore an effective existence. The right of a nation to independence derives not from a literary and ideal consciousness of its own being, still less from a more or less unconscious and inert acceptance of a *de facto* situation, but from an active consciousness, from a political will in action and ready to demonstrate its own rights: that is to say, from a state already coming into being. The State, in fact, as the universal ethical will, is the creator of right.

11. The nation as the State is an ethical reality which exists and lives in so far as it develops. To arrest its development is to kill it. Therefore the State is not only the authority which governs and gives the form of laws and the value of spiritual life to the wills of individuals, but it is also a power that makes its will felt abroad, making it known and respected, in other words, demonstrating the fact of its universality in all the necessary directions of its development. It is consequently organization and expansion, at least virtually. Thus it can be likened to the human will which knows no limits to its development and realizes itself in testing its own limitlessness.

12. The Fascist State, the highest and most powerful form of personality, is a force, but a spiritual force, which takes over all the forms of the moral and intellectual life of man. It cannot therefore confine itself simply to the functions of order and supervision as Liberalism desired. It is not simply a mechanism which limits the sphere of the supposed liberties of the individual. It is the form, the inner standard and the discipline of the whole person; its saturates the will as well as the intelligence. Its principle, the central inspiration of the human personality living in the civil community, pierces into the depths and makes its home in the heart of the man of action as well as of the thinker, of the artist as well as of the scientist: it is the soul of the soul.

13. Fascism, in short, is not only the giver of laws and the founder of institutions, but the educator and promoter of spiritual life. It wants to remake, not the forms of human life, but its content, man, character, faith. And to this end it requires discipline and authority that can enter into the spirits of men and there govern unopposed. Its sign, therefore, is the Lictors' rods, the symbol of unity, of strength and justice.

(ii) POLITICAL AND SOCIAL DOCTRINE

[. . .]
Fascism is today clearly defined not only as a regime but as a doctrine. And I mean by this that Fascism today, self-critical as well as critical of other movements, has an unequivocal point of view of its own, a criterion, and hence an aim, in face of all the material and intellectual problems which oppress the people of the world.

3. Above all, Fascism, in so far as it considers and observes the future and the development of humanity quite apart from the political considerations of the moment, believes neither in the possibility nor in the utility of perpetual peace. It thus repudiates the doctrine of Pacifism – born of a renunciation of the struggle and an act of cowardice in the face of sacrifice. War alone brings up to their highest tension all human energies and puts the stamp of nobility upon the peoples who have the courage to meet it. All other trials are substitutes, which never really put a man in front of himself in the alternative of life and death. A doctrine, therefore, which begins with a prejudice in favour of peace is foreign to Fascism; as are foreign to the spirit of Facism, even though acceptable by reason of the utility which they might have in given political situations, all internationalistic and socialistic systems which, as history proves, can be blown to the winds when emotional, idealistic and practical movements storm the hearts of peoples. . . .

4. The 'demographic' policy of the regime follows from these premises. Even the Fascist does in fact love his neighbour, but this 'neighbour' is not for him a vague and ill-defined concept; love for one's neighbour does not exclude necessary educational severities, and still less differentiations and distances. Fascism rejects universal concord, and, since it lives in the community of civilized peoples, it keeps them vigilantly and suspiciously before its eyes, it follows their states of mind and the changes in their interests and it does not let itself be deceived by temporary and fallacious appearances.

5. Such a conception of life makes Fascism the precise negation of that doctrine which formed the basis of the so-called Scientific or Marxian Socialism: the doctrine of historical Materialism, according to which the history of human civilizations can be explained only as the struggle of interest between the different social groups and as arising out of change in the means and instruments of production. That economic improvements – discoveries of raw materials, new methods of work, scientific inventions – should have an importance of their own, no one denies, but that they should suffice to explain human history to the exclusion of all other factors is absurd: Fascism believes, now and always, in holiness and in heroism, that is in acts in which no economic motive – remote or immediate – plays a part. With this negation of historical materialism, according to which men would be only by-products of history, who appear and disappear on the surface of the waves while in the depths the real directive forces are at work, there is also denied the immutable and irreparable 'class struggle' which is the natural product of this economic conception of history, and above all it is denied that the class struggle can be the primary agent of social changes. Socialism, being thus wounded in these two primary tenets of its doctrine, nothing of it is left save the sentimental aspiration – old as humanity – towards a social order in which the sufferings and the pains of the humblest folk could be alleviated. But here Fascism rejects the concept of an economic 'happiness' which would

be realized socialistically and almost automatically at a given moment of economic evolution by assuring to all a maximum prosperity. . . .

6. After Socialism, Fascism attacks the whole complex of democratic ideologies and rejects them both in their theoretical premises and in their applications or practical manifestations. Fascism denies that the majority, through the mere fact of being a majority, can rule human societies; it denies that this majority can govern by means of a periodical consultation; it affirms the irremediable, fruitful and beneficent inequality of men, who cannot be levelled by such a mechanical and extrinsic fact as universal suffrage. By democratic regimes we mean those in which from time to time the people is given the illusion of being sovereign, while true effective sovereignty lies in other, perhaps irresponsible and secret, forces. Democracy is a regime without a king, but with very many kings, perhaps more exclusive, tyrannical and violent than one king even though a tyrant. . . .

8. In face of Liberal doctrines, Fascism takes up an attitude of absolute opposition both in the field of politics and in that of economics. . . .

9. But the Fascist repudiations of Socialism, Democracy, Liberalism must not make one think that Fascism wishes to make the world return to what it was before 1789, the year which has been indicated as the year of the beginning of the liberal-democratic age. One does not go back-wards. . . . A party that governs a nation in a totalitarian way is a new fact in history. References and comparisons are not possible. Fascism takes over from the ruins of Liberal Socialistic democratic doctrines those elements which still have a living value. It preserves those that can be called the established facts of history, it rejects all the rest, that is to say the idea of a doctrine which holds good for all times and all peoples. If it is admitted that the nineteenth century has been the century of Socialism, Liberalism and Democracy, it does not follow that the twentieth must also be the century of Liberalism, Socialism and Democracy. Political doc-trines pass; peoples remain. It is to be expected that this century may be that of authority, a century of the 'Right', a Fascist century. If the nineteenth was the century of the individual (Liberalism means indi-vidualism) it may be expected that this one may be the century of 'collectivism' and therefore the century of the State. That a new doctrine should use the still vital elements of other doctrines is perfectly logical. No doctrine is born quite new, shining, never before seen. No doctrine can boast of an absolute 'originality'. It is bound, even if only historically, to other doctrines that have been, and to develop into other doctrines that will be. . . .

10. The keystone of Fascist doctrine is the conception of the State, of its essence, of its tasks, of its ends. For Fascism the State is an absolute before which individuals and groups are relative. Individuals and groups are 'thinkable' in so far as they are within the State. The Liberal State does not direct the interplay and the material and spiritual development of the groups, but limits itself to registering the results; the Fascist State has a

consciousness of its own, a will of its own, on this account it is called an 'ethical' State. . . .

11. From 1929 up to the present day these doctrinal positions have been strengthened by the whole economico-political evolution of the world. It is the State alone that grows in size, in power. It is the State alone that can solve the dramatic contradictions of capitalism. What is called the crisis cannot be overcome except by the State, within the State. . . . Fascism desires the State to be strong, organic and at the same time founded on a wide popular basis. The Fascist State has also claimed for itself the field of economics and, through the corporative, social and educational institutions which it has created, the meaning of the State reaches out to and includes the farthest off-shoots; and within the State, framed in their respective organizations, there revolve all the political, economic and spiritual forces of the nation. A State founded on millions of individuals who recognize it, feel it, are ready to serve it, is not the tyrannical State of the medieval lord. It has nothing in common with the absolutist States that existed either before or after 1789. In the Fascist State the individual is not suppressed, but rather multiplied, just as in a regiment a soldier is not weakened but multiplied by the number of his comrades. The Fascist State organizes the nation, but it leaves sufficient scope to individuals; it has limited useless or harmful liberties and has preserved those that are essential. It cannot be the individual who decides in this matter, but only the State.

12. The Fascist State does not remain indifferent to the fact of religion in general and to that particular positive religion which is Italian Catholicism. The State has no theology, but it has an ethic. In the Fascist State religion is looked upon as one of the deepest manifestations of the spirit; it is, therefore, not only respected, but defended and protected. The Fascist State does not create a 'God' of its own, as Robespierre once, at the height of the Convention's foolishness, wished to do; nor does it vainly seek, like Bolshevism, to expel religion from the minds of men; Fascism respects the God of the ascetics, of the saints, of the heroes, and also God as seen and prayed to by the simple and primitive heart of the people.

13. The Fascist State is a will to power and to government. In it the tradition of Rome is an idea that has force. In the doctrine of Fascism Empire is not only a territorial, military or mercantile expression, but spiritual or moral. One can think of an empire, that is to say a nation that directly or indirectly leads other nations, without needing to conquer a single square kilometre of territory. For Fascism the tendency to Empire, that is to say, to the expansion of nations, is a manifestation of vitality; its opposite, staying at home, is a sign of decadence: peoples who rise or re-rise are imperialist, peoples who die are renunciatory. Fascism is the doctrine that is most fitted to represent the aims, the states of mind, of a people, like the Italian people, rising again after many centuries of abandonment or slavery to foreigners. But Empire calls for discipline, co-ordination of forces, duty and sacrifice; this explains many aspects of

the practical working of the regime and the direction of many of the forces of the State and the necessary severity shown to those who would wish to oppose this spontaneous and destined impulse of the Italy of the twentieth century, to oppose it in the name of the superseded ideologies of the nineteenth, repudiated wherever great experiments of political and social transformation have been courageously attempted: especially where, as now, peoples thirst for authority, for leadership, for order. If every age has its own doctrine, it is apparent from a thousand signs that the doctrine of the present age is Fascism. That it is a doctrine of life is shown by the fact that it has resuscitated a faith. That this faith has conquered minds is proved by the fact that Fascism has had its dead and its martyrs.

Fascism henceforward has in the world the universality of all those doctrines which, by fulfilling themselves, have significance in the history of the human spirit.

(Michael Oakeshott, *The Social and Political Doctrines of Contemporary Europe*, Cambridge University Press, 1939)

I.12 Gaetano Salvemini, 'How the dictatorship arose' (1928)

In the municipal elections of 1920, the municipal administration had been won by the Socialists at Foiana della Chiana, as it had been in many other Communes. At the beginning of April, 1921, the Socialist Mayor received a letter from Marchese Perrone Compagni, General Secretary of the Fasci for Tuscany, in which the Mayor and his councillors were invited to resign within the week if they did not wish to expose themselves and their families to Fascist reprisals.[1] The Mayor and the Councillors did not obey.

On April 12, 1921, more than 200 Fascists collected in lorries from Arezzo, Florence and the intermediate towns, and made an 'expedition of propaganda' to the little town, i.e., they looted the town hall, the Chamber of Workers and the premises of the Peasants' Union, throwing the furniture into the street and burning it. They seized the Co-operative stores, distributing the goods to all and sundry and setting fire to what remained. On April 17, a second 'expedition of propaganda' was carried out. This time there were barely 20 Fascists in a single lorry. They confiscated the red flag which the 'Communists' usually ran up over the town hall instead of the national flag, burnt it together with the records of the Socialist club and then proceeded to the neighbouring village of Marciano on another 'propagandist trip'. On their return several Fascists stayed at Foiano to form a local 'Fascio' while the rest in the lorry took the road back to Arezzo.

[1] Examination of Galliano Gervasi during the trial at Arezzo, *Corriere della Sera*, October 17, 1924.

A short distance out of Foiano a group of about fifty peasants armed with guns, scythes, hatchets and pistols were lying in wait behind a hedge. The lorry was received with a hail of bullets. The driver fell wounded, the lorry swerved and ran against a tree. While the Fascists were thrown to the ground, the peasants in hiding leaped forward upon them. They cut off the head of the driver with a hatchet-blow. Two Fascists were killed and another had three fingers severed by an axe. The remainder managed to escape.

At the sound of the shots, the Carabineers, who till then had remained inactive, woke up and rushed out from Foiano together with those Fascists who had remained in the town. The peasants, seeing the Carabineers approaching, took to flight in their turn.

Now began the reprisals.

The farmhouses near the place of the ambush were set on fire. A peasant, Burri, who was discovered in an attic, was shot through the head with a revolver.

The next day reprisals continued on a larger scale. Five lorry-loads of Fascists left Florence in the early morning. Other lorries left Arezzo and the neighbouring towns and all concentrated in Foiano. The authorities, as usual, left the Fascists a free hand. The best-known 'Communists' of Foiano had already left their homes. The Fascists gave themselves up to ransacking, wrecking and burning private houses. A workman, Cino Milani, who had not bethought himself to escape, was dragged into the square: he was required to promise to resign from membership of the Socialist Party; he refused. He was required to declare that he deplored the ambush of the day before: he again refused. He was shot. A peasant, one Gherardi, guilty of being the brother of a 'Communist', was shot at and killed while he was trying to escape. The Fascists of Arezzo had brought with them as prisoner to Foiano the Socialist ex-Member of Parliament, Bernardini, editor of the Socialist paper of Arezzo. The prisoner was forced, under threat of death, to pronounce from the window of a house a speech against the 'violence of the Socialists', while the mass of Fascists howled and hooted in the street below. Thanks to this act of cowardice which dishonours his jailers no less than himself, his life was spared.

When they wearied of tormenting the people of Foiano, the Fascists repaired to the place of the 'ambush' of the day before. The peasant Caciolli was seriously wounded. Two other peasants, who were wounded as they fled, were not found; probably their injuries were not serious and they managed to hide. But this was not enough. In the night, towards one o'clock, the Fascists returned to this place; they ransacked the farmhouses, one by one, terrifying women, children and old people, and reduced other houses to smoking ruins. A woman, Luisa Bracciali, who was accused of having wounded a Fascist in the 'ambush' with a pitchfork, was found in her home and shot dead with revolvers. The peasant Nocciolini was killed whilst trying to flee. Another peasant,

Alfredo Rampi, hearing that the Fascists were on his track, killed himself.

Operations continued throughout the next day also, April 19. The house of the Mayor Nucci, who had fled, was invaded and set on fire. The Communist club of Bettole was sacked and burnt. Finally the Fascists collected a 'spontaneous' meeting of peasants, took down their names and declared the Fascio of Foiano founded. After having thus converted the 'Communists' of Foiano to the 'National faith', the Fascists, glorious and triumphant, abandoned the scene of their victory.

Needless to say the civil and military authorities were conspicuous by their absence. They were engaged in 'rounding up the Communists' who had hidden themselves in the country round Foiano. Of those guilty of the 'ambuscade' who had not been killed in the reprisals, four were sentenced to thirty years' imprisonment, three to twenty-five years, two to twenty years, six to ten years, and three to from seven to ten years.[1] None of the Fascists who took part in the operations described suffered in any way whatsoever.[2]

(Gaetano Salvemini, *The Fascist Dictatorship in Italy*, London, Jonathan Cape, 1928)

I.13 Report of the American Consul in Leipzig (21 Nov. 1938)

The shattering of shop windows, looting of stores and dwellings of Jews which began in the early hours of 10 November 1938, was hailed subsequently in the Nazi press as a 'spontaneous wave of righteous indignation throughout Germany, as a result of the cowardly Jewish murder of Third Secretary von Rath in the German Embassy at Paris'. So far as a very high percentage of the German populace is concerned, a state of popular indignation that would spontaneously lead to such excesses, can be considered as non-existent. On the contrary, in viewing the ruins and attendant measures employed, all of the local crowds observed were obviously benumbed over what had happened and aghast over the unprecedented fury of Nazi acts that had been or were taking place with bewildering rapidity throughout their city. . . .

At 3 a.m. on 10 November 1938 was unleashed a barrage of Nazi ferocity as had had no equal hitherto in Germany, or very likely anywhere else in the world since savagery began. Jewish buildings were smashed into and contents demolished or looted. In one of the Jewish sections an eighteen-year-old boy was hurled from a three-storey window to land with both legs broken on a street littered with burning beds and other household furniture and effects from his family's and other apartments.

[1] *Corriere della Sera*, December 13, 1924.
[2] In my account I have followed the version of *Corriere della Sera* of April 13, 19 and 20, 1921. I have not made use of anti-Fascist papers because the atrocious details they give could be suspected of exaggeration.

This information was supplied by an attending physician. It is reported from another quarter that among domestic effects thrown out of a Jewish building, a small dog descended four flights on to a cluttered street with a broken spine. Although apparently centred in poorer districts, the raid was not confined to the humble classes. One apartment of exceptionally refined occupants known to this office was violently ransacked, presumably in a search for valuables which was not in vain, and one of the marauders thrust a cane through a priceless medieval painting portraying a biblical scene. Another apartment of the same category is known to have been turned upside down in the frenzied pursuit of whatever the invaders were after. Reported loss by looting of cash, silver, jewellery, and otherwise easily convertible articles, has been apparent.

Jewish shop windows by the hundreds were systematically and wantonly smashed throughout the entire city at a loss estimated at several millions of marks. There are reports that substantial losses have been sustained on the famous Leipzig 'Grühl', as many of the shop windows at the time of the demolition were filled with costly furs that were seized before the windows could be boarded up. In proportion to the general destruction of real estate, however, losses of goods are felt to have been relatively small. The spectators who viewed the wreckage when daylight had arrived were mostly in such a bewildered mood that there was no danger of impulsive acts, and the perpetrators probably were too busy in carrying out their schedule to take off a whole lot of time for personal profit. At all events, the main streets of the city were a positive litter of shattered plate glass. According to reliable testimony, the debacle was executed by SS men and Stormtroopers not in uniform, each group having been provided with hammers, axes, crowbars and incendiary bombs.

Three synagogues in Leipzig were fired simultaneously by incendiary bombs and all sacred objects and records desecrated or destroyed, in most cases hurled through the windows and burned in the streets. No attempts whatsoever were made to quench the fires, the activity of the fire brigade being confined to playing water on adjoining buildings. All of the synagogues were irreparably gutted by flames, and the walls of the two that are close to the consulate are now being razed. The blackened frames have been centres of attraction during the past week of terror for eloquently silent and bewildered crowds. One of the largest clothing stores in the heart of the city was destroyed by flames from incendiary bombs, only the charred walls and gutted roof having been left standing. As was the case with the synagogues, no attempts on the part of the fire brigade were made to extinguish the fire, although apparently there was a certain amount of apprehension for adjacent property, for the walls of a coffee house next door were covered with asbestos and sprayed by the doughty firemen. It is extremely difficult to believe, but the owners of the clothing store were actually charged with setting the fire and on that basis were dragged from their beds at 6 a.m. and clapped into prison.

Tactics which closely approached the ghoulish took place at the Jewish cemetery where the temple was fired together with a building occupied by caretakers, tombstones uprooted and graves violated. Eyewitnesses considered reliable the report that ten corpses were left unburied at this cemetery for a whole week because all gravediggers and cemetery attendants had been arrested.

Ferocious as was the violation of property, the most hideous phase of the so-called 'spontaneous' action has been the wholesale arrest and transportation to concentration camps of male German Jews between the ages of sixteen and sixty, as well as Jewish men without citizenship. This has been taking place daily since the night of horror. This office has no way of accurately checking the numbers of such arrests, but there is very little question that they have run to several thousands in Leipzig alone. Having demolished dwellings and hurled most of the movable effects onto the streets, the insatiably sadistic perpetrators threw many of the trembling inmates into a small stream that flows through the Zoological Park, commanding horrified spectators to spit at them, defile them with mud and jeer at their plight. The latter incident has been repeatedly corroborated by German witnesses who were nauseated in telling the tale. The slightest manifestation of sympathy evoked a positive fury on the part of the perpetrators, and the crowd was powerless to do anything but turn horror-stricken eyes from the scene of abuse, or leave the vicinity. These tactics were carried out the entire morning of 10 November without police intervention and they were applied to men, women and children.

There is much evidence of physical violence, including several deaths. At least half-a-dozen cases have been personally observed, victims with bloody, badly bruised faces having fled to this office, believing that as refugees their desire to emigrate could be expedited here. As a matter of fact this consulate has been a bedlam of humanity for the past ten days, most of these visitors being desperate women, as their husbands and sons had been taken off to concentration camps.

Similarly violent procedure was applied throughout this consular district, the amount of havoc wrought depending upon the number of Jewish establishments or persons involved. It is understood that in many of the smaller communities even more relentless methods were employed than was the case in the cities. Reports have been received from Weissenfels to the effect that the few Jewish families there are experiencing great difficulty in purchasing food. It is reported that three Aryan professors of the University of Jena have been arrested and taken off to concentration camps because they had voiced disapproval of this insidious drive against mankind.

(J. Noakes and G. Pridham (eds) *Nazism 1919–1945*, vol. 2, *Nazism – State Economy and Society 1933–39*, University of Exeter, 1984)

I.14 Adolf Hitler, 'Memorandum on the Four-Year Plan' (Aug. 1936)

This memorandum was given to me personally by A.H. in 1944 with the following statement:

The lack of understanding of the *Reich* Ministry for Economics and the opposition of German business to all large-scale plans induced him to compose this memorandum at Obersalzberg.

He decided at that time to carry out a Four-Year Plan and to put Goering in charge of it. On the occasion of Goering's appointment as the official in charge of the Four-Year Plan he gave him this memorandum. There are only three copies, one of which he gave to me. . . .

[signed] ALBERT SPEER

THE POLITICAL SITUATION

Politics are the conduct and the course of the historical struggle of nations for life. The aim of these struggles is survival. Even ideological struggles have their ultimate cause and are most deeply motivated by nationally determined purposes and aims of life. But religions and ideologies are always able to impart particular bitterness to such struggles, and therefore also to give them great historical impressiveness. They leave their imprint on centuries of history. Nations and States living within the sphere of such ideological or religious conflicts cannot opt out of or dissociate themselves from these events. Christianity and the barbarian invasions determined the course of history for centuries. Mohammedanism convulsed the Orient as well as the Western world for half a millennium. The consequences of the Reformation have affected the whole of central Europe. Nor were individual countries – either by skill or by deliberate non-participation – able to steer clear of events. Since the outbreak of the French Revolution the world has been moving with ever-increasing speed towards a new conflict, the most extreme solution of which is Bolshevism; and the essence and goal of Bolshevism is the elimination of those strata of mankind which have hitherto provided the leadership and their replacement by world-wide Jewry.

No nation will be able to avoid or abstain from this historical conflict. *Since Marxism, through its victory in Russia, has established one of the greatest empires as a forward base for its future operations, this question has become a menacing one. Against a democratic world which is ideologically split stands a unified aggressive will, based on an authoritarian ideology.*

The military resources of this aggressive will are in the meantime rapidly increasing from year to year. One has only to compare the Red Army as it actually exists today with the assumptions of military men of ten or fifteen years ago to realize the menacing extent of this development. Only consider the results of a further development over ten, fifteen or twenty years and think what conditions will be like then.

Germany

Germany will as always have to be regarded as the focus of the Western world against the attacks of Bolshevism. I do not regard this as an agreeable mission but as a serious handicap and burden for our national life, regrettably resulting from our disadvantageous position in Europe. We cannot, however, escape this destiny. Our political position results from the following:

At the moment there are only two countries in Europe which can be regarded as standing firm against Bolshevism – Germany and Italy. The other nations are either corrupted by their democratic way of life, infected by Marxism and therefore likely to collapse in the foreseeable future, or ruled by authoritarian Governments, whose sole strength lies in their military resources; this means, however, that being obliged to protect their leadership against their own peoples by the armed hand of the Executive, they are unable to use this armed hand for the protection of their countries against external enemies. None of these countries would ever be capable of waging war against Soviet Russia with any prospects of success. In fact, apart from Germany and Italy, only Japan can be considered as a Power standing firm in the face of the world peril.

It is not the aim of this memorandum to prophesy the moment when the untenable situation in Europe will reach the stage of an open crisis. I only want, in these lines, to express my conviction that this crisis cannot and will not fail to occur, and that Germany has the duty of securing her existence by every means in the face of this catastrophe, and to protect herself against it, and that this obligation has a number of implications involving the most important tasks that our people have ever been set. *For a victory of Bolshevism over Germany would lead not to a Versailles Treaty but to the final destruction, indeed to the annihilation, of the German people.*

The extent of such a catastrophe cannot be estimated. How, indeed, would the whole of densely populated Western Europe (including Germany) after a collapse into Bolshevism, live through probably the most gruesome catastrophe which has been visited on mankind since the downfall of the states of antiquity. *In face of the necessity of warding off this danger, all other considerations must recede into the background as completely irrelevant.*

Germany's defensive capacity

Germany's defensive capacity is based upon several factors. I would give pride of place to the intrinsic value of the German people *per se*. The German nation with an impeccable political leadership, a firm ideology, a thorough military organization, certainly constitutes the most valuable factor of resistance in the world today. Political leadership is ensured by the National Socialist Party; ideological solidarity has, since the victory of National Socialism, been introduced to a degree that has never previously been attained. It must be constantly deepened and strengthened on the basis of this concept. This is the aim of the National Socialist education of our people.

The development of our military capacity is to be effected through the new Army. *The extent of the military development of our resources cannot be too large, nor its pace too swift.* It is a major error to believe that there can be any argument on these points or any comparison with other vital necessities. However well-balanced the general pattern of a nation's life ought to be there must at particular times be certain disturbances of the balance at the expense of other less vital tasks. *If we do not succeed in bringing the German Army as rapidly as possible to the rank of premier army in the world so far as its training, raising of units, armaments, and, above all, its spiritual education also is concerned, then Germany will be lost!* In this the basic principle applies that omissions during the months of peace cannot be made good in centuries.

Hence all other desires without exception must come second to this task. For this task involves life and the preservation of life, and all other desires – however understandable at other junctures – are unimportant or even mortally dangerous and are therefore to be rejected. Posterity will ask us one day, not what were the means, the reasons or the convictions by which we thought fit today to achieve the salvation of the nation, but *whether* in fact we achieved it. And on that day it will be no excuse for our downfall for us to describe the means which were infallible, but, alas, brought about our ruin.

Germany's economic situation

Just as the political movement among our people knows only one goal, the preservation of our existence, that is to say, the securing of all the spiritual and other prerequisites for the self-assertion of our nation, so neither has the economy any other goal than this. The nation does not live for the economy, for economic leaders, or for economic or financial theories; on the contrary, it is finance and the economy, economic leaders and theories, which all owe unqualified service in this struggle for the self-assertion of our nation. Germany's economic situation is, however, in the briefest outline as follows:

1. We are overpopulated and cannot feed ourselves from our own resources.

2. When our nation has six or seven million unemployed, the food situation improves because these people lack purchasing power. It naturally makes a difference whether six million people have 40 marks a month to spend, or 100 marks. It should not be overlooked that a third of all who earn their living is involved, that is to say that, taken as a proportion of the total population, through the National Socialist economic policy about 28 million people have been offered an increase in their standard of living of, on average, from at least 50 marks a month to at most 100–120 marks. This means an increased and understandable run on the foodstuffs market.

3. But if this rise in employment fails to take place, the effect of under-nourishment will be that a higher percentage of the population must gradually be deducted from the body of our nation, so far as its effective

contribution is concerned. Thus, despite the difficult food situation, the most important task of our economic policy is to see to it that all Germans are incorporated into the economic process, and so the prerequisites for normal consumption are created.

4. In so far as this consumption concerns articles of general use, it can be satisfied to a *large* extent by an increase in production. In so far as this consumption falls upon the foodstuffs market, it cannot be satisfied from the domestic German economy. For, although the output of numerous products can be increased without difficulty, the yield of our agricultural production can undergo no further substantial increase. It is equally impossible for us at present to manufacture artificially certain raw materials which we lack in Germany or to find other substitutes for them.

5. There is, however, no point in endless repetition of the fact that we lack foodstuffs and raw materials; what matters is the taking of those measures which can bring about a *final* solution for the *future* and a *temporary* easing of conditions during the *transition* period.

6. The final solution lies in extending our living space, that is to say, extending the sources of raw materials and foodstuffs of our people. It is the task of the political leadership one day to solve this problem.

7. The temporary easing of conditions can be achieved only within the framework of our present economy. In this connexion, the following must be noted:

(a) Since the German people will be increasingly dependent on imports for their food and must similarly, whatever happens, import a proportion at least of certain raw materials from abroad, every effort must be made to facilitate these imports.

(b) An increase in our own exports is possible in theory but in practice hardly likely. Germany does not export to a political or economic vacuum, but to areas where competition is very intense. Compared with the general international economic depression, our exports have fallen, not only *not more*, but in fact *less* than those of other nations and states. But since imports of food on the whole cannot be substantially reduced and are more likely to increase, an adjustment must be found in some other way.

(c) It is, however, impossible to use foreign exchange allocated for the purchase of raw materials to import foodstuffs without inflicting a heavy and perhaps even fatal blow on the rest. *But above all it is absolutely impossible to do this at the expense of national rearmament.* I must at this point sharply reject the view that by restricting national rearmament, that is today, the manufacture of arms and ammunition, we could bring about an 'enrichment' in raw materials which might then benefit Germany in the event of war. Such a view is based on a complete misconception, to put it mildly, of the tasks and military requirements that lie before us. For even a successful saving of raw materials by reducing, for instance, the production of munitions would merely mean that we should stockpile these raw materials in time of peace so as to manufacture them only in the event of war, that is to say, we should be depriving ourselves during the most critical months of munitions in exchange for raw copper, lead, or possibly iron. But in that case it would none the less be better for the nation to enter the war without a single kilogram of copper in stock but with full munition depots rather than with empty munition depots but so-called 'enriched' stocks of raw material.

War makes possible the mobilization of even the last remaining supplies of metal. For it then becomes not an *economic problem*, but solely a *question of will*. And the National Socialist leadership of the country will have not only the will but also the resolution and the toughness necessary to solve these problems in the event of war. But it is much more important to prepare for war in time of peace. Moreover, in this respect the following must be stated:

There can be no building up of a reserve of *raw materials* for the event of war, just as there can be no building up of foreign exchange reserves. The attempt is sometimes made today to represent matters as if Germany went to war in 1914 with well-prepared stocks of raw material. That is a lie. No country can assemble in advance the quantities of raw materials necessary for war lasting longer than, say, one year. But if any nation were really in a position to assemble those quantities of raw material needed for a year, then its political, military and economic leaders would deserve to be hanged. For they would in fact be setting aside the available copper and iron in preparation for the conduct of a war instead of manufacturing shells. But Germany went into the world war without any reserves whatsoever. What was available at that time in Germany in the way of apparent peacetime reserves was counterbalanced and rendered valueless by the miserable war stocks of ammunition. *Moreover, the quantities of war materials that are needed for a war are so large that there has* NEVER *in the history of the world been a real stockpiling for a period of any length!*, and as regards preparations in the form of piling up foreign exchange it is quite clear that:

1. War is capable of devaluing foreign exchange at any time, unless it is held in gold.

2. There is not the least guarantee that gold itself can be converted in time of war into raw materials. During the world war Germany still possessed very large assets in foreign exchange in a great many countries. It was not, however, possible for our cunning economic policy-makers to bring to Germany, in exchange for them fuel, rubber, copper or tin in any sufficient quantity. To assert the contrary is ridiculous nonsense. For this reason, and in order to secure the food supplies of our people, the following task presents itself as imperative:

It is not sufficient merely to establish from time to time raw material or foreign exchange balances, or to talk about the preparation of a war economy in time of peace; on the contrary, it is essential to ensure all the food supplies required in peacetime and, above all, those means for the conduct of a war which can be secured by human energy and activity. I therefore draw up the following programme for a final provision of our vital needs:

I. Parallel with the military and political rearmament and mobilization of our nation must go its economic rearmament and mobilization, and this must be effected in the same tempo, with the same determination, and if need be with the same ruthlessness as well. In future the interests of individual gentlemen can no longer play any part in these matters. There is only one interest, the interest of the nation; only one view, the bringing of Germany to the point of political and economic self-sufficiency.

II. For this purpose, foreign exchange must be saved in all those areas where our needs can be satisfied by German production, in order that it may be used for those requirements which can under no circumstances be fulfilled except by import.

III. Accordingly, German fuel production must now be stepped up with the utmost speed and brought to final completion within eighteen months. This task must be attacked and carried out with the same determination as the waging of a war, since it is on the discharge of this task, not upon the laying in of stocks of petroleum, that the conduct of the future war depends.

IV. The mass production of synthetic rubber must also be organized and achieved with the same urgency. From now on there must be no talk of processes not being fully determined and other such excuses. It is not a matter of discussing whether we are to wait any longer; otherwise time will be lost, and the hour of peril will take us all by surprise. Above all, it is not the job of the economic institutions of Government to rack their brains over methods of production. This has nothing whatever to do with the Ministry of Economics. Either we possess today a private industry, in which case its job is to rack its brains about methods of production; or we believe that it is the Government's job to determine methods of production, and in that case we have no further need of private industry.

V. The question of the cost of producing these raw materials is also quite irrelevant, since it is in any case better for us to produce expensive tyres in Germany which we can use, than to sell theoretically cheap tyres, but tyres for which the Minister of Economics cannot allocate any foreign exchange, and which therefore cannot be produced for lack of raw materials and consequently cannot be used at all. If we really are obliged to build up our domestic economy on autarkic lines, which we are – for lamenting and harping on our foreign exchange plight will certainly not solve the problem – then the price of raw materials individually considered no longer plays a decisive part.

It is further necessary to increase German iron production to the utmost limits. The objection that with German ore, which has a 26 per cent ferrous content, we cannot produce pig iron as cheaply as with the 45 per cent Swedish ores, etc., is irrelevant; we are not faced with the question of what we would *rather* do, but what we *can* do. The objection, moreover, that in that event all the German blast-furnaces would have to be converted is equally irrelevant, and, what is more, this is no concern of the Ministry of Economics. The job of the Ministry of Economics is simply to set the national economic tasks; private industry has to fulfil them. But if private industry thinks itself incapable of doing this, then the National Socialist State will know how to resolve the problem on its own. In any case, for a thousand years Germany had no foreign iron ores. Even before the war, more German iron ores were being processed than during the period of our worst decline. *Nevertheless, if there is still the possibility of our importing cheaper ores, well and good. But the future of the national economy and, above all, of the conduct of war, must not depend on this.*

Moreover, the distillation of potatoes into alcohol must be prohibited forthwith. Fuel must be obtained from the ground, not from potatoes. Instead it is our duty to use any arable land that may become available either for human or animal foodstuffs or for the cultivation of fibrous materials.

It is further necessary for us to make our supplies of *industrial* fats independent of imports as quickly as possible. This can be done by using our coal. This problem has been solved by chemical means and the technique is actually crying out to be put into practice. Either German industry will grasp the new economic tasks or else it will show itself incapable of surviving any longer in this modern age in which a Soviet State is setting up a gigantic plan. *But in that case it will not be Germany that will go under, but at most a few industrialists.* Moreover, the extraction of other ores must be increased, *regardless of cost*, and, in particular, the production of light metals must be increased to the utmost limits, in order to produce a substitute for certain other metals.

Finally, it is also necessary for the rearmament programme to make use even now whenever possible of those materials which must and will replace high-grade metals in time of war. *It is better to consider and resolve these problems in time of peace than to wait for the next war and only then, in the midst of a multitude of tasks, to try to undertake these economic researches and experiments with methods.*

In short, I consider it necessary that now, with iron determination, a 100 per cent self-sufficiency should be attained in every sphere where it is feasible, and that not only should the national requirements in these most essential raw materials be made independent of other countries, but we should also thus save the foreign exchange which in peacetime we need for our imports of foodstuffs. *In this connexion, I want to emphasize that in these tasks I see the only true economic mobilization and not in the throttling of armament industries in peacetime in order to save and stockpile raw materials for war.*

But I further consider it necessary to make an immediate investigation of the outstanding debts in foreign exchange owed to German business abroad. There is no doubt that the outstanding claims of German business abroad are quite enormous. Nor is there any doubt that behind this in some cases there lies concealed the contemptible desire to possess, whatever happens, certain reserves abroad which are thus withheld from the grasp of the domestic economy. I regard this as deliberate sabotage of our national self-assertion, that is to say, of the defence of the *Reich*, and I therefore consider it necessary for the *Reichstag* to pass the following two laws:

1. A law providing the death penalty for economic sabotage, and

2. A law making the whole of Jewry liable for all damage inflicted by individual specimens of this community of criminals upon the German economy, and thus upon the German people.

Only the fulfilment of these tasks, in the form of a Several Years Plan for rendering our national economy independent of foreign countries, will make it possible for the first time to demand sacrifices from the German people in the economic sphere and in that of foodstuffs. For then the nation will have a right to demand of their leaders whom they blindly acknowledge, that they should not only talk about the problems in this field but tackle them with unparalleled and determined energy, not only point them out but solve them.

Nearly four precious years have now gone by. There is no doubt that by now we could have been completely independent of foreign countries in the spheres of fuel supplies, rubber supplies, and partly also iron ore supplies. Just as we are now producing 700,000 or 800,000 tons of petroleum, we could be producing 3 million tons. Just as we are today manufacturing a few thousand tons of rubber, we could already be producing 70,000 or 80,000 tons per annum. Just as we have stepped up the production of iron ore from 2½ million tons to 7 million tons, we could process 20 or 25 million tons of German iron ore and even 30 millions if necessary. There has been time enough in four years to find out what we cannot do. Now we have to carry out what we can do.

I thus set the following tasks:

I. The German armed forces must be operational within four years.

II. The German economy must be fit for war within four years.

(J. Noakes and G. Pridham (eds) *Nazism 1919–1945*, vol. 2, *Nazism – State, Economy and Society 1933–39*, University of Exeter, 1984)

I.15   Anatoli Lunacharsky, 'The tasks of the state cinema in the RSFSR'[1] (1919)

[Anatoli Lunacharsky (1875–1933) was the People's Commissar for Enlightenment from 1917 to 1929.]

The state cinema in Russia faces quite unusual tasks. It is not simply a matter of nationalizing production and film distribution and the direct

[1] Russian Soviet Federated Socialist Republic, the name applied to the whole country between 1917 and 1924, but to the Russian Republic alone after 1924.

control of cinemas. It is a matter of fostering a completely new spirit in this branch of art and education.

In the present impoverished state of the Russian economy we cannot count on producing films of a purely artistic, literary or even scientifically objective character and competing with foreign firms or replacing Russian private films. For the present, while trade is significantly restricted, we might perhaps borrow this kind of material from films that have already been made or imported from abroad; but this situation will not of course last for ever.

We must do what nobody else is either able or willing to do. We should remember that a socialist government must imbue even film shows with a socialist spirit.

There is absolutely no doubt that in this respect far more newsreel footage must be shot and there is no need for me to say more.

Furthermore, the main task of cinema in both its scientific and feature divisions is that of propaganda.

Generally speaking, every art, as Tolstoy once remarked, is above all a means of instilling the artist's emotions into the masses. Education in the wider sense of the word consists in the dissemination of ideas among minds that would otherwise remain a stranger to them. Cinema can accomplish both these things with particular force: it constitutes, on the one hand, a visual clarion for the dissemination of ideas and, on the other hand, if we introduce elements of the refined, the poetic, the pathetic etc., it is capable of touching the emotions and thus becomes an apparatus of agitation. We must pay attention to these aspects above all. If there is a place where a stupid fear of tendentiousness becomes even more absurd, that place is cinema. Generally speaking, tendentiousness is harmful only if it is petty; the great tendentiousness of a religious idea or of a broad socialist idea that approximates to it can only produce works of art, and it was not for nothing that Chekhov complained that the art of his time had been deprived of God and that no amount of talent on the part of the artist and no outward mastery can, even in isolation, act as a substitute for a life-giving idea.

A Communist government has such a life-giving idea and, with the minimum of attention and experience, this idea can be very easily conveyed in the appropriate artistic guise.

It seems to me that we must first of all produce a cultural-historical picture. It is impossible to imagine a richer source for cinema than the cultural history of mankind as a whole. This is, in the literal sense of the word, an inexhaustible source, and it is worth tapping it, starting with the life of primeval man so that the head really spins at the wealth of images that can be realized most fully through cinema.

But we must not be carried away by the full panoply of the past: we must concentrate only on moments that are important for agitation and propaganda. We must convey the history of the beginnings of the growth of the state in such a way that basic Communist ideas on the criminal nature and at the same time on the necessity of each state, on the development of man and his different forms, on the unique form of the state – the dictatorship of the poor or of the proletariat – are made clear to every viewer.

Just as important is the history of the Church, including the depiction of cults – the cruellest and most senseless – and also of all the abuses committed by the Christian Church but, with historical objectivity, we must clearly distinguish its democratic and positive aspects. It is very easy, having given due credit to the positive and idealistic aspects of Christianity, to show how they have been systematically falsified by ecclesiastics in the service of the state and the wealthy classes.

The history of political conflicts, in particular the history of the great French Revolution, and all kinds of important events of our recent revolutionary history, from the Decembrists to the October Revolution of 1917, must also be treated with all due care.

While in no way denying the enormous importance of a broader range of themes, depicting, for instance, the history of science (an unusually rich theme), including the history of inventions or the history of the highest culture, I think that, with our limited time and resources, we must not hesitate too much, and in choosing between two pictures of roughly the same importance and value we must make the one that can speak to the mind and the heart more vividly from the standpoint of revolutionary propaganda.

(Richard Taylor (ed. and trans.) *The Film Factory: Russian and Soviet Cinema in Documents 1896–1939*, co-edited and intro. by Ian Christie, London, Routledge and Kegan Paul, 1988, pp. 47 and 49)

I.16 Pavel Petrov-Bytov, 'We have no Soviet cinema' (21 April 1929)

[Pavel Petrov-Bytov (1895–1960) was a film director.]

We call our cinema Soviet. Do we have the right to call it that at present? In my view we do not.

When people talk about Soviet cinema they brandish a banner on which is written: *The Strike, The Battleship Potemkin, October, The Mother, The End of St Petersburg* and they add the recent *New Babylon, Zvenigora* and *The Arsenal. Do 120 million workers and peasants march beneath this banner? I quite categorically state that they do not.* And never have done. I am not denying the virtues of these films. These virtues do of course exist and they are not negligible. Great formal virtues. We must study these films just as we study the bourgeois classics. But making them the banner of Soviet cinema is premature. It is not with these films that we must initiate Soviet cinema.

Anyone who knows the workers and peasants will understand me without argument. We must know them first of all. More than once I have had to listen to high-flown declarations even, to their shame, from Party members: 'The mass is stupid, the mass understands nothing. Yes, our country is uncultured.' The workers and peasants as a mass are uncultured. So what? Should we turn away from them disdainfully, make our high-art films and not worry about whether they understand us or not? Some people do hold that point of view. They say that the masses do not understand now but they will in five to ten years' time. This is a patronizing point of view. Who is to do the rough labour of raising the masses to a level where they can understand these films? _The principal task of Soviet cinema is to raise the cultural level of the masses now, urgently, immediately_. We must think of the future but for ninety per cent of the time we must think of the present.

We must think of the negative aspects of life and link cinema to other methods of eradicating them. Is so-called Soviet cinema performing this task? Yes, it is, but only at five per cent capacity. . . . Why so little? Because the people who make up Soviet cinema are ninety-five per cent alien, aesthetes or unprincipled. Generally speaking none of them have any experience of life. Can these people, who are capable of understanding abstract problems but not life, serve the masses? Yes they can if they are born again or regenerated. If their hearts beat in unison, with the masses. If the joys and sorrows of these masses are as dear and close to them. If they get to know the minutiae of the daily life of these masses. If, with all these qualities, they are progressive people, fraternally inveighing against the vices and failings of these masses.

If they are regenerated in this way, then there will be honour and a role for them in Soviet cinema. If not, the workers and peasants will show them their proper place. So far they have not been regenerated but they shout from the house-tops: 'We shall lead the masses behind us.' _I am sorry, but you will not lead with 'Octobers' and 'New Babylons' if only because people do not want to watch these films. Before you lead the masses behind you, you must know them. For this you must either be from the masses yourself or have studied them thoroughly , and not just studied but also experienced what these masses themselves experience._

The public-spirited artist who works on the masses and leads them must, before being an artist, spend a couple of years in the worker's 'school of life' and two years in the peasant's, or he must come from this milieu. No books can take the place of this. As well as theory we need practice. Before we talk about life we must get to know it. We can say a great deal about this. We can cite as much evidence as we want. Can the FEKS[1] and Eisenstein say that they know the masses? No, they cannot. Because they lead the masses behind them? But you have to talk to them in their native language and not in the language of the Formalists. We have to produce new forms but we do not have to be like the Frenchman explaining in his own language the meaning of 'art for art's sake' to a

[1] Factory of the Eccentric Actor.

Russian. The Russian will spit and walk out, just as the public is walking out of *New Babylon*.

When we talk to the masses in the language of *New Babylon* we are in so doing surrendering them to the power of street singers, Harry Piel and *Happy Canaries*. Is this what Soviet cinema wants? After this should we aestheticize, revelling in formal achievements, or should we, as revolutionaries, abandon our conceit and talk in the language that the masses use, only gradually teaching them new words? It is obvious that we must do the latter.

'New content requires new forms.' It would be more accurate to say that the new content of our creative identity requires more vivid means of expression to communicate the feelings and thoughts of the artist. But do not transform the Russian language into Babylonian at a stroke. Let the Babylonians learn Russian first, i.e. get to know the needs, the feelings and thoughts of the masses, and only then let them learn Babylonian. It is not enough to approach the masses from above and stand in the vanguard. No. You must find your own way through the masses, so that the sorrows and needs of these masses leave the blood and guts of living flesh on your body. It is only then, being in the vanguard, that you will be able to understand the masses and lead them behind you.

We have no workers' and peasants' cinema.

I state this boldly. Let anyone prove otherwise.

What do we have to offer the peasant woman, thinking with her ponderous and sluggish brain about her husband who has gone to make a living in the town, about the cow that is sick in the dirty cow-shed with tuberculosis of the lungs, about the starving horse that has broken its leg, about the child that is stirring in her womb? What are we providing for her? What are we proposing to provide? *New Babylon*? *The Happy Canary*? What Babylonian barbarism on our part! What stupid parasitic self-satisfaction at the summits of culture!

What can we offer the peasant? Which one of us knows the thoughts and feelings that trouble him? Who will direct him and teach him to feel and think in a new way? Which films will help him to escape from the idiocy of rural life? Which films will teach him to reorganize his life in a new way? *New Babylon*? *The Happy Canary*? And we dare to call ourselves public-spirited? Parasites: that is our name.

'What have you done for me?' the worker asks. 'For goodness sake: *October*, *New Babylon*, *The Happy Canary*,' we answer familiarly. He does not say a word but swings his hand and punches us. I do not know why he has not done it before. It is long overdue. We have nothing to offer our own dear worker and peasant. There is nothing. Name something we can offer them. It is not with *Octobers* and *New Babylons* that we must begin to build Soviet cinema. Does Soviet cinema need *New Babylons*? Let them be. We need them like Soviet diplomacy needs tail-coats.

For the peasants we have to make straightforward realistic films with a simple story and plot. We must touch the thoughts and feelings that are close and intelligible to the peasant and gradually direct them on to socialist rails. We must talk in his own sincere language about the cow that is sick with tuberculosis, about the dirty cow-shed that must be transformed into one that is clean and bright, about the child that is stirring in the peasant woman's womb, about crèches for the child, about rural hooligans, the *kolkhoz*, and so on. These films do not constitute a vulgarization. In them a great artist opens up an artistic depth that our aestheticizing directors will be unable to cope with.

Certain effete directors call this tinkering with the everyday and flee to the heady heights of aestheticism, turning their noses up at the dung heap that is called everyday life. But in order to clear this heap away you have to tinker with it. You will not do anything with it unless you remove from it everything that is base. Whoever does not do this and calls this work 'tinkering with the everyday' deserves to be suspected: he is an anarchist or, more accurately, a parasite. But, in order to fight the shortcomings of human life, we must know the so-called popular soul. We must take account of the thoughts and feelings of the mass that we wish to emancipate from its uncultured state.

I repeat, we must speak in their own language, the one that they understand. We must speak truthfully and sincerely. Our hearts and minds must be with them. The artist himself must not imitate the masses from above but must think and feel fundamentally and positively at one with the masses and be in the vanguard. It is only then that we shall avoid vulgar epigonism and the falsity that is found in the works of directors who ingratiate themselves with the Soviet audience. These artists get nothing but reproaches from this audience because what they are doing does not pour out of them organically, they are taking over by force an ideology that is alien to them.

The interests of the artist and the masses correspond fundamentally and positively. The culture and merits of the artist *vis-à-vis* the masses must be measured not by his works that are highly cultured but also intelligible to the masses, but by the works through which he has helped to raise the cultural level of the masses. *Every film must be useful, intelligible and familiar to the millions – otherwise neither it nor the artist who made it are worth twopence.*

We are surrounded by such obscenity, such dirt, poverty, coarseness and thickheadedness. People are looking for a place to rest from this vile filth. They are running away from life. Divorcing themselves from it. But we artists must not be advocates of the doctrine of 'art for art's sake'. No. With the help of art that is not divorced from the masses we shall fight all the base aspects of life so that not only art but life itself shall become beautiful.

(Richard Taylor (ed. and trans.) *The Film Factory: Russian and Soviet Cinema in Documents 1896–1939*, co-edited and intro. by Ian Christie, London, Routledge and Kegan Paul, 1988, pp. 259, 261–2)

I.17   Adolf Hitler, speech from the 'Twilight Rally' sequence of *Triumph of the Will* (1935)

A year ago we first met on this ground in response to the first general call from the Political Executive of the National Socialist Party. Two hundred thousand men are gathered here who have come following no other command but that of their hearts and their loyalty. It was the great need of our people which moved us, united us in battle and helped us grow to maturity through our struggles. Those countries whose people have not suffered the same misery cannot hope to understand. To them what links hundreds of thousands together and makes them endure misery, suffering and hardship seems strange and mysterious. They cannot conceive of such concord without a compulsory state command. They are mistaken. It is not the State that commands us, but we who command the State. The State did not create us, rather we created the State. No, the Movement lives and stands securely founded on rock. And as long as one of us can still breathe, he will continue to further the cause and uphold it. Then, as in years gone by, drum will answer drum and flag join flag, groups and communities will come together until finally the mighty column of the united Nation, the people once so divided, will follow on behind.

To let slip what was so hard fought for with so much sorrow, so much sacrifice and so much misery, would be sacrilege. One cannot betray a lifetime's work and ideals. It would be unthinkable if there was no divine purpose behind all this and indeed our commands come from no earthly leader but from the Lord who has created our nation. Let us therefore dedicate ourselves this evening, every hour and every day, to think only of Germany – of the people and the State – of our German people, our German State. *Sieg heil! Sieg heil! Sieg heil!*

(translation provided by the Imperial War Museum)

I.18   John Reith, 'The best of everything' (1924)

The policy of the Company being to bring the best of everything into the greatest number of homes, it follows that if this policy be carried out, that many educative influences must have been stirred.

It was early realized that there were very great educational possibilities in broadcasting. It was also realized that in this direction it was advisable to proceed with caution. Entertainment was the stated function of the Company, and many apparently considered that all its operations and the whole of the time available should be confined to purposes of entertainment alone. I have endeavoured to indicate how narrow a conception this is; in fact it is impossible of execution. It is impossible to occupy all the available hours in transmissions which would normally be described as of an entertaining nature. Entertainment, pure and simple, quickly grows tame; dissatisfaction and boredom result. If hours are to be occupied agreeably, it would be a sad reflection on human intelligence if it were contended that entertainment, in the accepted sense of the term, was the only means for doing so. The suspicious and the hesitant have, however, to be dealt with gently. Short lectures were introduced, lectures intended to cover a wide range of subjects of general interest, delivered in a popular manner. In certain quarters these were hailed as the most interesting part of the programme. No doubt mistakes were made. Subjects were not always of sufficient interest; the lecturers were not always sufficiently attractive. As time went on efforts were made to co-ordinate these talks, and to arrange them on some sort of systematic basis. Greater attention is now being paid to the choice of subject and speaker.

Already series of talks have been given on various subjects, and this idea will be developed in so far as it is found practicable or acceptable. It will be necessary to decide whether a speaker or a subject is of interest enough to warrant being broadcast simultaneously all over the country. It may be that one lecturer may be heard by several stations, and another lecturer on the same subject by the remainder. It is our object that there should be a recognition of the local standing of suggested speakers, but that there should also be taken into account the status of the lecturer from a national point of view. A man should be of pre-eminent and recognized position if he is to speak to the whole country, outweighing the advantages of local authorities on the same subject. There are many who would prefer to hear a professor from their nearest University, or a local man of affairs, rather than a man of greater status from any other town; and so the relative merits have to be assessed.

(John Reith, *Broadcast over Britain*, reprinted in A. Smith (ed.) *British Broadcasting*, Newton Abbott, David and Charles, 1974, pp. 44–5)

I.19 John Reith, on the BBC's coverage of the General Strike, May 1926 (15 May 1926)

The responsibility of keeping the country in touch with the progress of events, as practically the sole means of general communication, was an onerous one, and that it has been discharged with almost no error of judgement or failure of any kind is, in view of the multiplicity of interests and the extent of the operations, a conclusive achievement in itself. I feel that some explanation is due to the staff with regard to our position during the Emergency. Under the Emergency Regulations, the Government would have been within its powers if it had taken over our organization literally, making Broadcasting an official medium comparable with the Government newspaper. There were indeed considerable efforts from some quarters to have this done. I felt it would be unfortunate from every point of view, the Government's, the country's and our own. By the terms of our Licence, even apart from Emergency Regulations, we were bound to broadcast official announcements, but, largely due to the sympathetic and enlightened attitude adopted throughout by the Deputy

Chief Civil Commissioner, Mr J. C. C. Davidson, in charge of official news, the BBC was not definitely commandeered. We were given direct access to all official news, allowed to exercise editorial discretion with regard to it, and were also permitted to preserve, apart from this, an appreciable degree of impartiality in the broadcasting of general news. I may say that the Prime Minister and the Home Secretary in particular approved of our being left with a considerable measure of independence. This indicated a gratifying trust in the Company's loyalty and judgement.

There could be no question about our supporting the Government in general, particularly since the General Strike had been declared illegal in the High Court. This being so, we were unable to permit anything which was contrary to the spirit of that judgement, and which might have prolonged or sought to justify the Strike. The broadcasting of official communiqués issued by the Government would have been expected and demanded irrespective of its political complexion. But as it was we were able to give listeners authentic impartial news of the situation to the best of our ability.

The arguments used against definite commandeering included the following: that we had secured and held the goodwill and even affection of the people; that we had been trusted to do the right thing at all times; that we were a national institution and a national asset; that if commandeered or unduly hampered or manipulated the immediate purpose of such action would not only have been unserved but actually prejudiced; that it was not a time for dope, even if people could have been doped; that those hostile to the Government would only have been more hostile; that if we had suppressed news of any unfortunate situation arising, it might only have led to the panic of ignorance, which is more dangerous than a knowledge of facts. But, on the other hand, since the BBC was a national institution, and since the Government in this crisis were acting for the people, apart from any Emergency powers or clause in our Licence, the BBC was for the Government in the crisis too: and that we had to assist in maintaining the essential services of the country, the preservation of law and order, and of the life and liberty of the individual and of the community.

It was unfortunate that we were unable to define our position. The matter was discussed several times at Cabinet meetings, but embarrassing as the situation was, it was less undesirable than a definite commandeering. Had we been commandeered we could have done nothing in the nature of impartial news, nor could we have in any way helped inspire appreciation of the fact that a prolongation of the stoppage was a sure means of reducing the standard of living, which it was the avowed intention of the Trade Unions to improve. Nor could we have initiated or emphasized statements likely to counteract a spirit of violence and hostility. We felt we might contribute, perhaps decisively, to the attitude of understanding without which goodwill could not be restored.

It was urged therefore as cardinally important even during the crisis, to maintain the BBC tradition and preserve its prestige, and as for the future when the trouble was over, that it would be a calamity if public confidence in the BBC had been dissipated through actions, negative or positive, during the Emergency. Its pioneer work for nearly four years might have been undermined and its great influence shaken.

From the above you will realize that the position was one of extreme delicacy and embarrassment throughout. It was impossible to give the lead which we should have liked, but it is a satisfaction to find an almost universal appreciation and recognition of the services rendered, and it may be only ourselves who feel that we might have done more with a freer hand.

The only definite complaint may be that we had no speaker from the Labour side. We asked to be allowed to do so, but the decision eventually was that since the Strike had been declared illegal this could not be allowed.

This is a highly confidential document, but I shall be glad if you will read the contents or such part of them as you consider necessary or advisable, to those under you.

(John Reith, confidential memorandum to senior BBC staff, 15 May 1926, reprinted in A. Briggs, *The Birth of Broadcasting*, London, Oxford University Press, 1961, pp. 364–6)

I.20 Parliamentary discussion on censorship and restriction of liberty (7 Dec. 1938)

Mr Mander: . . . I now pass to the subject of news reels. This is a very important new medium. There do not exist with regard to it the same traditions as those which have been established with regard to the Press over a long period of years in this country. Some of those responsible for news reels try to realize their usefulness as a very important organ of information. Others are not so careful about that side of it, and are perhaps interested more in the purely commercial side. There is no doubt that the difficulties with regard to alleged censorship which exists here are not altogether, but very largely, the fault of the cinema people and the exhibitors themselves. If they would only show a little more courage, if they would only stand up and say, 'We are not going to be interfered with by the Board of Censors on political matters', they have, to a large extent, got the matter in their own hands. I hope that in future they will take a firmer line when any attempts are made to interfere with them. But I do assert that there is, in connection with the news reels, a definite political censorship which is hostile to the Opposition and friendly to the Government. I do not necessarily say that the Government themselves are directly influencing it, but I say that such a thing exists and that there is no question about it.

There is, of course, the British Board of Film Censors of which Lord Tyrrell is the chairman and Mr Brooke Wilkinson secretary. It is an unofficial body, and it is extremely convenient that that should be so, because, of course, the Government can say, 'They have nothing to do with us; they can do anything they like.' But that does not prevent useful contacts being established with the Government all the same. This Board of Film Censors is supposed to deal with questions of morals only, but on many occasions there has been political action. Before I proceed to give examples of that I would like to make a brief reference to a new type of film which is coming into use, what is called the 'non-flam' film. These films are outside the Act and can be shown in any hall in the country. There is great anxiety among those connected with them lest an attempt should be made to impose some sort of control or censorship upon them, and it would be a great relief to many of them if the Home Secretary were able to say tonight that it was not the desire of the Government that they should be interfered with or controlled in any way, and that they would be allowed to carry on in accordance with the law, without any form of censorship, unofficial or otherwise, such as they fear is contemplated at the moment. I hope this fear can be shown to be groundless.

I pass to a brief reference to a case mentioned in the newspapers yesterday of the filming of scenes of the *Relief of Lucknow*. According to the information in the Press generally, the producers of the film were informed by the Board of Censors that owing to the official attitude there would be no hope of a certificate for it, and that it was being banned on the intervention of the India Office. I do not know anything more than that statement in the Press, but, no doubt, the Home Secretary will be able to deal with that point. It may be a good thing that this film should not be made. I do not know enough about it to express an opinion, but if that is so, let us be told, publicly and openly, that the Government have intervened and think it desirable that the film should not be made, rather than that there should be any suggestion that it is only an unofficial body which has intervened. If there is a proper censorship, let us know about it. Do not let us hide behind the pretence that such a thing as a censorship does not exist.

The first case of political censorship to which I would refer was in reference to the Peace Film which was got up in 1936 by some people associated with the League of Nations Union to put forward a point of view in which at one time the Home Secretary himself was very much interested. It was held up by the British Board of Film Censors as controversial. As a result of Press exposure, it was widely shown throughout the country. Then there was the case of one of the *March of Time* films called *Arms and the League*. This took place at the time of the resignation of the late Foreign Secretary, and the film was not shown after the Board of Censors had expressed their view. Then there was another *March of Time* film called *Threat to Gibraltar* showing the threatened grip by the Fascists on the Mediterranean, owing to the situation in Spain. That, again, was banned owing to the intervention of the Board.

The next one was *Crisis in Algeria*, showing the possibilities of a North

African *coup* by a Fascist state. That again was badly cut. Many other cuts took place in such films as *Inside Nazi Germany*, *Nazi Conquest No. 1 (Austria)*, and *Croix de Feu*. In November 1937 there was a film called *Spanish Earth*, which was cut because it contained the outrageous suggestion that Germany and Italy were intervening in Spain. The most important of the films is *Britain's Dilemma*, which some hon. Members of this House, I know, have seen. It was shown in the United States under that name, and it was very much appreciated, I understand, by everybody. It was based on events in Europe in relation to the policy laid down in *Mein Kampf*. It dealt with the well known events of the retreat from the League, Manchuria, Abyssinia, Spain, China, and it stopped short at Czechoslovakia. Here, after a number of cuts had been made, it was re-titled *Britain and Peace*, but the cuts were made because it was considered dangerous to show in this country what had happened in those instances, in which everybody on this side of the House believed the Government to have been wholly wrong, but apparently it was not desired that more than one point of view should be shown.

Mr Fleming: In all those instances that the hon. Member has mentioned is it the case that the cuts were ordered at the instance of the British Board of Film Censors?

Mr Mander: Yes, that is so. The British Board of Film Censors on one occasion indicated to those who were thinking of making a film that it would not be desirable to show anything of an anti-Fascist nature because it would not be possible to convince the Italian Government that the British Government were not in control of the films here and, therefore, that it was not Government propaganda. That is a very deplorable suggestion. I will ask the House to observe that in all these examples which I have given, in every case where cuts have been made nothing anti-Government, nothing anti-Fascist, is permitted, but anything that is favourable to the policy that the Government are pursuing is allowed to go forward. I venture to say that it is not the job of the British Board of Film Censors to deal with political matters of this kind at all. It is monstrous that they should be permitted to carry on this subtle kind of unofficial political censorship. Who asks them to be political? I do not say by any means that it is always done at the direct instigation of the Government – that is not one of my charges tonight, but I believe that a great deal is done on what they believe would be acceptable or otherwise to the Government, according to their own ideas – but I do believe there is pressure by Government Departments or by their friends at times. It is widely alleged in the Press and elsewhere that the Conservative Central Office is not wholly disinterested in or without knowledge of what is going on.

I may, perhaps, be permitted to quote from a resolution which was sent to me recently, since this Motion was put down, by the News Theatres Association, a body representing from 80 to 90 per cent of the news theatre interests in this country, and the resolution was as follows:

News Theatres in association have instructed me [that is, the Secretary] to say that they would resist by every legitimate means within their power the censorship of the news reel, or other screen news, which some might desire to impose – either officially or unofficially, from outside or inside the industry.

I am desired to place it on record that, should the occasion arise, the members of this association would be more than prepared to join forces with the public, the industry, the Press, and others concerned to preserve the complete liberty of the 'Screen Press'.

I suggest that the Home Secretary could render a very great service in connection with this whole matter if he was able to say in his speech tonight that, so far as the Government are concerned, they do not wish to exercise any influence whatsoever on the British Board of Film Censors, that that board must be guided wholly by its duty of censorship on moral grounds, that if on any occasion the Government do feel called upon to intervene, they will openly say so, but that otherwise it must be clearly understood that the Government are not interested. I seriously appeal to the Home Secretary to make such a statement tonight, if he feels able to do so, because I am sure that it would clear up a great deal of apprehension and misunderstanding that certainly exist now.

I now come to the last but most interesting case. During the crisis four out of the five news reel theatres played down the Czechoslovakian point of view, but Paramount gave it space and gave a number of pictures of happy life in Czechoslovakia. One hon. Member of this House told me that he had seen it and that he had immediately notified his friends and had urged them to see it, because, he said, 'I do not suppose this will be tolerated for very long.' It was not tolerated for more than one day. In order to give the point of view of Czechoslovakia – because, after all, I suppose the people of this country have some right to hear that side – Paramount invited Mr Wickham Steed and Mr A. J. Cummings to speak during the reel. The film was issued on the evening of 21st September, and it was withdrawn on 22nd September. A telegram was sent by British Paramount News to all its theatres, saying:

Please delete Wickham Steed and A. J. Cummings' speeches from to-day's Paramount news. We have been officially requested to do so.

Later on they denied that they had been officially requested to do so and said they had done it at their own discretion, but, unfortunately for them, the Chancellor of the Exchequer had given the whole show away, and I would remind the House of what took place. I asked the Prime Minister on 23rd November:

Why representations were recently made by His Majesty's Government to the American Embassy for the withdrawal from a Paramount news reel of items contributed by Mr Wickham Steed and Mr A. J. Cummings?

Sir J. SIMON: His Majesty's Government considered that certain passages in the news reel referred to, which was being shown at the time of the Prime Minister's conversations with Herr Hitler at Godesberg, might have a prejudicial effect upon the negotiations. The Ambassador of the United States, I understand, thought it right to communicate this consideration to a member of the Hays organisation which customarily deals with matters of this kind and which brought it to the attention of Paramount News, who, from a sense of public duty in the general interest, decided to make certain excisions from the news reel.

He was asked various other questions, but the only relevant reply was:

I do not know of the other cases, but in the present case His Majesty's Government are grateful to the Ambassador of the United States, and I am glad that the Ambassador and ourselves were in complete accord. [OFFICIAL REPORT, 23rd November, 1938; cols. 1727–8; Vol. 341.]

It is very interesting to find such an accommodating Ambassador – very remarkable. The matter was raised again by me later, and the Prime Minister then gave the impression to the House that no such incident had ever taken place. He said, however, at the third time of asking:

The attention of the American Ambassador was drawn to certain items, and he was asked to look into the matter. [OFFICIAL REPORT, 1st December, 1938; col. 584, Vol. 342.]

There you get a perfectly clear and open case of political censorship by the Government of the day in the interests of the foreign policy that they were pursuing, and it was a foreign policy which was detested by probably half the nation. It is not as if you were dealing with a case where you had national unity and 95 per cent of the people thinking one thing. That would have been very different. [HON. MEMBERS: 'Why?'] If hon. Members say 'Why?' I will agree that it is not desirable to have any censorship at all, under any circumstances, but I submit that you must have a sense of proportion. If they wish no censorship at all, I am fully in agreement with them.

What were the words that were withdrawn? What was it that was said by these two gentlemen? I will tell the House. In the course of an objective narrative of events Paramount introduced Mr Wickham Steed as a former editor of the *Times* and a friend of President Masaryk. We know that he is one of the most distinguished journalists in the world today. He then introduced Mr Cummings in the following terms:

British Paramount News, seeking still further independent and informed opinion, interviewed the famous foreign affairs journalist, Mr A. J. Cummings; and for the man-in-the-street's viewpoint sought the popular broadcasting taxi-driver, Mr Herbert Hodge.

That is what Mr Wickham Steed said:

Has England surrendered? Who is 'England'? – the Government or Parliament or the people? The British Parliament has not surrendered for it has not been convened, and still less have the British people. Our Government, together with that of France, is trying to make a present to Hitler – for use against us when he may think the time has come – of the 3,000,000 men and the thousands of aeroplanes that he would need to overcome Czechoslovak resistance. Hitler does not want to fight – oh, no! He only wants to get without fighting more than he would be able to get by fighting. And we seem to be helping him to get it. And all this because British and French Ministers feared to take a risk when they could have taken it successfully and believed they could diminish the risk by helping Hitler to gain a triumph – when he was at his wit's end – instead of standing up to him.

I turn to Herbert Hodge and A. J. Cummings, and the dialogue went in this way:

HODGE: Well, Mr Cummings, what do you think of the news? Everybody's saying to me that England has surrendered to Hitler. Do you think that's right?

CUMMINGS: Well, beyond a doubt, Hitler has won an overwhelming diplomatic triumph for German domination in Europe. Nothing in future will stop him but a mass war.

HODGE: I think most of us, although we want peace with all our hearts, would be prepared to go to war if it was a case of either going to war or allowing Hitler to dominate Europe.

I thought that was the policy of the Government. The dialogue continues:

CUMMINGS: The fact is our statesmen have been guilty of what I think is a piece of yellow diplomacy.

Perhaps that is what the Government did not like.

If in good time we had made a joint declaration with France and with Russia making clear our intentions, and stating emphatically and in express terms that we would prevent the invasion of Czechoslovakia, I'm certain that Hitler would not have faced that formidable combination. If we were not prepared to go to the extreme limit we should certainly not have engaged in a game of bluff with the finest poker player in Europe.

HODGE: What worries me about it all, Mr Cummings, is whether we've simply postponed war for another year or two against a much stronger Hitler of the future.

CUMMINGS: I am afraid we've only postponed war; and frankly, I am very fearful about what is yet in store for millions of young men of military age in all the countries of Europe.

I can see nothing improper in these statements. They represented the views of a very large proportion of people in this House and the country, but the Government censored them. They would not allow them to be said. They took every step in their power to prevent the opposition point of view being presented. The other side of it was not interfered with. We could have plenty of pictures of the Prime Minister and we could hear all the 'try, try and try again' slogans, and things of that kind. There was no limit to that, but anything that represented the opposition point of view was not to be allowed to be shown in the cinemas of this country. That was a most improper action by the Government.

I hope that the ventilation of this subject tonight, even if the Government try to make out that a great deal of it is not quite as represented, must do a great deal to stop the growth of censorship, direct or indirect, and to prevent it arising in future. I venture to hope that we shall show, in spite of the spread of dictatorship in so many great countries, that we are still a true democracy, that we are prepared to hear all views and to have every aspect of political matters laid before us, and, to the best of our ability, choose that which we think is wisest. If ever this country were to be gagged and bound and our centuries-long liberties interfered with, we may have peace, but it would not be England. I hope that by passing this

Motion tonight unanimously we shall show we are the freest people in the world.

Mr R. Acland: I beg to second the Motion.

8.32 p.m.

Mr Beechman: I beg to move, in line 5, at the end, to add:

but is fully satisfied that His Majesty's Government have maintained these traditions unimpaired.

(*Hansard*, House of Commons, 7 December 1938, cols 1270–8)

I.21 Extracts from the reply of the Allied and Associated Powers to the Observations of the German Delegation on the Conditions of Peace (16 June 1919)

The Allied and Associated Powers . . . feel it necessary to begin their reply by a clear statement of the judgment passed upon the war by practically the whole of civilized mankind.

In the view of the Allied and Associated Powers the war which began on August 1st, 1914, was the greatest crime against humanity and the freedom of peoples that any nation, calling itself civilized, has ever consciously committed. For many years the rulers of Germany, true to the Prussian tradition, strove for a position of dominance in Europe. They were not satisfied with that growing prosperity and influence to which Germany was entitled, and which all other nations were willing to accord her, in the society of free and equal peoples. They required that they should be able to dictate and tyrannize to a subservient Europe, as they dictated and tyrannized over a subservient Germany.

In order to attain their ends they used every channel in their power through which to educate their own subjects in the doctrine that might was right in international affairs. They never ceased to expand German armaments by land and sea, and to propagate the falsehood that this was necessary because Germany's neighbours were jealous of her prosperity and power. They sought to sow hostility and suspicion instead of friendship between nations. They developed a system of espionage and intrigue which enabled them to stir up internal rebellion and unrest and even to make secret offensive preparations within the territory of their neighbours whereby they might, when the moment came, strike them down with greater certainty and ease. They kept Europe in a ferment by threats of violence and when they found that their neighbours were resolved to resist their arrogant will, they determined to assert their predominance in Europe by force. As soon as their preparations were complete, they encouraged a subservient ally to declare war against Serbia at 48 hours' notice, knowing full well that a conflict involving the control of the Balkans could not be localized and almost certainly meant a general war. In order to make doubly sure, they refused every attempt at conciliation and conference until it was too late, and the world war was inevitable for which they had plotted, and for which alone among the nations they were fully equipped and prepared.

Germany's responsibility, however, is not confined to having planned and started the war. She is no less responsible for the savage and inhuman manner in which it was conducted.

Though Germany was herself a guarantor of Belgium, the rulers of Germany violated, after a solemn promise to respect it, the neutrality of this unoffending people. Not content with this, they deliberately carried out a series of promiscuous shootings and burnings with the sole object of terrifying the inhabitants into submission by the very frightfulness of their action. They were the first to use poisonous gas, notwithstanding the appalling suffering it entailed. They began the bombing and long-distance shelling of towns for no military object, but solely for the purpose of reducing the morale of their opponents by striking at their women and children. They commenced the submarine campaign with its piratical challenge to international law, and its destruction of great numbers of innocent passengers and sailors, in mid ocean, far from succour, at the mercy of the winds and the waves, and the yet more ruthless submarine crews. They drove thousands of men and women and children with brutal savagery into slavery in foreign lands. They allowed barbarities to be practised against their prisoners of war from which the most uncivilized people would have recoiled.

The conduct of Germany is almost unexampled in human history. The terrible responsibility which lies at her doors can be seen in the fact that not less than seven million dead lie buried in Europe, while more than twenty million others carry upon them the evidence of wounds and sufferings, because Germany saw fit to gratify her lust for tyranny by resort to war.

The Allied and Associated Powers believe that they will be false to those who have given their all to save the freedom of the world if they consent to treat this war on any other basis than as a crime against humanity and right. . . .

Justice, therefore, is the only possible basis for the settlement of the accounts of this terrible war. Justice is what the German Delegation asks for and says that Germany had been promised. Justice is what Germany shall have. But it must be justice for all. There must be justice for the dead and wounded and for those who have been orphaned and bereaved that Europe might be freed from Prussian despotism. There must be justice for the peoples who now stagger under war debts which exceed £30,000,000,000 that liberty might be saved. There must be justice for those millions whose homes and land, ships and property German savagery has spoliated and destroyed.

That is why the Allied and Associated Powers have insisted as a cardinal feature of the Treaty that Germany must undertake to make reparation to the very uttermost of her power; for reparation for wrongs inflicted is of the essence of justice. That is why they insist that those individuals who are most clearly responsible for German aggression and for those acts of barbarism and inhumanity which have disgraced the German conduct of the war, must be handed over to a justice which has not been meted out to them at home. That, too, is why Germany must submit for a few years to certain special disabilities and arrangements. Germany has ruined the industries, the mines and the machinery of neighbouring countries, not during battle, but with the deliberate and calculated purpose of enabling her industries to seize their markets before their industries could recover from the devastation thus wantonly inflicted upon them. Germany has despoiled her neighbours of everything she could make use of or carry away. Germany has destroyed the shipping of all nations on the high seas, where there was no chance of rescue for their passengers and crews. It is only justice that restitution should be made and that these wronged peoples should be safeguarded for a time from the competition of a nation whose industries are intact and have even been fortified by machinery stolen from occupied territories. If these things are hardships for Germany, they are hardships which Germany has brought upon herself. Somebody must suffer for the consequences of the war. Is it to be Germany, or only the peoples she has wronged?

Not to do justice to all concerned would only leave the world open to fresh calamities. If the German people themselves, or any other nation, are to be deterred from following the footsteps of Prussia, if mankind is to be lifted out of the belief that war for selfish ends is legitimate to any state, if the old era is to be left behind and nations as well as individuals are to be brought beneath the reign of law, even if there is to be early reconciliation and appeasement, it will be because those responsible for concluding the war have had the courage to see that justice is not deflected for the sake of convenient peace.

It is said that the German Revolution ought to make a difference and that the German people are not responsible for the policy of the rulers whom they have thrown from power.

The Allied and Associated Powers recognize and welcome the change. It represents a great hope for peace, and for a new European order in the future. But it cannot affect the settlement of the war itself. The German Revolution was stayed until the German armies had been defeated in the field, and all hope of profiting by a war of conquest had vanished. Throughout the war, as before the war, the German people and their representatives supported the war, voted the credits, subscribed to the war loans, obeyed every order, however savage, of their government. They shared the responsibility for the policy of their government, for at any moment, had they willed it, they could have reversed it. Had that policy succeeded they would have acclaimed it with the same enthusiasm with which they welcomed the outbreak of the war. They cannot now pretend, having changed their rulers after the war was lost, that it is justice that they should escape the consequences of their deeds.

(*Papers Relating to the Foreign Relations of the United States. The Paris Peace Conference*, vol. XIII, Washington, 1947, pp. 44–9)

I.22   Jan Smuts, letter to Lloyd George (26 March 1919)

. . . I am seriously afraid that the peace to which we are working is an impossible peace, conceived on a wrong basis; that it will not be accepted by Germany, and, even if accepted, that it will prove utterly unstable, and only serve to promote the anarchy which is rapidly overtaking Europe. . . .

To my mind certain points seem quite clear and elementary:
1. We cannot destroy Germany without destroying Europe;
2. We cannot save Europe without the co-operation of Germany.

Yet we are now preparing a peace which must destroy Germany, and yet we think we shall save Europe by so doing! The fact is, the Germans are, have been, and will continue to be, the *dominant factor* on the Continent of Europe, and no permanent peace is possible which is not based on that fact. The statesmen of the Vienna Congress were wiser in their generation; they looked upon France as necessary to Europe. And yet we presume to look down upon them and their work! My fear is that the Paris Conference may prove one of the historic failures of the world; that the statesmen connected with it will return to their countries broken, discredited men, and that the Bolshevists will reap where they have sown. . . .

Take again the territorial terms we are preparing. I note that Danzig, an ancient German town with a German population, has to be handed over to Poland together with some millions of Germans, some of them in solid blocks of old Prussian territory. It is rumoured that in addition to Alsace-Lorraine the Saar Valley is also going to France; and that Germany is to be further dismembered by the constitution of a separate state west of the Rhine. I am simply amazed at all this. Are we in our sober senses, or suffering from shell-shock? What has become of Wilson's Fourteen Points, or of your repeated declarations against the humiliation and dismemberment of Germany? I note the stand you have made against some of these things; but that is not enough. We shall be judged, not by our protests, but by our acts.

All these territorial arrangements I look upon as most dangerous, and indeed fatal from the point of view of securing present and future peace. If the Germans are like the rest of us they simply will not accept such terms, and will throw back on their despoilers the responsibility for the resulting chaos. And for the future there is the legacy of revenge.

The fact is, neither Poland nor Bohemia will be politically possible without German goodwill and assistance. They ought to be established on a basis which will secure German co-operation in their future success; and Germany ought to undertake definite liabilities in the peace treaty to assist and protect them militarily and otherwise against Russia and Hungary and against each other. Instead of dismembering and destroying Germany, she ought in a measure to be taken into the scope of our policy, and be made responsible for part of the burden which is clearly too heavy for us to bear. Are we going to defend Poland and Bohemia as we have defended the Ukraine against the Bolshevists? If it is necessary for Germany to be made to bear her share of the heavy burden of the new Europe, she ought not to be despoiled and treated as an international pariah, but rather to be taken in hand by the Allies and helped to her feet again. Unless this is done, I fear we are ploughing the sands of the sea at this Conference. Without German goodwill, neither Poland nor Bohemia will show any stable vitality, and they will become simply problems and burdens for the future politics of Europe. . . .

My view is that, in trying to break Germany in order to create and territorially satisfy these smaller States, we are labouring at a task which is bound to fail. We shall get no peace treaty now, and Europe will know no peace hereafter. And in the coming storms these new States will themselves be the first to founder. It is not through breaking Germany that we shall save them; but, on the contrary, they can only be saved by Germany sharing with us the responsibility for their defence and maintenance. But in that case, Poland will have to be satisfied with rights of way to the Baltic, instead of annexing German territory.

I do not know how it stands with the two important questions of punishment for war crimes and exaction of reparations. Here too, however, I would look at the matter from a large point of view, and not ask the impossible. In particular a large indemnity should only be asked on our promise to supply raw materials to re-start German industry. While such a promise would probably induce Germany to accept the liability to pay a very large sum, payment could only be made if German industry is put in a position to supply the goods.

To conclude: even at this late hour I would urge that we revise our attitude towards Germany, and, while making her pay heavily, and also making her undertake burdens for the defence and assistance of Central Europe which we have neither the men nor the means to undertake ourselves, treat her in a different spirit from that in which our proposals have so far been framed; avoid all appearance of dismembering her or subjecting her to indefinite economic servitude and pauperism, and make her join the League of Nations from the beginning. Her complete economic exhaustion and disarmament would prevent her from becoming a military or naval danger in this generation, and her appeasement now may have the effect of turning her into a bulwark against the oncoming Bolshevism of Eastern Europe. My experience in South Africa has made me a firm believer in political magnanimity, and your and Campbell-Bannerman's great record still remains not only the noblest, but also the *most successful*, page in recent British statesmanship. On the other hand, I fear, I greatly fear our present panic policy towards Germany will bring failure on this Conference, and spell ruin for Europe. Yours very sincerely,

s. J. C. Smuts

(W. K. Hancock and J. van der Poel (eds) *Selections from the Smuts Papers*, Cambridge University Press, 1966, pp. 83–7)

I.23   Adolf Hitler, extracts from *Mein Kampf* (1925)

Extract (a)

In 1919, when the Peace Treaty was imposed on the German nation, there were grounds for hoping that this instrument of unrestricted oppression would help to reinforce the outcry for the freedom of Germany. Peace treaties which make demands that fall like a whiplash on the people turn out not infrequently to be the signal of a future revival.

To what purpose could the Treaty of Versailles have been exploited?

In the hands of a willing Government, how could this instrument of unlimited blackmail and shameful humiliation have been applied for the purpose of arousing national sentiment to its highest pitch? How could a well-directed system of propaganda have utilized the sadist cruelty of that treaty so as to change the indifference of the people to a feeling of indignation and transform that indignation into a spirit of dauntless resistance?

Each point of that Treaty could have been engraved on the minds and hearts of the German people and burned into them, until sixty million men and women would find their souls aflame with a feeling of rage and shame; and a torrent of fire would burst forth as from a furnace, and one common will would be forged from it, like a sword of steel. Then the people would join in the common cry: 'To arms again!'

Yes. A treaty of that kind can be used for such a purpose. Its unbounded oppression and its impudent demands were an excellent propaganda weapon to arouse the sluggish spirit of the nation and restore its vitality.

Then, from the child's story-book to the last newspaper in the country, and every theatre and cinema, every pillar where placards are posted and every free space on the hoardings should be utilized in the service of this one great mission, until the faint-hearted cry, 'Lord, deliver us', which our patriotic associations send up to Heaven today would be transformed into an ardent prayer: 'Almighty God, bless our arms when the hour comes. Be just, as Thou has always been just. Judge now if we deserve our freedom. Lord, bless our struggle.'

All opportunities were neglected and nothing was done.

Who will be surprised now if our people are not such as they should be or might be? The rest of the world looks upon us only as its valet, or as a kindly dog that will lick its master's hand after he has been whipped.

Of course the possibilities of forming alliances with other nations are hampered by the indifference of our own people but much more by our Governments. They have been, and are, so corrupt that now, after eight years of indescribable oppression, there exists only a faint desire for liberty.

In order that our nation may undertake a policy of alliances, it must restore its prestige among other nations, and it must have an authoritative Government that is not a drudge in the service of foreign states and the taskmaster of its own people, but rather the herald of the national will.

If our people had a Government which would look upon this as its mission, six years would not have passed before a courageous foreign policy on the part of the *Reich* would find a corresponding support among the people, whose desire for freedom would be encouraged and intensified thereby.

Extract (b)

I shall briefly deal with the question of how far our territorial aims are justified according to ethical and moral principles. This is all the more necessary here because in our so-called nationalist circles there are all kinds of plausible phrase-mongers who try to persuade the German people that the great aim of their foreign policy ought to be to right the wrongs of 1918, while at the same time they consider it incumbent on them to assure the whole world of the brotherly spirit and sympathy of the German people towards all other nations.

In regard to this point I should like to make the following statement: To demand that the 1914 frontiers should be restored is a glaring political absurdity that is fraught with such consequences as to make the claim itself appear criminal. The confines of the *Reich* as they existed in 1914 were thoroughly illogical; because they were not really complete, in the sense of including all the members of the German nation. Nor were they reasonable, in view of the geographical exigencies of military defence. They were not the consequence of a political plan which had been well considered and carried out. But they were temporary frontiers established in virtue of a political struggle that had not been brought to a finish; and indeed they were partly the chance result of circumstances.

One would have just as good a right, and in many cases a better right, to choose some other oustanding year than 1914 in the course of our history and demand that the objective of our foreign policy should be the re-establishment of the conditions then existing. . . .

If we are once convinced that the future of Germany calls for the sacrifice, in one way or another, of all that we have and are then we must set aside considerations of political prudence and devote ourselves wholly to the struggle for a future that will be worthy of our country.

For the future of the German nation the 1914 frontiers are of no significance. They did not serve to protect us in the past, nor do they offer any guarantee for our defence in the future. With these frontiers the German people cannot maintain themselves as a compact unit, nor can they be assured of their maintenance. From the military viewpoint these frontiers are not advantageous or even such as not to cause anxiety. And while we are bound to such frontiers it will not be possible for us to improve our present positions in relation to the other World Powers, or rather in relation to the real World Powers. We shall not lessen the discrepancy between our territory and that of Great Britain, nor shall we reach the magnitude of the United States of America. Not only that, but we cannot substantially lessen the importance of France in international politics.

One thing alone is certain: The attempt to restore the frontiers of 1914, even if it turned out successful, would demand so much bloodshed on the part of our people that no future sacrifice would be possible to carry out effectively such measures as would be necessary to assure the future existence of the nation. On the contrary, under the intoxication of such a superficial success further aims would be renounced, all the more so because the so-called 'national honour' would seem to be revindicated and new ports would be opened, at least for a certain time, to our commercial development.

Against all this we National Socialists must stick firmly to the aim that we have set for our foreign policy; namely, that the German people must be assured the territorial area which is necessary for it to exist on this earth. And only for such action as is undertaken to secure those ends can it be lawful in the eyes of God and our German posterity to allow the blood of our people to be shed once again. . . .

The German frontiers are the outcome of chance and are only temporary frontiers that have been established as the result of political struggles which took place at various times.

The same is also true of the frontiers which demarcate the territories on which other nations live. And just as only an imbecile could look on the physical geography of the globe as fixed and unchangeable – for in reality it represents a definite stage in a given evolutionary epoch which is due to the formidable forces of nature and may be altered tomorrow by more powerful forces of destruction and change – so, too, in the lives of the nations the confines which are necessary for their sustenance are subject to change.

State frontiers are established by human beings and may be changed by human beings.

The fact that a nation has acquired an enormous territorial area is no reason why it should hold that territory perpetually. At most, the possession of such territory is a proof of the strength of the conqueror and the weakness of those who submit to him. And in this strength alone lives the right of possession.

If the German people are imprisoned within an impossible territorial area and for that reason are face to face with a miserable future, this is not by the command of Destiny and the refusal to accept such a situation is by no means a violation of Destiny's laws. For just as no Higher Power has promised more territory to other nations than to the German, so it cannot be blamed for an unjust distribution of the soil. The soil on which we now live was not a gift bestowed by Heaven on our forefathers. But they had to conquer it by risking their lives. So also in the future our people will not obtain territory, and therewith the means of existence, as a favour from any other people, but will have to win it by the power of a triumphant sword.

Today we are all convinced of the necessity of regulating our situation in regard to France; but our success here will be ineffective in its broad results if the general aims of our foreign policy will have to stop at that. It can have significance for us only if it serves to cover our flank in the struggle for that extension of territory which is necessary for the existence of our people in Europe. For colonial acquisitions will not solve that question. It can be solved only by the winning of such territory for the settlement of our people as will extend the area of the Motherland and thereby will not only keep the new settlers in the closest communion with the land of their origin but will guarantee to this territorial ensemble the advantages which arise from the fact that in their expansion over greater territory the people remain united as a political unit.

The Nationalist Movement must not be the advocate for other nations, but the protagonist for its own nation. Otherwise it would be something superfluous and, above all, it would have no right to clamour against the action of the past; for then it would be repeating the action of the past. The old German policy suffered from the mistake of having been determined by dynastic considerations. The new German policy must not follow the sentimentality of cosmopolitan patriotism. Above all, we must not form a police guard for the famous 'poor small nations'; but we must be the soldiers of the German nation.

We National Socialists have to go still further. The right to territory may become a duty when a great nation seems destined to go under unless its territory be extended. And that is particularly true when the nation in question is not some little group of negro people but the Germanic mother of all the life which has given cultural shape to the modern world. Germany will either become a World Power or will not continue to exist at all. But in order to become a World Power it needs that territorial magnitude which gives it the necessary importance today and assures the existence of its citizens.

Therefore we National Socialists have purposely drawn a line through the line of conduct followed by pre-war Germany in foreign policy. We put an end to the perpetual Germanic march towards the South and West of Europe and turn our eyes towards the lands of the East. We finally put a stop to the colonial and trade policy of pre-war times and pass over to the territorial policy of the future.

But when we speak of new territory in Europe today we must principally think of Russia and the border States subject to her.

(Adolf Hitler, *Mein Kampf*, trans. J. Murphy, London, Hurst and Blackett, 1939, pp. 514–16, 528–33)

I.24   Extracts from the Hossbach Memorandum (Nov. 1937)

MINUTES OF THE CONFERENCE IN THE REICH CHANCELLERY, BERLIN, NOVEMBER 5, 1937, FROM 4:15 to 8:30 P.M.
Present: The Führer and Chancellor,
    Field Marshal von Blomberg, War Minister,
    Colonel General Baron von Fritsch, Commander in Chief, Army,
    Admiral Dr. h. c. Raeder, Commander in Chief, Navy,
    Colonel General Goering, Commander in Chief, *Luftwaffe*,
    Baron von Neurath, Foreign Minister,
    Colonel Hossbach.

The Führer began by stating that the subject of the present conference was of such importance that its discussion would, in other countries, certainly be a matter for a full Cabinet meeting, but he – the Führer – had rejected the idea of making it a subject of discussion before the wider circle of the *Reich* Cabinet just because of the importance of the matter. His exposition to follow was the fruit of thorough deliberation and the experiences of his 4½ years of power. He wished to explain to the gentlemen present his basic ideas concerning the opportunities for the development of our position in the field of foreign affairs and its requirements, and he asked, in the interests of a long-term German policy, that his exposition be regarded, in the event of his death, as his last will and testament.

The Führer then continued:

The aim of German policy was to make secure and to preserve the racial community [*Volksmasse*] and to enlarge it. It was therefore a question of space. . . .

German policy had to reckon with two hate-inspired antagonists, Britain and France, to whom a German colossus in the centre of Europe was a thorn in the flesh, and both countries were opposed to any further strengthening of Germany's position either in Europe or overseas; in support of this opposition they were able to count on the agreement of all their political parties. Both countries saw in the establishment of German military bases overseas a threat to their own communications, a safe-guarding of German commerce, and, as a consequence, a strengthening of Germany's position in Europe. . . .

Germany's problem could only be solved by means of force and this was never without attendant risk. The campaigns of Frederick the Great for Silesia and Bismarck's wars against Austria and France had involved unheard-of risk, and the swiftness of the Prussian action in 1870 had kept

Austria from entering the war. If one accepts as the basis of the following exposition the resort to force with its attendant risks, then there remain still to be answered the questions 'when' and 'how'. In this matter there were three cases [*Fälle*] to be dealt with:

Case 1: Period 1943–1945: after this date only a change for the worse, from our point of view, could be expected.

The equipment of the army, navy, and *Luftwaffe*, as well as the formation of the officer corps, was nearly completed. Equipment and armament were modern; in further delay there lay the danger of their obsolescence. In particular, the secrecy of 'special weapons' could not be preserved forever. The recruiting of reserves was limited to current age groups; further drafts from older untrained age groups were no longer available.

Our relative strength would decrease in relation to the rearmament which would by then have been carried out by the rest of the world. If we did not act by 1943–45, any year could, in consequence of a lack of reserves, produce the food crisis, to cope with which the necessary foreign exchange was not available, and this must be regarded as a 'waning point of the regime'. Besides, the world was expecting our attack and was increasing its counter-measures from year to year. It was while the rest of the world was still preparing its defences [*sich abriegele*] that we were obliged to take the offensive.

Nobody knew today what the situation would be in the years 1943–45. One thing only was certain, that we could not wait longer.

On the one hand there was the great *Wehrmacht*, and the necessity of maintaining it at its present level, the ageing of the movement and of its leaders; and on the other, the prospect of a lowering of the standard of living and of a limitation of the birth rate, which left no choice but to act. If the Führer was still living, it was his unalterable resolve to solve Germany's problem of space at the latest by 1943–45. The necessity for action before 1943–45 would arise in cases 2 and 3.

Case 2: If internal strife in France should develop into such a domestic crisis as to absorb the French Army completely and render it incapable of use for war against Germany, then the time for action against the Czechs had come.

Case 3: If France is so embroiled by a war with another state that she cannot 'proceed' against Germany.

For the improvement of our politico-military position our first objective, in the event of our being embroiled in war, must be to overthrow Czechoslovakia and Austria simultaneously in order to remove the threat to our flank in any possible operation against the West. In a conflict with France it was hardly to be regarded as likely that the Czechs would declare war on us on the very same day as France. The desire to join in the war would, however, increase among the Czechs in proportion to any weakening on our part and then her participation could clearly take the form of an attack towards Silesia, towards the north or towards the west.

If the Czechs were overthrown and a common German–Hungarian frontier achieved, a neutral attitude on the part of Poland could be the more certainly counted on in the event of a Franco-German conflict. Our agreements with Poland only retained their force as long as Germany's strength remained unshaken. In the event of German set-backs a Polish action against East Prussia, and possibly against Pomerania and Silesia as well, had to be reckoned with.

On the assumption of a development of the situation leading to action on our part as planned, in the years 1943–45, the attitude of France, Britain, Italy, Poland, and Russia could probably be estimated as follows:

Actually, the Führer believed that almost certainly Britain, and probably France as well, had already tacitly written off the Czechs and were reconciled to the fact that this question would be cleared up in due course by Germany. Difficulties connected with the Empire, and the prospect of being once more entangled in a protracted European war, were decisive considerations for Britain against participation in a war against Germany. Britain's attitude would certainly not be without influence on that of France. An attack by France without British support, and with the prospect of the offensive being brought to a standstill on our western fortifications, was hardly probable. Nor was a French march through Belgium and Holland without British support to be expected; this also was a course not to be contemplated by us in the event of a conflict with France, because it would certainly entail the hostility of Britain. It would of course be necessary to maintain a strong defence [eine Abriegelung] on our western frontier during the prosecution of our attack on the Czechs and Austria. And in this connection it had to be remembered that the defence measures of the Czechs were growing in strength from year to year, and that the actual worth of the Austrian Army also was increasing in the course of time. Even though the populations concerned, especially of Czechoslovakia, were not sparse, the annexation of Czechoslovakia and Austria would mean an acquisition of foodstuffs for 5 to 6 million people, on the assumption that the compulsory emigration of 2 million people from Czechoslovakia and 1 million people from Austria was practicable. The incorporation of these two States with Germany meant, from the politico-military point of view, a substantial advantage because it would mean shorter and better frontiers, the freeing of forces for other purposes, and the possibility of creating new units up to a level of about 12 divisions, that is, 1 new division per million inhabitants.

Italy was not expected to object to the elimination of the Czechs, but it was impossible at the moment to estimate what her attitude on the Austrian question would be; that depended essentially upon whether the Duce were still alive.

The degree of surprise and the swiftness of our action were decisive factors for Poland's attitude. Poland – with Russia at her rear – will have little inclination to engage in war against a victorious Germany.

Military intervention by Russia must be countered by the swiftness of our operations; however, whether such an intervention was a practical contingency at all was, in view of Japan's attitude, more than doubtful.

Should case 2 arise – the crippling of France by civil war – the situation thus created by the elimination of the most dangerous opponent must be seized upon *whenever it occurs* for the blow against the Czechs.

The Führer saw case 3 coming definitely nearer; it might emerge from the present tensions in the Mediterranean, and he was resolved to take advantage of it whenever it happened, even as early as 1938. . . .

If Germany made use of this war to settle the Czech and Austrian questions, it was to be assumed that Britain – herself at war with Italy – would decide not to act against Germany. Without British support, a warlike action by France against Germany was not to be expected.

(*Documents on German Foreign Policy, 1918–1945*, series D, vol. 1, London, HMSO, 1949, pp. 29–30)

I.25   Adolf Hitler, speech to the *Reichstag* (7 March 1936)

In order to prevent any doubt as to their intentions, and to make clear the purely defensive character of this measure, as well as to give expression to their lasting desire for the true pacification of Europe between nations of equal rights and mutual respect, the German Government declare themselves prepared to negotiate immediately new agreements for the establishment of a system of European security on the basis of the following proposals:

1. The German Government declare themselves prepared to negotiate with France and Belgium for the establishment of a bilateral demilitarized zone and to assent to other proposals with regard to the extent and effects of such a zone, under the stipulation of complete parity.

2. In order to assure the inviolability and integrity of the frontiers in the West, the German Government propose the conclusion of a non-aggression pact between Germany, France and Belgium with duration which they are prepared to fix at 25 years.

3. The German Government desire to invite England and Italy to sign this treaty as guarantor Powers.

4. The German Government are willing to include the Government of the Netherlands in this treaty system should the Government of the Netherlands desire it, and the other treaty partners approve.

5. For the further strengthening of these security arrangements between the Western Powers, the German Government are prepared to conclude an air pact which shall be designed automatically and effectively to prevent the danger of sudden attacks from the air.

6. The German Government repeat their offer to conclude with States bordering on Germany in the East non-aggression pacts similar to that concluded with Poland. Since the attitude of the Lithuanian Government

has undergone a certain modification as regards Memel, the German Government withdraw the exception which they once had to make with regard to Lithuania, and declare themselves ready to sign a non-aggression pact with Lithuania also, under the stipulation of an effective organisation of the guaranteed autonomy of the Memel territory.

7. With the achievement, at last, of Germany's equality of rights and the restoration of full sovereignty over the whole territory of the German *Reich*, the German Government regard the chief reason for their withdrawal from the League of Nations as eliminated. Germany is therefore prepared to enter the League of Nations again.

(F. J. Berber (ed.) *Locarno: A Collection of Documents*, issued under the auspices of the German Academy of Political Science, Berlin, and the Institute of International Affairs, Hamburg; London, William Hodge, 1936, pp. 224–5)

I.26 R. Barrington-Ward, editorial in *The Times* (9 March 1936)

A CHANCE TO REBUILD

Herr Hitler's invasion of the Rhineland is a challenge, abrupt in form and deliberate in fact, to the voluntary agreement which has maintained the inviolability of the eastern frontiers of France and Belgium for the last eleven years. The Locarno Treaty, which embodied this understanding, was designed to inaugurate a process. Locarno was intended to call mutual good faith and confidence into play among the signatories. Certain penal and discriminatory clauses in the main Peace Treaties preserved the mood of war-bitterness and war-exhaustion in which they were drafted, maintained an unstable equilibrium, and threatened the durability of the settlement as a whole. They were to yield to negotiation and consent, and to disappear, leaving the peace of Europe refounded upon something more lasting than a preponderance of force. The Locarno agreement was in some ways ahead of its time. So much so that, whatever the reasons in detail, it was never in fact allowed to create the conditions requisite to that frank understanding between France and Germany which was and is the first essential of European stability. But the agreement in another respect was not ahead of its time. It embodied the clauses of the Versailles Treaty which imposed demilitarization upon the German side only of the Franco-German frontier. Thus, having failed as the starting point of a process of appeasement it survived only, in German eyes, as an additional guarantee of one of the 'inequalities' in which the Nazi movement of resurgence and revolt had its birth. In the view, not of Nazidom alone, but of all Germans, the sacrifice offered in Germany's free acceptance of the 'inequality' had proved vain.

Herr Hitler's action thus strikes the Locarno arrangement in its weakest joint. For some time past it has been widely admitted both in France and in this country that discriminatory demilitarization in the Rhineland was not destined to endure for ever. How it might end was less certain. It has now been ended by an act which, in the terms of Herr Hitler's declaration to the *Reichstag* on Saturday, is aimed not so much at the intentions of Locarno as at the particular servitude which is borrowed from the Versailles Treaty. It is none the less plainly the breach of a treaty freely negotiated and constantly reaffirmed. The more sensationally minded have described it also during the week-end as an act of 'aggression'. If it be that as well, there is still a distinction to be drawn between the march of detachments of German troops, sent to re-occupy territory indisputably under German sovereignty, and an act which carries fire and sword into a neighbour's territory. Anger and panic would, at the best, be over-hasty interpreters of the event. No one in this country can or will wish to dispute that the engagements of Locarno have been grossly violated and that the obligations of the guarantor may now be invoked. With these facts taken for granted, it becomes the task of the guarantor and the guaranteed Powers in council to examine jointly and dispassionately the whole meaning of the move which confronts them. . . .

For Germany the demilitarized zone, no longer an offering to neighbourly relations, has become more than a badge of inferior status, a source of military weakness to a Power which might one day become involved in war on both fronts again. Though aircraft and mechanization must largely have diminished the value of any demilitarized zone, the reasoning persists.

This age-old clash of suspicions lies behind the story. Is Germany, who has now repudiated a freely negotiated treaty, ever to be trusted? Is France, who has brought Russia in to redress the balance of manpower in the West, ever to be satisfied? The greatest mission of statesmanship is still to break this vicious circle of distrust, and the statesman as well as the judge must be heard in the Paris meeting tomorrow. The Locarno Treaty distinguishes non-justiciable from justiciable issues between the signatories. In the background is such an issue. Herr Hitler has endeavoured to give to his default, flagrant and indefensible in itself, a constructive political implication. A breach of a treaty is not to be condoned or explained away. But those who are called to sit in judgement upon it will fall short of what is due to their peoples if they fail to test it not only by the text of the treaty but also by its consequences. What is the right advantage to be wrung from it? Is this but the latest and worst blow to the sanctity of international law? Will the ends for which treaties exist be vindicated here solely by the machinery of penalty and enforcement? . . .

Such is the settlement which Herr Hitler proposes as the price of his armed re-entry into the Rhineland. There are glaring gaps in it to be filled, deep obscurities to be examined. But the questions for statesmanship are whether the Locarno Treaty is to be made the means or the bar to the exploration of this offer, and whether Europe will be safer and its economic recovery nearer according as the Locarno Powers agree to examine or determine to reject it. The offer, let it be observed, is made subject to no condition that can be ruled out as arbitrary or inadmissable. A double zone of demilitarization in the West may no longer be practicable, but the demand for equality is not the less reasonable in itself. Nor is the demand for full autonomy in the Memel territory. . . .

There cannot indeed be two minds about the objective, for all the difficulties with which the method of its presentation has hedged it at the moment. British opinion will be nearly unanimous in its desire to turn an untoward proceeding to account and, far from weakening the régime of treaties, to seize the opportunity of broadening and strengthening the collective system which opens with the German offer of re-entry. What upholds the League serves French no less than British interests. More than that. Where French security is at stake, the two are found to coincide. It is one of the self-evident facts of Europe, over and above specific undertakings, that any threat to French or Belgian territory engages Britain. If this was not clear formerly, it is clear to the great majority in this island now, though the truth was already explicit in the Locarno Treaty itself. The whole meaning of collective security has gained in clarity through experience. . . . France and Britain alike have reason for indignation and food for suspicions. But, since neither stands alone, they have the more power, even while they are faced with an admitted offence against the law of Europe, to take a steady measure of the undertakings which Germany has offered in extenuation. The old structure of European peace, one-sided and unbalanced, is nearly in ruins. It is the moment, not to despair, but to rebuild.

(*The Times*, 9 March 1936)

I.27 Eric Dunstan, commentary to *The Rhine* (12 March 1936)

We live in momentous times. To the Rhineland, which under the Versailles Treaty was to be for ever demilitarized, there return German troops, cheered and lionized by the civilian population.

Cologne Cathedral, so familiar to the British Army of Occupation, witnesses the march of soldiers again – soldiers of Germany, sent into the Rhineland as an accomplished fact by Hitler.

It was the day before the anniversary of Heroes' Day which Hitler chose for his *coup*. Germany's mourning for her war dead is expressed by a national ceremony on March 8th in the Opera House, and consciousness of having regained full sovereignty exalted the hearts of the participants in the solemn occasion.

On the previous day, Hitler had arrived at the *Reichstag*'s temporary building and reviewed his guard of honour before entering.

The words of the epoch-making speech were carried to the waiting crowds; and when he returned to the Chancellery, he had to acknowledge again and again the cheers of his delighted compatriots.

The world, though shocked by Germany's repudiation of the terms of the Locarno Treaty, into which her representatives entered freely and without the constraint exercised at Versailles, hopes that out of the difficult situation may be rebuilt a new peace system on a surer foundation. Meanwhile Germany resumes her watch on the Rhine.

(British Movietone News, vol. 7, no. 353a)

I.28 Neville Chamberlain, extract from speech to House of Commons (24 March 1938)

His Majesty's Government have expressed the view that recent events in Austria have created a new situation, and we think it right to state the conclusions to which consideration of these events has led us. We have already placed on record our judgment upon the action taken by the German Government. I have nothing to add to that. But the consequences still remain. There has been a profound disturbance of international confidence. In these circumstances the problem before Europe, to which in the opinion of His Majesty's Government it is their most urgent duty to direct their attention, is how best to restore this shaken confidence, how to maintain the rule of law in international affairs, how to seek peaceful solutions to questions that continue to cause anxiety. Of these the one which is necessarily most present in many minds is that which concerns the relations between the Government of Czechoslovakia and the German minority in that country; and it is probable that a solution of this question, if it could be achieved, would go far to re-establish a sense of stability over an area much wider than that immediately concerned.

Accordingly, the Government have given special attention to this matter, and in particular they have fully considered the question whether the United Kingdom, in addition to those obligations by which she is already bound by the Covenant of the League and the Treaty of Locarno, should, as a further contribution towards preserving peace in Europe, now undertake new and specific commitments in Europe, and in particular such a commitment in relation to Czechoslovakia. I think it is right that I should here remind the House what are our existing commitments, which might lead to the use of our arms for purposes other than our own defence and the defence of territories of other parts of the British Commonwealth of Nations. They are, first of all, the defence of France and Belgium against unprovoked aggression in accordance with our existing obligations under the Treaty of Locarno, as reaffirmed in the arrangement which was drawn up in London on 19th March, 1936. We have also obligations by treaty to Portugal, Iraq and Egypt. Those are our definite obligations to particular countries. . . .

The question now arises, whether we should go further. Should we forthwith give an assurance to France that, in the event of her being called upon by reason of German aggression on Czechoslovakia to implement her obligations under the Franco-Czechoslovak Treaty, we would immediately employ our full military force on her behalf? Or, alternatively, should we at once declare our readiness to take military action in resistance to any forcible interference with the independence and integrity of Czechoslovakia, and invite any other nations, which might so desire, to associate themselves with us in such a declaration?

From a consideration of these two alternatives it clearly emerges that under either of them the decision as to whether or not this country would find itself involved in war would be automatically removed from the discretion of His Majesty's Government, and the suggested guarantee would apply irrespective of the circumstances by which it was brought into operation, and over which His Majesty's Government might not have been able to exercise any control. This position is not one that His Majesty's Government could see their way to accept, in relation to an area where their vital interests are not concerned in the same degree as they are in the case of France and Belgium; it is certainly not the position that results from the Covenant. For these reasons His Majesty's Government feel themselves unable to give the prior guarantee suggested. . . .

It remains for his Majesty's Government to state their attitude in regard to the proposal made by the Government of the USSR that an early conference should be held for the purpose of discussion with certain other Powers of the practical measures which in their opinion the circumstances demand. His Majesty's Government would warmly welcome the assembly of any conference at which it might be expected that all European nations would consent to be represented, and at which it might therefore be found possible to discuss matters in regard to which anxiety is at present felt. In present circumstances, however, they are obliged to recognize that no such expectation can be entertained, and the Soviet Government do not, in fact, appear to entertain it. Their proposal would appear to involve less a consultation with a view to settlement than a concerting of action against an eventuality that has not yet arisen. Its object would appear to be to negotiate such mutual undertakings in advance to resist aggression as I have referred to, which, for the reasons I have already given, His Majesty's Government for their part are unwilling to accept. Apart from this, His Majesty's Government are of opinion that the indirect, but none the less inevitable, consequence of such action as is proposed by the Soviet Government would be to aggravate the tendency towards the establishment of exclusive groups of nations, which must, in the view of His Majesty's Government, be inimical to the prospects of European peace.

Great Britain has repeatedly borne witness to the principles on which she considers the peace of the world depends. We do not believe that any stable order can be established unless by one means or other recognition can be secured for certain general principles. The first is that differences between nations should be resolved by peaceful settlement and not by methods of force. The second, admittedly of no less importance, is that a peaceful settlement, to be enduring, must be based on justice. Holding these views successive British Governments have accepted the full obligations of the Covenant of the League of Nations, and done their best to discharge them; they have acceded to special instruments designed to pledge the nations afresh to refrain from resort to aggressive war; and they have reinforced the general obligations thus undertaken by specific undertakings within the framework of the League towards countries with whom they enjoy special relations or in which they have special interest. On the other side they have constantly lent, and are prepared to continue to lend, their influence to the revision of relations between nations, established by treaty or otherwise, which appeared to demand review. They will continue, whether by way of action through the League or by direct diplomatic effort, to exert all their influence on the side of bringing to peaceful and orderly solutions any issues liable to interrupt friendly relations between nations.

So far as Czechoslovakia is concerned, it seems to His Majesty's Government that now is the time when all the resources of diplomacy should be enlisted in the cause of peace. They have been glad to take note of and in no way under-rate the definite assurances given by the German Government as to their attitude. On the other side they have observed with satisfaction that the Government of Czechoslovakia are addressing themselves to the practical steps that can be taken within the framework of the Czechoslovak constitution to meet the reasonable wishes of the German minority. For their part, His Majesty's Government will at all times be ready to render any help in their power, by whatever means might seem most appropriate, towards the solution of questions likely to cause difficulty between the German and Czechoslovak Governments.

(Neville Chamberlain, *The Struggle for Peace*, London, Hutchinson, 1939)

II
WORLD WAR II AND ITS CONSEQUENCES

II.1 'Order concerning the exercise of martial jurisdiction and procedure in the area "Barbarossa" and special military measures' (13 May 1941)

The application of martial law aims in the first place at *maintaining discipline*.

The fact that the operational areas in the East are so far-flung, the battle strategy which this necessitates, and the peculiar qualities of the enemy, confront the courts martial with problems which, being short-staffed, they cannot solve while hostilities are in progress, and until some degree of pacification has been achieved in the conquered areas, unless jurisdiction is confined, in the first instance, to its main task.

This is possible only if *the troops* take ruthless action themselves against any threat from the enemy population.

For these reasons I herewith issue the following order effective for the area 'Barbarossa' (area of operations, army rear area, and area of political administration):

I. Treatment of offences committed by enemy civilians:

1. Until further notice the military courts and the courts martial will not be competent for *crimes committed by enemy civilians*.

2. *Guerillas* should be disposed of ruthlessly by the military, whether they are fighting or in flight.

3. Likewise *all other attacks by enemy civilians on the Armed Forces*, its members and employees, are to be suppressed at once by the military, using the most extreme methods, until the assailants are destroyed.

4. Where such measures have been neglected or were not at first possible; *persons suspected of criminal action will be brought at once before an officer. This officer will decide whether they are to be shot.*

On the orders of an officer with the powers of at least a Battalion Commander, *collective despotic measures* will be taken without delay against *localities* from which cunning or malicious attacks are made on the Armed Forces, if circumstances do not permit of a quick identification of individual offenders.

5. It is *expressly forbidden* to keep suspects in *custody* in order to hand them over to the courts after the reinstatement of civil courts.

6. The C-in-Cs of the Army Groups may by agreement with the competent Naval and Air Force Commanders *reintroduce military jurisdiction for civilians*, in areas which are sufficiently settled.

For the *area of the 'Political Administration'* this order will be given by the Chief of the Supreme Command of the Armed Forces.

II. Treatment of offences committed against inhabitants by members of the Armed Forces and its employees.

1. With regard to *offences* committed *against enemy civilians* by *members of the Wehrmacht* and its employees *prosecution is not obligatory* even where the deed is at the same time a military crime or offence.

2. When *judging such offences*, it must be borne in mind, whatever the circumstances, that the collapse of Germany in 1918, the subsequent sufferings of the German people and the fight against National Socialism which cost the blood of innumerable supporters of the movement, were caused primarily by Bolshevik influence and that no German has fogotten this fact.

3. Therefore the judicial authority will decide in such cases whether a disciplinary penalty is indicated, or whether *legal measures* are necessary. In the case of offences against inhabitants it will order a *court martial* only if *maintenance of discipline or security of the Forces* call for such a measure. This applies for instance to serious offences originating in lack of self-control in sexual matters, or in a criminal disposition, and to those which indicate that the troops are threatening to get out of hand. Offences which have resulted in senseless destruction of billets or stores of other captured material to the disadvantage of our Forces should as a rule be judged no less severely.

The order to institute proceedings requires in every single case the signature of the Judicial Authority.

4. *Extreme caution* is indicated in assessing the credibility of statements made by enemy civilians.

III. Within their sphere of competence Military Commanders are *personally* responsible for seeing that:

1. Every commissioned officer of the units under their command is instructed promptly and in the most emphatic manner on principles set out under I above.

2. Their legal advisers are notified promptly of these instructions and of *verbal information in which the political intentions of the High Command were explained to C-in-Cs.*

3. Only those court sentences are confirmed which are in accordance with the political intentions of the High Command.

IV. *Security.*

Once the camouflage is lifted this decree will be treated as 'Most Secret'.

By order
Chief of the Supreme Command of the Armed Forces
[signed] Keitel

(*Nazi Conspiracy and Aggression: A Collection of Documentary Evidence and Guide Materials Prepared by the American and British Prosecuting Staffs for Presentation before the International Military Tribunal at Nürnberg,* 8 vols, US Government Printing Office, 1946–48, vol. vi, pp. 873–5)

II.2 'Top secret: supplement to Order No. 33' (23 Ju

TOP SECRET
By officer only

Fuehrer HQ. 23 july 1941

Chief, High Command of the Armed Forces
No. 441254/41, Top Secret, by officer only
Armed Forces Operational Staff/Dept. L (1 Op)

14 copies
Copy No. 2

Supplement to Order No. 33

On 22 July, the Fuehrer after receiving the Commander of the Army issued the following order with a view to supplementing and enlarging Order No. 33:

[1 to 5: strategic measures]

6. In view of the vast size of the occupied areas in the East, the forces available for establishing security in these areas will be sufficient only if all resistance is punished not by legal prosecution of the guilty, but by the spreading of such terror by the occupying forces as is alone appropriate to eradicate every inclination to resist amongst the population.

The respective Commanders, with the troops available to them, are to be held responsible for maintaining peace within their areas. The Commanders must find the means of keeping order within the regions where security is their responsibility [*Sicherungsräume*], not by demanding more security forces, but by applying suitable, draconian measures.

[Signed] Keitel

(*Nazi Conspiracy and Aggression: A Collection of Documentary Evidence and Guide Materials Prepared by the American and British Prosecuting Staffs for Presentation before the International Military Tribunal at Nürnberg*, 8 vols, US Government Printing Office, 1946–48, vol. viii, p. 876)

II.3 Generaloberst Franz Halder, affidavit at Nürnberg (22 Nov. 1945)

Nürnberg, Germany
22 November, 1945

I, Franz Halder, being first duly sworn, depose and say as follows:
That, on the 1st day of April 1938, I took over in the Supreme Command of the German Army the position of First Quartermaster General, responsible for working out plans for operations under the direction of the Chief of Staff. . . .

I, furthermore, state and affirm that in March 1941, before the start of the Russian campaign which happened in June of that year, Hitler called the Chiefs of Command of the three parts of the armed forces and also high commanders to a conference in the Armed Forces' Chancery. At that meeting, Hitler first gave us the reasons for his resolution to attack Russia. In that conference, Hitler said as follows: 'The aggressive intentions of Russia have been proved by the Bolshevistic claim to world rulership and to world supremacy and Russia's tendency and attitude toward Finland: Russia's policy in the Balkans and the age-old policy of Russia in the Dardanelles (Hitler had reference here to the last visit of Molotov). Russia has continuously been strengthening her forces along the demarcation line which separates us from Russia. We must count on an attack by Russia as a certainty. Furthermore, there exist secret agreements between Russia and England and, because of these secret agreements, England has rejected Germany's peace offers. Russia is the last resort that England has on the Continent and we therefore have to anticipate Russia's attack against us.' His talk concerning Russia continues as follows: 'The war against Russia will be such that it cannot be conducted in a knightly fashion. This struggle is a struggle of ideologies and racial differences and will have to be conducted with unprecedented, unmerciful, and unrelenting harshness. All officers will have to rid themselves of obsolete ideologies. I know that the necessity for such means of waging war is beyond the comprehension of you Generals but I cannot change my orders and I insist absolutely that my orders will be executed without contradiction. The Kommissars are the bearers of those ideologies of Russia and are directly opposed to National Socialism. Therefore they, the Kommissars, will be liquidated. For the German soldiers who are guilty in this fight of breaking international law, provided that breaking of civil law, such as murder, rape or robbery are not involved, then their breach of international law shall be excused. Russia has not participated in the Hague Convention, therefore has no rights under it. Russia has proved that she will not recognize members of the SS and the German Police as members of any German military organization.' When this talk given by Hitler was over, listeners on the part of the army were of course outraged by this speech of Hitler's and some officers turned to Field Marshal von Brauchitsch and gave expression to their feelings concerning it. Von Brauchitsch then assured them that he was going to fight against this resolution and that the orders as given by Hitler could not be executed in their form. Immediately after the discussion, von Brauchitsch wrote down the way he understood the directives that were given by Hitler regarding the treatment of Kommissars and also regarding the type of warfare that would be employed in Russia and then submitted his notes to the OKW, with a recommendation that we, of the OKW, could never execute such orders.

Although the German General Staff included in its operational plan against Russia, the normal provisions for the care of captured prisoners, including the provision for the moving of same to the German home area, Hitler issued an order to the armies operating against Russia that no

Russian prisoners would be evacuated to the German home area. The reasons were obvious. Hitler wanted no contamination of German people by the Bolshevists. I, therefore, declared that the German General Staff of OKH was not in a position to solve the Russian prisoner of war problem, for OKH then had close to a million of such prisoners of war. I informed Keitel. Keitel appreciated the tremendous problem, suddenly thrust upon OKH, and agreed to take over all Russian prisoners who were delivered to him back of the Operational boundary line. In this purpose he received part of my personnel who had been employed by me on this task. Subsequently, Keitel accepted all Russian prisoners who were delivered by OKH to him. Under Keitel's command there was organized back of the Operational line, zones or territories for the reception and care of such Russian prisoners of war. I later made a trip to Smolensk, and while there one of the Commanders, Oberst Freiherr von Bachtelsheim, of a zone or territory created by OKW, came to me and informed me of the terrible conditions under which the Russian prisoners in his zone were forced to live. The prisoners had no roofs over their heads; they had no blankets, little nourishment, and insufficient medical care. They died; almost whole camps died of typhus. I caused a report of this to be made to General Wagner, who is now dead, and I know Keitel had this matter brought to his attention, for General Wagner reported this condition to OKW.

[signed]   Franz Halder
FRANZ HALDER

Certified by
  CURTIS L. WILLIAMS, Col, IGD

(*Nazi Conspiracy and Aggression: A Collection of Documentary Evidence and Guide Materials Prepared by the American and British Prosecuting Staffs for Presentation before the International Military Tribunal at Nürnberg*, 8 vols, US Government Printing Office, 1946–48, vol. viii, pp. 643 and 645–7)

II.4   Milovan Djilas, extract from *Wartime* (1977)

Covered with orchards and rising from the confluence of two mountain streams, the still undamaged town of Foča seemed to offer charming and peaceful prospects. But the human devastation inside it was immeasurable and inconceivable. In the spring of 1941 the Ustashi – among them a good number of Moslem toughs – had killed many Serbs. Then the Chetniks occupied the little town and proceeded to slaughter the Moslems. The Ustashi had selected twelve only sons from prominent Serbian families and killed them, while in the village of Miljevina they had slit the throats of Serbs over a vat – apparently, so as to fill it with blood instead of fruit pulp. The Chetniks had slaughtered groups of Moslems whom they tied together on the bridge over the Drina and threw into the river. Many of our people saw groups of corpses floating, caught on some rock or log. Some even recognized their own families. Four hundred Serbs and three thousand Moslems were reported killed in the region of Foča. Yet, judging by the devastation of a large number of villages, it seems that many more Serbs were killed. In the hotel in which I was put up – not, of course, until after our sanitation corps had steamed my clothing – I was shown a room with a bullet-riddled ceiling; the room in which Major Sergei Mikailovich, the Russian émigré who conducted the massacre of the Moslems, had boozed and caroused.

How did it all come about? The killing of Serbs was carried out methodically – first the leaders and the more prosperous citizens, then others right down the line – by small groups of déclassé failures, largely led by the Ustashi: returned exiles from Italy or Hungary. Men and movements had come to the fore whose vision of the future called for the extermination of other faiths and peoples.

In the beginning, at any rate, the Chetnik massacres of Moslems demonstrated the revenge and bitterness of those whose relatives the Ustashi had killed. Still weak, horrified by the massacre of the Serbs, the Communists at first collaborated with the Chetniks, but tried to dissuade them from punishing all Moslems and Croats. But the Chetnik leadership was taken over largely by officers who believed in the higher nationalist aim of exterminating the Moslems. Characteristically, the Chetniks were not united or consistent in this either. For us Communists the Ustashi were a totally alien enemy force, and the Chetniks a conglomeration of Serbian liberal nationalists, terrified peasant masses, Serb chauvinists, and fascists. At the start, the various Chetnik movements differed from province to province: in Bosnia and Croatia they stood for self-defence against extermination; in Serbia, for the restoration of the monarchy and hegemony over other peoples; in Montenegro, for counter-revolution. But all had their roots in ancestral traditions, in village life, and in national and religious myths. In such soil and such a consciousness – particularly after the Ustashi massacres of Serbs – the urge to exterminate other faiths and peoples was ever present. Yet tradition preserved some tolerance and humanity, so that enlightened and liberal ideas also survived. Not many Chetnik officers, let alone the Chetnik peasant masses, were obsessed with the ideology of extermination. Therefore we Communists tried to differentiate between traditional ideas and Greater Serbian chauvinism, and to attract or at least neutralize certain segments, particularly among the peasantry.

What about the people of Foča? What did they feel? There were few of them around – occasionally an old man, but mostly women and children. They rarely ventured out, except to go to meetings. There was no ray of warmth or curiosity in their expressions, which remained apathetic, dull, inhuman. They were emaciated and yellowed, and dressed in rags.

The Partisan authorities were moderate but determined. There was hardly anyone around to prosecute, so they put their energies into making use of local supplies. For example, they invented a bread made of dried pears and barley which was indescribably vile, though it contained vital nutrients. Recuperated Communist forces bubbled with life and activity in this half-dead little town, amid a people whom senseless extermination had made indifferent to death. Partisan institutions in Foča did not have the formal dignity of those in Užice, but were more supple and realistic. Not that there was any lack of statutes and decrees in Foča. There were jokes about Pijade's decrees concerning people's committees – the very institutions which learned conformists in Yugoslav universities today hold up as the model beginnings of the new 'constitutional' order. Arso Jovanović worked up a statute for the proletarian brigades, but that too proved unrealistic. However, even these activities – in addition to the practical ones of establishing local authorities and winning over supporters – demonstrated our inexhaustible efforts in building a new order.

[. . .]

An assembly was called. The peasants – some four hundred of them, largely from the district of Nikšić, my ancestral home – didn't know why they had been summoned. If they had, many wouldn't have shown up. We set up two men with submachine-guns on a mound in the middle of the meeting ground, just in case. Sava was also there, greeting the peasants and joking with them. He knew many by name.

Standing on a boulder, I spoke for nearly an hour. Had anyone recorded that speech, probably I too would laugh at it and wonder at its demagoguery and frankness. First I made them laugh, which dispelled their distrust. Then I praised their heroism and self-sacrifice, even above the heroism and self-sacrifice of their ancestors. We were no better equipped than the insurgents of olden times against the Turks, yet we had to face an enemy who fought with planes and tanks. I told them that we were their children, reminded them of their murdered relatives, brothers, sons, and neighbours: our blood and lives could not be separated, even if they renounced this glorious struggle – the most glorious and most difficult in the memory of our mountains. I threw in verses from the folk epics and Njegoš, and I lashed out at the Chetniks: we could understand, I said, why they were against us Communists, but we couldn't understand why those lackeys murdered with the invader's own guns their brothers who rose up against that invader. And though victory was certain for us and the great Allies, I said finally, the fickle fortunes of war might indeed force us to abandon this or that village. Even so, we would never abandon the war throughout the homeland, and that was why we were forming regular units. These units needed weapons and we had none to give them except those borne by heroes: heroes who for reasons of their own – always just and honourable ones – were unable to join the units which would go wherever the peoples of Yugoslavia might summon them. I added, half in jest, that it would be good for them to give up their rifles, just in case the Chetniks came into their villages; they could tell them that the Communists would not have disarmed them if they had any confidence in them.

The peasants calmly gave up their rifles, though here and there individuals scowled. But I don't think my speech would have had such success, had Uzdomir not fallen [to an Italian attack].

[. . .]

Before his departure for the new territories [in June 1942] Tito issued an order which prescribed the severest punishment for the least offence against the population or against property. The Communists implemented the order, and the army, hungry and in rags, accepted the order with selfless pride. This ideological sharpening had led to a clarification of feelings toward the people. On the second day of the march, a Montenegrin peasant woman whose cow had been seized by the Partisans came to the Supreme Staff. Tito was horrified: 'Don't our comrades know that in the village a cow is like a member of the household?' So I went from unit to unit until I found a cow good enough to satisfy the woman.

[. . .]

Suddenly darkness fell over the mountain and it began to shower. By afternoon the sky had cleared, and the Fourth Brigade surrounded the village of Rakitnica. The brigade staff had moved ahead. We stopped just short of the village, from which bullets began to fly, until the brigade rushed forward across the wet pastures and grain fields. The hair of our girls streamed behind them. With the other staff members, I hastened to the village in bold excitement. The Moslem peasants met us apprehensively. We captured a gendarme and shot him, as his wife wailed with an infant in her arms. Peasants can instantly gauge what kind of an army they are dealing with; these villagers understood that we prohibited looting, and soon showered us with complaints about it. A patrol brought in a Montenegrin, a mustachioed fellow from Morača. He admitted nothing.

'We can still see the cream on your mustache!' I said.

'I was hungry,' he said.

'We'll have you shot as an example!'

'Comrade Djido, don't let me die shamefully over a jug of milk, but in battle as befits a man.'

'Take care, next time.'

Ashamed, I let him go. A few days later, two Montenegrins from the First Proletarian Brigade were shot for a similar offence.

[. . .]

There were no informers in Driniće or the surrounding villages. Not once did the planes that constantly cruised overhead threaten us. There were no political groups in the villages save the Communists – an ideal situation; the Communists and the people, solidarity in sacrifice and hope. The local Communists told us with malicious joy how the Ustashi had first killed off the bourgeoisie in the towns – priests, merchants, political party leaders – so that we were left with the people pure and simple. The Chetniks who showed up there with the Italians were left stranded and weak when the Italians drew back into 'their' Dalmatia. The local Chetnik leaders, Radić and Drenović, therefore collaborated with the Ustashi, who went on slaughtering Serbs wherever they could. Serbian peasant wisdom was incapable of interpreting this collaboration as cowardice or treason, but simply saw it as madness and degeneracy.

The special suffering and turmoil of the Serbs of Krajina and Lika gained historical significance when they took up arms as a people – the only group to do so. Thus even in the intellectual offices of *Borba*, Tito's article in *Proleter* of December 1942 was received with enthusiasm.

The Serbian people have given the greatest contribution in blood to the struggle against the invader and his traitorous assistants Pavelić, Nedić, Pećanac, as well as Draža Mihailović and his Chetniks. . . . The Serbian people know well why our national tragedy occurred and who the main culprit was, and it is for this reason that they are fighting so heroically. It is therefore the sacred duty of all the other peoples of Yugoslavia to take part in the same measure, if not even more, with the Serbian people in this great war of liberation against the invader and all his minions.[1]

The editorial staff of *Borba* instantly drew close to the peasants, not only because of vital everyday connections, but because of something new in our perception of them: we finally recognized the enormous 'new' role of the peasantry in the revolution and in revolutionary wars. In our case the workers, such as there were, were not in the ranks of the Partisans, except for small class-conscious groups or party functionaries. Our army was predominantly peasant. This was a frequent topic of discussion in the Central Committee, of course, with the aim of giving this a Marxist explanation and Marxist generalization.

The peasants of Drinće also understood that something important was happening in their village. Yet they didn't receive us so cordially merely because we appreciated their contribution, but because they knew that the Communists, as the military and intellectual backbone of the struggle, kept them from chaos and destruction. The Communists immediately instituted an authority and fellowship: an order, an economy, transportation, schools. And for the young and for women, they offered prospects of enlightenment.

[. . .]

Though we largely took refuge in backward regions, we still were astounded at the backwardness of the peasants, especially the women, on Vlašić. Many of them had never even been in the nearby towns. They wore hand-woven dresses open down to the navel, so that their breasts flopped out. They greased their hair with butterfat, parted it in the middle, then tucked it up over their foreheads. Their vocabulary was meagre, except concerning livestock and the like. The quartermaster of the Supreme Staff, a rascal quite typical of the Serbian towns, exchanged

---

[1] Josip Broz Tito, *Borba za oslobodjenje Jugoslavije* [The struggle for the liberation of Yugoslavia] (Belgrade: Kultura, 1947), pp. 138–9.

all kinds of trinkets with the peasant women for excellent cheese. During the trading they would naively question him.

'Honestly, now, are these real gold?'

And he would say in mock seriousness: 'They are, so help me God and all the saints!'

We laughed at this scoundrel, and probably not even the deceived peasant women were angry: even if they weren't gold, the trinkets glittered. Here was an opportunity made to order for our feminists: they pleaded with the brothers and husbands to permit their women to attend meetings, and the women did go to them, in groups and all dressed up as on feast days. The men were on a markedly higher level than the women, for they had seen something of the world in the army, on jobs, and through trade. Yet the relationship between the sexes was based more on a natural division of labour than on sexual servitude. Several armies had already passed through this village, but the peasants greeted ours as their own; we spoke their language and fought against the German evildoers.

(Milovan Djilas, *Wartime*, trans. Michael B. Petrovich, New York, Harcourt Brace Jovanovich, 1977, pp. 139–41, 166–7, 187, 189, 205–6, 309)

II.5 'The Atlantic Charter', joint statement by President of the United States and Prime Minister of Great Britain (1941)

The following statement signed by the President of the United States and the Prime Minister of Great Britain is released for the information of the Press:

The President of the United States and the Prime Minister, Mr Churchill, representing His Majesty's Government in the United Kingdom, have met at sea.

They have been accompanied by officials of their two Governments, including high ranking officers of their Military, Naval and Air Services.

The whole problem of the supply of munitions of war, as provided by the Lease-Lend Act, for the armed forces of the United States and for those countries actively engaged in resisting aggression has been further examined.

Lord Beaverbrook, the Minister of Supply of the British Government, has joined in these conferences. He is going to proceed to Washington to discuss further details with appropriate officials of the United States Government. These conferences will also cover the supply problems of the Soviet Union.

The President and the Prime Minister have had several conferences. They have considered the dangers to world civilization arising from the policies of military domination by conquest upon which the Hitlerite government of Germany and other governments associated therewith have embarked, and have made clear the stress which their countries are respectively taking for their safety in the face of these dangers.

They have agreed upon the following joint declaration:

Joint declaration of the President of the United States of America and the Prime Minister, Mr Churchill, representing His Majesty's Government in the United Kingdom, being met together, deem it right to make known certain common principles in the national policies of their respective countries on which they base their hopes for a better future for the world.

First, their countries seek no aggrandizement, territorial or other;

Second, they desire to see no territorial changes that do not accord with the freely expressed wishes of the peoples concerned;

Third, they respect the right of all peoples to choose the form of government under which they will live; and they wish to see sovereign rights and self government restored to those who have been forcibly deprived of them;

Fourth, they will endeavour, with due respect for their existing obligations, to further the enjoyment by all States, great or small, victor or vanquished, of access, on equal terms, to the trade and to the raw materials of the world which are needed for their economic prosperity;

Fifth, they desire to bring about the fullest collaboration between all nations in the economic field with the object of securing, for all, improved labour standards, economic advancement and social security;

Sixth, after the final destruction of the Nazi tyranny, they hope to see established peace which will afford to all nations the means of dwelling in safety within their own boundaries, and which will afford assurance that all the men in all the lands may live out their lives in freedom from fear and want;

Seventh, such a peace should enable all men to traverse the high seas and oceans without hindrance;

Eighth, they believe that all of the nations of the world, for realistic as well as spiritual reasons must come to the abandonment of the use of force. Since no future peace can be maintained if land, sea or air armaments continue to be employed by nations which threaten, or may threaten, aggression outside of their frontiers, they believe, pending the establishment of a wider and permanent system of general security, that the disarmament of such nations is essential. They will likewise aid and encourage all other practicable measures which will lighten for peace-loving peoples the crushing burden of armaments.

(Joseph M. Siracusa (ed.) *The American Diplomatic Revolution*, Milton Keynes, Open University Press, 1978)

II.6 Josef Stalin, extract from speech to the Moscow Soviet and representatives of Moscow Party and public organizations on the 25th anniversary of the October Revolution (6 Nov. 1942)

It may now be regarded as beyond dispute that in the course of the war imposed upon the nations by Hitlerite Germany, a radical demarcation of forces and the formation of two opposite camps have taken place: the camp of the Italo-German coalition, and the camp of the Anglo-Soviet-American coalition.

It is equally beyond dispute that these two opposite coalitions are guided by two different and opposite programmes of action.

The programme of action of the Italo-German coalition may be characterized by the following points: race hatred; domination of the 'chosen' nations; subjugation of other nations and seizure of their territories; economic enslavement of the subjugated nations and spoliation of their national wealth; destruction of democratic liberties; universal institution of the Hitler regime. The programme of action of the Anglo-Soviet-American coalition is: abolition of racial exclusiveness; equality of nations and inviolability of their territories; liberation of the enslaved nations and restoration of their sovereign rights; the right of every nation to manage its affairs in its own way; economic aid to war-ravaged nations and assistance in establishing their material welfare; restoration of democratic liberties; destruction of the Hitler regime. . . .

It is said that the Anglo-Soviet-American coalition has every chance of winning, and would certainly win if it did not suffer from an organic defect which might weaken and disintegrate it. This defect, in the opinion of these people, is that this coalition consists of heterogeneous elements having different ideologies, and that this circumstance will prevent them from organizing joint action against the common enemy.

I think that this assertion is wrong.

It would be ridiculous to deny the difference in the ideologies and social systems of the countries that constitute the Anglo-Soviet-American co-alition. But does this preclude the possibility, and the expediency, of joint action on the part of the members of this coalition against the common enemy who threatens to enslave them? Certainly not. Moreover, the very existence of this threat imperatively dictates the necessity of joint action among the members of the coalition in order to save mankind from reversion to savagery and medieval brutality. Is not the programme of action of the Anglo-Soviet-American coalition a sufficient basis upon which to organize a joint struggle against Hitler tyranny and to vanquish it? I think it is quite sufficient.

(Robert V. Daniels (ed.) *A Documentary History of Communism*, vol. 2, Hanover and London, University Press of New England on behalf of the University of Vermont, 1984)

II.7 'The Crimea Declaration: a statement issued by the Prime Minister, President Roosevelt and Marshal Stalin at Yalta' (12 Feb. 1945)

PLANS FOR THE FINAL DEFEAT OF THE COMMON ENEMY

For the past eight days, Mr Winston S. Churchill, Prime Minister of Great

Britain, Mr Franklin D. Roosevelt, President of the United States, and Marshal J. V. Stalin, Chairman of the Council of People's Commissars of the USSR, have met, with the Foreign Secretaries, Chiefs of Staff, and other advisers, in the Crimea.

[. . .]

The following statement is made by the Prime Minister of Great Britain, the President of the United States, and the Chairman of the Council of People's Commissars of the Union of Soviet Socialist Republics, on the result of the Crimea Conference:

1. DEFEAT OF GERMANY

We have considered and determined the military plans of the three Allied Powers for the final defeat of the common enemy. The Military Staffs of the three allied nations have met in daily meetings throughout the Conference. These meetings have been most satisfactory from every point of view, and have resulted in closer co-ordination of the military effort of the three allies than ever before.

The fullest information has been interchanged. The timing, scope, and co-ordination of new and even more powerful blows to be launched by our armies and air forces into the heart of Germany from the East, West, North, and South have been fully agreed and planned in detail.

Our combined military plans will be made known only as we execute them, but we believe that the very close working partnership among the three Staffs attained at this Conference will result in shortening the war. Meetings of the three Staffs will be continued in the future whenever the need arises.

Nazi Germany is doomed. The German people will only make the cost of their defeat heavier to themselves by attempting to continue a hopeless resistance.

2. THE OCCUPATION AND CONTROL OF GERMANY

We have agreed on common policies and plans for enforcing the unconditional surrender terms which we shall impose together on Nazi Germany after German armed resistance has been finally crushed. These terms will not be made known until the final defeat of Germany has been accomplished.

Under the agreed plan the forces of the three Powers will each occupy a separate zone of Germany. Co-ordinated administration and control has been provided for under the plan through a Central Control Commission consisting of the Supreme Commanders of the three Powers with headquarters in Berlin.

It has been agreed that France should be invited by the three Powers, if she should so desire, to take over a zone of occupation, and to participate as a fourth member of the Control Commission. The limits of the French zone will be agreed by the four Governments concerned through their representatives on the European Advisory Commission.

It is our inflexible purpose to destroy Germany militarism and Nazism and to ensure that Germany will never again be able to disturb the peace of the world. We are determined to disarm and disband all German armed forces; break up for all time the German General Staff that has repeatedly contrived the resurgence of German militarism; remove or destroy all German military equipment; eliminate or control all German industry that could be used for military production; bring all war criminals to justice and swift punishment and exact reparation in kind for the destruction wrought by the Germans; wipe out the Nazi Party, Nazi laws, organizations and institutions; remove all Nazi and militarist influences from public office and from the cultural and economic life of the German people; and take in harmony such other measures in Germany as may be necessary to the future peace and safety of the world.

It is not our purpose to destroy the people of Germany, but only when Nazism and militarism have been extirpated will there be hope for a decent life for Germans and a place for them in the comity of nations.

3. REPARATION BY GERMANY

We have considered the question of the damage caused by Germany to the Allied Nations in this war, and recognized it as just that Germany be obliged to make compensation for this damage in kind to the greatest extent possible. A Commission for the Compensation of Damage will be established. The Commission will be instructed to consider the question of the extent and methods for compensating damage caused by Germany to the Allied countries. The Commission will work in Moscow.

4. UNITED NATIONS' CONFERENCE

We are resolved upon the earliest possible establishment with our Allies of a general international organization to maintain peace and security. We believe that this is essential both to prevent aggression and to remove the political, economic, and social causes of war through the close and continuing collaboration of all peace-loving peoples. The foundations were laid at Dumbarton Oaks.

On the important question of voting procedure, however, agreement was not there reached. The present Conference has been able to resolve this difficulty.

We have agreed that a Conference of United Nations should be called to meet at San Francisco, in the United States, on April 25th, 1945, to prepare the Charter of such an organization along the lines proposed in the informal conversations at Dumbarton Oaks. The Government of China and the Provisional Government of France will be immediately consulted and invited to sponsor invitations to the Conference jointly with the Governments of the United States, Great Britain, and the Union of Soviet

Socialist Republics. As soon as the consultation with China and France has been completed the text of the proposals on voting procedure will be made public.

5. DECLARATION ON LIBERATED EUROPE

We have drawn up and subscribed to a Declaration on Liberated Europe. This Declaration provides for concerting the policies of the three Powers and for joint action by them in meeting the political and economic problems of Liberated Europe in accordance with democratic principles. The text of the Declaration is as follows:

The Premier of the Union of Soviet Socialist Republics, the Prime Minister of the United Kingdom, and the President of the United States of America have consulted with each other in the common interests of the peoples of their countries and those of Liberated Europe. They jointly declare their mutual agreement to concert during the temporary period of instability in Liberated Europe the policies of their three Governments in assisting the peoples liberated from the domination of Nazi Germany, and the peoples of the former Axis satellite States of Europe, to solve by democratic means their pressing political and economic problems.

The establishment of order in Europe and the rebuilding of national economic life must be achieved by processes which will enable the liberated peoples to destroy the last vestiges of Nazism and Fascism and to create democratic institutions of their own choice.

This is a principle of the Atlantic Charter – the right of all peoples to choose the form of government under which they will live – the restoration of sovereign rights and self-government to those peoples who have been forcibly deprived of them by the aggressor nations.

To foster the conditions in which the liberated peoples may exercise these rights, the three Governments will jointly assist the people in any European liberated State or former Axis satellite State in Europe where, in their judgment, conditions require:

 (*a*) to establish conditions of peace;

 (*b*) to carry out emergency measures for the relief of distressed people;

 (*c*) to form interim Governmental authorities broadly representative of all democratic elements in the population and pledged to the earliest possible establishment through free elections of Governments responsive to the will of the people; and

 (*d*) to facilitate where necessary the holding of such elections.

The three Governments will consult the other United Nations and provisional authorities or other Governments in Europe when matters of direct interest to them are under consideration.

When, in the opinion of the three Governments, conditions in any European liberated State or any former Axis satellite State in Europe make such action necessary, they will immediately consult together on the measures necessary to discharge the joint responsibilities set forth in this Declaration.

By this Declaration we re-affirm our faith in the principles of the Atlantic Charter, our pledge in the Declaration by the United Nations, and our determination to build in co-operation with other peace-loving nations a world order under law, dedicated to peace, security, freedom, and the general well-being of all mankind.

In issuing this Declaration the three Powers express the hope that the Provisional Government of the French Republic may be associated with them in the procedure suggested.

6. POLAND

We came to the Crimea Conference resolved to settle our differences about Poland. We discussed fully all aspects of the question. We re-affirm our common desire to see established a strong, free, independent, and democratic Poland. As a result of our discussions we have agreed on the conditions in which a new Polish Provisional Government of National Unity may be formed in such a manner as to command recognition by the three major Powers. The agreement reached is as follows:

A new situation has been created in Poland as a result of her complete liberation by the Red Army.

This calls for the establishment of a Polish Provisional Government which can be more broadly based than was possible before the recent liberation of Western Poland. The Provisional Government which is now functioning in Poland should, therefore, be reorganized on a broader democratic basis with the inclusion of democratic leaders from Poland itself and from Poles abroad. This new Government should then be called the Polish Provisional Government of National Unity.

Mr Molotov, Mr Harriman, and Sir A. Clark Kerr are authorized as a Commission to consult in the first instance in Moscow with members of the present Provisional Government and with other Polish democratic leaders from within Poland and from abroad, with a view to the re-organization of the present Government along the above lines.

This Polish Provisional Government of National Unity shall be pledged to the holding of free and unfettered elections as soon as possible on the basis of universal suffrage and secret ballot. In these elections all demo-cratic and anti-Nazi parties shall have the right to take part and to put forward candidates.

When a Polish Provisional Government of National Unity has been properly formed in conformity with the above, the Government of the Union of Soviet Socialist Republics, which now maintains diplomatic relations with the present Provisional Government of Poland, and the Government of the United Kingdom and the Government of the United States will establish diplomatic relations with the new Polish Provisional Government of National Unity, and will exchange Ambassadors by whose reports the respective Governments will be kept informed about the situation in Poland.

The three heads of Government consider that the Eastern frontier of

Poland should follow the Curzon Line, with digressions from it in some regions of five to eight kilometres in favour of Poland. They recognize that Poland must receive substantial accessions of territory in the North and West. They feel that the opinion of the new Polish Provisional Government of National Unity should be sought in due course on the extent of these accessions, and that the final delimitation of the Western frontier of Poland should thereafter await the Peace Conference.

7. YUGOSLAVIA

We have agreed to recommend to Marshal Tito and Dr Subasitch that the agreement between them should be put into effect immediately, and that a new Government should be formed on the basis of that agreement. We also recommend that as soon as the new Government has been formed it should declare that:

(1) The Anti-Fascist Assembly of National Liberation (*Avnoj*) should be extended to include members of the last Yugoslav Parliament (*Skupshtina*) who have not compromised themselves by collaboration with the enemy, thus forming a body to be known as a temporary Parliament, and

(2) Legislative Acts passed by the Assembly of National Liberation will be subject to subsequent ratification by a Constituent Assembly.

There was also a general review of other Balkan questions.

8. MEETINGS OF FOREIGN SECRETARIES

Throughout the Conference, besides the daily meetings of the Heads of Governments and the Foreign Secretaries, separate meetings of the three Foreign Secretaries and their advisers have also been held daily.

These meetings have proved of the utmost value, and the Conference agreed that permanent machinery should be set up for regular consultation between the three Foreign Secretaries. They will, therefore, meet as often as may be necessary, probably about every three or four months. These meetings will be held in rotation in the three capitals, the first meeting being held in London after the United Nations Conference on World Organizations.

9. UNITY FOR PEACE AS FOR WAR

Our meeting here in the Crimea has reaffirmed our common determination to maintain and strengthen in the peace to come that unity of purpose and of action which has made victory possible and certain for the United Nations in this war. We believe that this is a sacred obligation which our Governments owe to our peoples and to all the peoples of the world.

Only with continuing and growing co-operation and understanding among our three countries and among all the peace-loving nations can the highest aspiration of humanity be realized – a secure and lasting peace which will, in the words of the Atlantic Charter, 'afford assurance that all the men in all the lands may live out their lives in freedom from fear and want'.

Victory in this war and establishment of the proposed International Organization will provide the greatest opportunity in all history to create in the years to come the essential conditions of such a peace.

(Signed) WINSTON S. CHURCHILL;
FRANKLIN D. ROOSEVELT;
J. V. STALIN.

(*Victory: War Speeches of Winston S. Churchill 1945*, compiled by Charles Eade, London, Cassell, 1946)

BOMBING — CENTRAL FEATURE

II.8 Extract from the report by the Police President of Hamburg on the raids on Hamburg in July and August 1943 (1 Dec. 1943)

The rapidity with which the fires and firestorms developed, made every plan and every prospect of defence by the inhabitants purposeless. Houses, which in previous raids might have been preserved by the courageous efforts of Self Protection and other personnel, now fell victims to the flames. Before the necessity of flight could be realized, often every path to safety was cut off.

After the alarm, Self Protection personnel in their shelters, fireguards of the Extended Self Protection and Works Air Protection Services in the places assigned to them, awaited the beginning and development of the raid. HE bombs and land mines in waves shook the houses to their foundations. Only very shortly after the first HE bombs had fallen an enormous number of fires caused by a great concentration of incendiary bombs – mixed with HE bombs – sprang up. People who now attempted to leave their shelters to see what the situation was or to fight the fires were met by a sea of flame. Everything round them was on fire. There was no water and with the huge number and size of the fires all attempts to extinguish them were hopeless from the start.

Many members of the Self Protection Service on their patrols or when courageously fighting the fires, were either buried by HE bombs or cut off by the rapid spread of the fires. The same fate overtook many fireguards in Extended Self Protection or Works Air Protection establishments while bravely doing their duty. One eyewitness report says: 'None knew where to begin firefighting'. The constant dropping of HE bombs and land mines kept driving people back into the shelters. The heat, which was becoming unbearable, showed plainly that there was no longer any question of putting out fires but only of saving their lives. Escape from the sea of flame seemed already impossible. Women, especially, hesitated to risk flight from the apparently safe shelter through the flames into the unknown. The continual falling of HE and incendiary bombs increased their fears. So people waited in the shelters until the heat and the obvious danger compelled some immediate action, unless action was forced upon them by rescue measures from outside. In many cases they were no longer able to act by themselves. They were already unconscious or dead from carbon monoxide poisoning. The house had collapsed or all the exits had been blocked. The fire had become a hurricane which made it impossible in most cases to reach the open. The firestorm raging over many square kilometres had cut off innumerable people without hope of rescue. Only those got away who had risked an early escape or happened to be so near the edge of the sea of fire that it was possible to rescue them. Only where the distance to water or to open spaces of sufficient size, was short, was flight now possible, for to cover long distances in the red-hot streets of leaping flames was impossible.

Many of these refugees even then lost their lives through the heat. They fell, suffocated, burnt or ran deeper into the fire. Relatives lost one another. One was able to save himself, the others disappeared. Many wrapped themselves in wet blankets or soaked their clothes and thus reached safety. In a short time clothes and blankets became hot and dry. Anyone going any distance through this hell found that his clothes were in flames or the blanket caught fire and was blown away in the storm.

Numbers jumped into the canals and waterways and remained swimming or standing up to their necks in water for hours until the heat should die down. Even these suffered burns on their heads. They were obliged to wet their faces constantly or they perished in the heat. The firestorm swept over the water with its heat and its showers of sparks so that even thick wooden posts and bollards burned down to the level of the water. Some of these unfortunate people were drowned. Many jumped out of windows into the water or the street and lost their lives.

The number of deaths is still not finally settled. This is not due to faulty methods of investigation but solely to the unimaginable immensity of the destruction and the limited amount of staff available. The fact that even now up to 100 bodies are found and recovered on some days, will give some idea of the situation. The destruction was so immense that of many people literally nothing remains. From a soft stratum of ash in a large air raid shelter the number of persons who lost their lives could only be estimated by doctors at 250 to 300. Exact information will only be available when everyone at that time resident in Hamburg if still alive, has reported himself.

The scenes of terror which took place in the firestorm area are indescribable. Children were torn away from their parents' hands by the force of the hurricane and whirled into the fire. People who thought they had escaped fell down, overcome by the devouring force of the heat and died in an instant. Refugees had to make their way over the dead and dying. The sick and the infirm had to be left behind by rescuers as they themselves were in danger of burning.

This sad fate, which befell Hamburg, exceeded in effect and extent any catastrophic fire – with the exception of Tokyo – of the past. It is distinguished in the first place by the fact that never before in a city of a million inhabitants everyone, prepared and equipped for fire-fighting, supported by great experience and great success in fire-fighting in many earlier raids, was waiting at the signal of the sirens for duty and the necessity of fighting the fire. In earlier cases it developed as a rule gradually during many hours or days from a small incipient fire. Here a population ready and prepared for the alarm were literally overwhelmed by the fire which reached its height in under an hour.

Even taking the conditions of those days into consideration, the fire in Hamburg in 1842, bears only a faint likeness to the fire in Hamburg in 1943. The catastrophes of Chicago and San Francisco, the fire in the Paris Opera house, all these events, of which the scenes of fantastic and gruesome terror have been described by contemporaries, pale beside the extent and the uniqueness of the Hamburg fire of 1943. Its horror is revealed in the howling and raging of the firestorms, the hellish noise of exploding bombs and the death cries of martyred human beings as well as in the big silence after the raids. Speech is impotent to portray the measure of the horror, which shook the people for ten days and nights and the traces of which were written indelibly on the face of the city and its inhabitants.

And each of these nights convulsed by flames was followed by a day which displayed the horror in the dim and unreal light of a sky hidden in smoke. Summer heat intensified by the glow of the firestorms to an unbearable degree; dust from the torn earth and the ruins and debris of damaged areas which penetrated everywhere; showers of soot and ashes; more heat and dust; above all a pestilential stench of decaying corpses and smouldering fires weighed continually on the exhausted men.

And these days were followed by more nights of more horror, yet more smoke and soot, heat and dust and more death and destruction. Men had not time to rest or salvage property according to any plan or to search for their families. The enemy attacked with ceaseless raids until the work of destruction was complete. His hate had its triumph in the firestorms which destroyed mercilessly men and material alike.

The Utopian picture of a city rapidly decaying, without gas, water, light and traffic connections, with stony deserts which had once been flourishing residential districts, had become reality.

The streets were covered with hundreds of corpses. Mothers with their children, youths, old men, burnt, charred, untouched and clothed, naked with a waxen pallor like dummies in a shop window, they lay in every posture, quiet and peaceful or cramped, the death-struggle shown in the expression on their faces. The shelters showed the same picture, even more horrible in its effect, as it showed in many cases the final distracted struggle against a merciless fate. Although in some places shelterers sat quietly, peacefully and untouched as if sleeping in their chairs, killed without realization or pain by carbon monoxide poisoning, in other shelters the position of remains of bones and skulls showed how the occupants had fought to escape from their buried prison.

No flight of imagination will ever succeed in measuring and describing the gruesome scenes of horror in the many buried air-raid shelters. Posterity can only bow its head in honour of the fate of these innocents, sacrificed by the murderous lust of a sadistic enemy.

The conduct of the population, which at no time and nowhere showed panic or even signs of panic, as well as their work, was worthy of the magnitude of this disaster. It was in conformity with the Hanseatic spirit and character, that during the raids, friendly assistance and obligation found expression and after the raids an irresistible will to rebuild.

(Sir Charles K. Webster and Noble Frankland, *The Strategic Air Offensive against Germany, 1939–1945*, vol. 4, London, HMSO, 1961)

II.9 Sybil Bannister, extracts from *I Lived Under Hitler* (1957)

(a) May 1943

Except for a short stay in Wuppertal-Barmen in 1941, this was my first visit to West Germany since the beginning of the war. As usual, it was a relief to get away from the factious borderlands and to come into the heart of the country; not that they had no troubles – in fact they now had more than we had in the East – but particularly when threatened from outside, there was a solidarity and singleness of purpose. The knowledge that they were all in the same boat, and would stick together whatever happened, gave strength to each individual.

Besides the war in general, there were two things which were obviously lowering their vitality; one was the food shortage, and the other the continued air-raids, although the big raids had not yet begun. The food shortage was as yet not desperately acute. There were enough goods in the shops to supply the full complement on the ration cards, but this was just *not* enough. It is easy to go short for a few days or a few weeks without noticing many ill effects, but when it runs into months, the need accumulates until a permanent state of hunger and enervation ensues. Later on, the shorter the ration became, the worse the need grew, until finally near-starvation level was reached.

At that time, in May 1943, coming straight from the country in the East where we had unlimited supplies of milk, potatoes, and vegetables, into a town in an industrial centre in the West, it was remarkable to note what a difference the deficiency in these foods made to the possibility of varying the menu and still more of satisfying appetites. Meats, fats, sugar, bread, flour, cereals, everything else was now available in the East only in the same quantities as in the West.

(b) *January 1945*

As we steamed into Hamburg *Hauptbahnhof* [Central Station] the jagged ruins of the town rose stark and eerie against the chill light of dawn. Was this the ghost of the city I had visited ten years ago when I had witnessed that memorable performance of *Die Walküre*? Had Wotan in reality encircled Brünnhilde with consuming fire? The town itself was now the stage where scenes were enacted more dramatic than could ever be derived by any playwright.

It seemed impossible to believe that so many human beings could still exist in these shattered houses, still less survive the bombing which had, eighteen months previously, reduced the second largest German city to a vast pile of rubble. But communal life was not broken. The survivors had crawled out of their cellars, buried their dead if they could find the corpses and started afresh. Much reconstruction had already been done. A few streets, with their rows of new shop-windows, appeared to be normal until you looked more closely and noticed that above and behind the bright façade there were gaping walls hiding the burnt-out interim. Some buildings had been repaired on the lower floors whilst the walls of the top stories projected above like fantastic monuments. Many large areas were so completely devastated that repairs were out of the question. As I travelled down to Wandsbeker Chaussee by tram (the main thoroughfare northwards) except for little shacks scattered along the side of the road, which the shopkeepers had erected to replace their once prosperous stores, I would see nothing, far and wide, but broken bricks, dust and ashes.

I had been advised to get out at the Wandsbekerchausseebahnhof. There I asked the way to Manfred's house. It was in a small street which had once had fair-sized detached houses on each side, with pretty gardens. Not being so much on top of each other as the blocks of flats and larger buildings nearer the centre of the town, some of them had escaped total destruction. . . .

I prowled round Manfred's house but found no signs of occupation . . . I was just passing on when I saw a boy of about thirteen beating a carpet in the garden. I asked him if he knew where I would find Herr and Frau Petersen. 'Oh no! They live in Bromberg and we haven't seen them for a long time.' I said, 'I have just come from Bromberg, and the Petersens left before me. We had to leave because the Russians were encircling the town. . . .'

'. . . Just a moment, please. I will call mother.' He dashed off into the ruins. Surely, I thought, they cannot be living in that heap of crushed masonry! But yes indeed! As I drew nearer and made a closer inspection, I saw that what had been the garage next to the house had been repaired and converted into a small bungalow. Frau Lippert appeared and asked me in. The garage was divided by a partition. The children (two daughters and the boy) slept in one side in bunks. Father and Mother Lippert slept in the other compartment which was also used as a dining-sitting-room. At one end there was an all-purpose stove, and somewhere at the back there was a pantry. Thus, in this humble dwelling, one of Hamburg's wealthiest merchants housed with his family, only too thankful to have survived the terror raids and to have a roof over their heads.

(Sybil Bannister, *I Lived Under Hitler: An Englishwoman's Story*, London, Rockliffe, 1957, pp. 141, 203–4)

II.10 Extracts from *Protocol of the Proceedings of the Berlin Conference* (2 Aug. 1945)

II THE PRINCIPLES TO GOVERN THE TREATMENT OF GERMANY IN THE INITIAL CONTROL PERIOD

A Political Principles

1. In accordance with the Agreement on Control Machinery in Germany, supreme authority in Germany is exercised, on instructions from their respective Governments, by the Commanders-in-Chief of the armed forces of the United States of America, the United Kingdom, the Union of Soviet Socialist Republics and the French Republic, each in his own zone of occupation, and also jointly, in matters affecting Germany as a whole, in their capacity as members of the Control Council.

2. So far as is practicable, there shall be uniformity of treatment of the German population throughout Germany.

3. The purposes of the occupation of Germany by which the Control Council shall be guided are:

   (i) The complete disarmament and demilitarization of Germany and the elimination or control of all German industry that could be used for military production. To these ends:

     (a) All German land, naval and air forces, the SS, SA, SD and Gestapo, with all their organizations, staffs and institutions, including the General Staff, the Officers' Corps, Reserve Corps, military schools, war veterans' organizations and all other military and semi-military organizations, together with all clubs and associations which serve to keep alive the military tradition in Germany, shall be completely and finally abolished in such manner as permanently to prevent the revival or reorganization of German militarism and Nazism;

     (b) All arms, ammunition and implements of war and all specialized facilities for their production shall be held at the disposal of the Allies or destroyed. The maintenance and production of all aircraft and all arms, ammunition and implements of war shall be prevented.

   (ii) To convince the German people that they have suffered a total military defeat and that they cannot escape responsibility for what they have brought upon themselves, since their own ruthless warfare and the fanatical Nazi resistance have destroyed German economy and made chaos and suffering inevitable.

(iii) To destroy the National Socialist Party and its affiliated and super-vised organizations, to dissolve all Nazi institutions, to ensure that they are not revived in any form, and to prevent all Nazi and militarist activity or propaganda.

(iv) To prepare for the eventual reconstruction of German political life on a democratic basis and for eventual peaceful co-operation in international life by Germany.

4. All Nazi laws which provided the basis of the Hitler régime or established discrimination on grounds of race, creed, or political opinion shall be abolished. No such discriminations, whether legal, adminis-trative or otherwise, shall be tolerated.

5. War criminals and those who have participated in planning or carrying out Nazi enterprises involving or resulting in atrocities or war crimes shall be arrested and brought to judgment. Nazi leaders, influential Nazi supporters and high officials of Nazi organizations and institutions and any other persons dangerous to the occupation or its objectives shall be arrested and interned.

6. All members of the Nazi party who have been more than nominal participants in its activities and all other persons hostile to Allied purposes shall be removed from public and semi-public office, and from positions of responsibility in important private undertakings. Such persons shall be replaced by persons who, by their political and moral qualities, are deemed capable of assisting in developing genuine democratic institutions in Germany.

7. German education shall be so controlled as completely to eliminate Nazi and militarist doctrines and to make possible the successful develop-ment of democratic ideas.

8. The judicial system will be reorganized in accordance with the principles of democracy, of justice under law, and of equal rights for all citizens without distinction of race, nationality or religion.

9. The administration in Germany should be directed towards the de-centralization of the political structure and the development of local responsibility. To this end:

(i) local self-government shall be restored throughout Germany on democratic principles and in particular through elective councils as rapidly as is consistent with military security and the purposes of military occupations;

(ii) all democratic political parties with rights of assembly and of public discussion shall be allowed and encouraged throughout Germany;

(iii) representative and elective principles shall be introduced into regional, provincial and State (*Land*) administration as rapidly as may be justified by the successful application of these principles in local self-government;

(iv) for the time being, no central German Government shall be established. Notwithstanding this, however, certain essential central German administrative departments, headed by State Secretaries, shall be established, particularly in the fields of finance, transport, communications, foreign trade and industry. Such departments will act under the direction of the Control Council.

10. Subject to the necessity for maintaining military security, freedom of speech, press and religion shall be permitted, and religious institutions shall be respected. Subject likewise to the maintenance of military security, the formation of free trade unions shall be permitted.

B Economic Principles

11. In order to eliminate Germany's war potential, the production of arms, ammunition and implements of war as well as all types of aircraft and sea-going ships shall be prohibited and prevented. Production of metals, chemicals machinery and other items that are directly necessary to a war economy, shall be rigidly controlled and restricted to Germany's approved post-war peace-time needs to meet the objectives stated in paragraph 15. Productive capacity not needed for permitted production shall be removed in accordance with the reparations plan recommended by the Allied Commission on reparations and approved by the Governments concerned or, if not removed, shall be destroyed.

12. At the earliest practicable date, the German economy shall be decentralized for the purpose of eliminating the present excessive concentration of economic power as exemplified in particular by cartels, syndicates, trusts and other monopolistic arrangements.

13. In organizing the German economy, primary emphasis shall be given to the development of agriculture and peaceful domestic industries.

14. During the period of occupation Germany shall be treated as a single economic unit. To this end common policies shall be established in regard to:
   (a) mining and industrial production and its allocation;
   (b) agriculture, forestry and fishing;
   (c) wages, prices, and rationing;
   (d) import and export programmes for Germany as a whole;
   (e) currency and banking, central taxation and customs;
   (f) reparation and removal of industrial war potential;
   (g) transportation and communications.

In applying these policies account shall be taken, where appropriate, of varying local conditions.

15. Allied controls shall be imposed upon the German economy but only to the extent necessary:
   (*a*) to carry out programmes of industrial disarmament and demilitarization, of reparations, and of approved exports and imports;
   (*b*) to assure the production and maintenance of goods and services

required to meet the needs of the occupying forces and displaced persons in Germany and essential to maintain in Germany average living standards not exceeding the average of the standards of living of European countries. (European countries means all European countries excluding the United Kingdom and the Union of Soviet Socialist Republics);

(c) to ensure in the manner determined by the Control Council the equitable distribution of essential commodities between the several zones so as to produce a balanced economy throughout Germany and reduce the need for imports;

(d) to control German industry and all economic and financial international transactions, including exports and imports, with the aim of preventing Germany from developing a war potential and of achieving the other objectives named herein;

(e) to control all German public or private scientific bodies, research and experimental institutions, laboratories, etc. connected with economic activities.

16. In the imposition and maintenance of economic controls established by the Control Council, German administrative machinery shall be created and the German authorities shall be required to the fullest extent practicable to proclaim and assume administration of such controls. Thus it should be brought home to the German people that the responsibility for the administration of such controls and any breakdown in these controls will rest with themselves. Any German controls which may run counter to the objectives of occupation will be prohibited.

17. Measures shall be promptly taken:
    (a) to effect essential repair of transport;
    (b) to enlarge coal production;
    (c) to maximize agricultural output;
    (d) to effect emergency repair of housing and essential utilities.

18. Appropriate steps shall be taken by the Control Council to exercise control and the power of disposition over German-owned external assets not already under the control of United Nations which have taken part in the war against Germany.

19. Payment of reparations should leave enough resources to enable the German people to subsist without external assistance. In working out the economic balance of Germany the necessary means must be provided to pay for imports approved by the Control Council in Germany. The proceeds of exports from current production and stocks shall be available in the first place for payment for such imports.

The above clause will not apply to the equipment and products referred to in paragraph 4 (a) and 4 (b) of the Reparations Agreement.

XII ORDERLY TRANSFER OF GERMAN POPULATIONS

The Three Governments, having considered the question in all its aspects, recognize that the transfer to Germany of German populations, or elements thereof, remaining in Poland, Czechoslovakia and Hungary, will have to be undertaken. They agree that any transfers that take place should be effected in an orderly and humane manner.

Since the influx of a large number of Germans into Germany would increase the burden already resting on the occupying authorities, they consider that the Control Council in Germany should, in the first instance, examine the problem, with special regard to the question of the equitable distribution of these Germans among the several zones of occupation. They are accordingly instructing their respective representatives on the Control Council to report to their Governments as soon as possible the extent to which such persons have already entered Germany from Poland, Czechoslovakia and Hungary, and to submit an estimate of the time and rate at which further transfer could be carried out having regard to the present situation in Germany.

The Czechoslovak Government, the Polish Provisional Government and the Control Council in Hungary are at the same time being informed of the above and are being requested meanwhile to suspend further expulsions pending an examination by the Governments concerned of the report from their representatives on the Control Council.

(*Protocol of the Proceedings of the Berlin Conference*, London, HMSO, 1947)

II.11   Interview with resistance worker (M. Pestourie) by Dr H. R. Kedward (24 June 1969)

In 1940 I was a bachelor aged 20 with a peasant background on both sides of the family. My father had died when he was 32 as a result of his injuries in the First World War. My brother was mobilized in 1939 and captured and made a prisoner of war in 1940. As a result I had to leave the job I had in a transport firm in Brive and return to the family farm of seventeen hectares in the Lot. I had been a member of the Young Communists since 1937 and a member of the party since 1938.

When war had been declared I felt the same kind of shock as the rest of my generation. I was convinced that war was inevitable after the refusal of Britain and France to form an anti-Fascist pact with Russia. During the *drôle de guerre* I saw the bourgeoisie use the pretext of the Nazi-Soviet pact to revenge themselves on the working class by turning the French people against the PCF.

I was stupefied by the signing of the Armistice, even though my party had led me to expect it. I felt a deep anger and resentment against those who had produced the disaster and the humiliation. I would quite happily have used violence at once against the traitors.

By and large the great majority of the communist militants in Brive remained faithful to the party. I myself had confidence in the USSR, and this allowed me to understand the pact. But we had to think things out for ourselves as the liaisons with the party were broken and we had to take the initiative at the grass roots. The pact had traumatized public opinion and the party was even more isolated than it had been at the time of Munich. Our first reaction was one of self-defence against all this suspicion and hostility. There were several different ideas about the situation within the party and many comrades were at first influenced by the public hostility. They were honest party members who just didn't understand. Several of them had been soldiers in the 1914–18 War and were affected by the government propaganda of 1939–40, which declared that this was another patriotic war. But it wasn't, and they could soon see that. It was an imperialist war in 1939 and *not* a war against Fascism. You could see that by the way in which the working class were opposed by a hostile bourgeois government. And then comrades came back from the front and told us that the whole war was a bluff. No one was fighting against Hitler; there was no intention at all to wage war against him.

So from the start our Resistance was a class struggle, a struggle against Fascism which we had started before the war. Once we were invaded we added propaganda for the liberation of the country to the class war.

You mustn't forget that we were very dispersed in 1939–40, not just because of persecution but also because of mobilization and all the prisoners of war. So we had to start our activity by making lists. Our job was to find out who was still there and to contact them. We contacted the wives when the husbands were missing. We had to show we still existed. This was Resistance because it was illegal. Only then did we go on to reform the party in groups of three. I remember investigating the *Lycée* at Cahors and schools in Brive during 1941–2, still looking for Communists but also good republicans who were not necessarily members of the party. Bit by bit we built up an underground organization.

At that time we didn't hear of any other movements, though we knew of de Gaulle's broadcast. Gaullism spread much faster than we did. It had the benefit of the radio, and there were many popular ways of showing you were a Gaullist. I remember people coming out of mass in our village in the Lot and just saying '*Vive de Gaulle*' to each other.

Pétain's influence did enormous damage to the Resistance. His hold over the families of prisoners of war was very strong. The trouble was that people's bitterness about the defeat didn't make them want to do something active to change the situation but made them even more submissive to Pétain. They also thought he was playing a double game and was getting ready to defeat the Germans. The officers in the Armistice Army believed that, and in Brive they thought he would call for armed Resistance when the Germans invaded the southern zone. They were bitterly disillusioned.

(H. R. Kedward, *Resistance in Vichy France*, London, Oxford University Press, 1978)

II.12   Interview with resistance worker (M. Chauliac) by Dr H. R. Kedward (20 Sept. 1970)

I was 36 in 1940 and was an engineer in Montpellier. I was a Catholic and was married with three children. I was on the municipal council and was well-known in the town. I was a dissident from the Socialist Party along with Marcel Déat, and had been in favour of the Munich agreement of 1938 and against the war. I suppose I was a pacifist, more or less.

During the war I was attached to aircraft control in the air force, but mainly dealing with civil aviation. In June 1940 I tried to cross to Algiers from Bordeaux but was overtaken by the Armistice. I returned to Montpellier, where, to begin with, I was fairly undecided what to do. Mers-el-Kébir was a severe blow. But I rejected the defeatism of Déat and also that of the Communists. I had read *Mein Kampf* and was strongly opposed to Nazism.

In Montpellier I resigned as a municipal councillor before the Vichy suppression of local government. I was hostile to Pétain and never thought he was playing a double game. Before the war I was an official of the *Fédération des Officiers de Réserve Républicains*, which was left-wing, and on the whole most of us refused to join Pétain's *Légion*.

My resistance was a progressive activity, starting from talking to friends whose attitudes I was confident about. I knew the professors in the University who were hostile to the Armistice and collaboration, and I became involved with Renouvin's activities and with *Combat*. I recruited mainly among my friends, though by 1943 there were a lot of Jews under my command in the *Armée Secrète* (AS). Resistance was not a movement of the people until August 1944.

The clandestine press was very important, so too was the fact that there were all types of people in the Resistance. There was a great fraternity of different jobs and different political backgrounds.

The Armistice Army missed a great chance in November 1942. It refused to give the arms it had camouflaged to the Resistance, but rather threw them into rivers and ponds or surrendered them. Nevertheless, we had organized the first armed *maquis* in the area before the end of 1942, in fact before the total occupation of the southern zone.

(H. R. Kedward, *Resistance in Vichy France*, London, Oxford University Press, 1978)

II.13   Interview with resistance worker (M. Malafosse) by Dr H. R. Kedward (20 Sept. 1970)

When war broke out I was an artillery officer in the reserve. I volunteered shortly afterwards to go on the Norwegian campaign, and on the way back in April 1940 I passed through England. From that point I knew the determination of the English.

I was 27 at the time, had received my doctorate in law at Montpellier, and was a barrister at Béziers. I had no party politics, but I had rejected the Munich agreement of 1938 because I knew what Hitler's game was. Those responsible for the French defeat were firstly the General Staff, secondly the French people, and thirdly Daladier, who admitted that he couldn't get rid of incompetent generals. As a barrister I was asked to talk to the troops I was with about the German danger. They didn't know what it was. The average Frenchman thought the French army was the strongest in the world. Once it was defeated he thought nothing else could possibly resist. I myself was totally opposed to Pétain's Armistice decision since he knew the power of England and the USA.

When I arrived back in France in mid-May 1940, I was sent to Chantilly, but the Germans were already on their way. I was then sent to Briançon to fight against the Italians. When the Armistice was declared, I was told to surrender our arms to the Italians. I refused to do so.

I returned to the bar at Béziers but still had the spirit of adventure. I had volunteered for Norway and I had volunteered for the anti-tank units. My anti-Vichy ideas were soon well-known in Béziers. I made no secret of them in the corridors of the law courts. In 1940 I had no colleagues who shared my opinion and by 1942 there were still very few. They were almost all Pétainist.

In October 1940 I had my first conversation with another barrister, André Boyer in Marseille. By the spring of 1941 we were in contact with London, and I was part of the network Brutus, seeking out military information. It was difficult in the southern zone because there were no Germans. I also distributed propaganda from *Combat* and defended Communists in Béziers. I defended Solié because I had known him before the war. But I had been very critical of the Nazi-Soviet pact, and before the invasion of Russia the Communist Party in the area did nothing, *qua* party. But individuals did do something as individual Communists.

I myself was of independent means and had plenty of money. This was an important facility in my Resistance activity. I became a Resister, I suppose, because I was against Hitler, but chance had a lot to do with it. I was also a patriot, and more and more of a democrat. We recruited mainly among workers.

(H. R. Kedward, *Resistance in Vichy France*, London, Oxford University Press, 1978)

II.14 'Programme of the CNR (Conseil National de la Résistance)' (15 March 1944)

1. To establish the Provisional Government of the Republic formed by General de Gaulle for the defence of the political and economic independence of the nation and to re-establish France in the full power and grandeur of her universal mission;

2. To ensure the punishment of traitors and the expulsion from government and private occupations of all who have had dealings with the

enemy or who have been actively associated with the policies of the collaborationist governments;

3. To secure the confiscation of the possessions of traitors and black marketeers, by the establishment of a progressive tax on the spoils of war and more generally on the profits taken at the expense of the people and of the nation during the occupation, along with the confiscation of all enemy possessions including the shares acquired in all types of French and colonial enterprises since the armistice by the Axis Governments and their citizens, with the restoration of these shares to the inalienable national patrimony.

4. To assure:
—the establishment of the widest democracy and a voice to the French people, by the establishment of universal suffrage; full liberty of thought, conscience and expression;
—the freedom of the press, its integrity and independence, with respect to the state, the monied interests, and foreign influence; freedom of association, assembly and demonstration;
—the sanctity of the home and privacy of correspondence;
—respect for the human person;
—absolute equality of all citizens before the law.

5. United as to the goal to be attained, united as to the means required to achieve this goal, the speedy liberation of the country, the representatives of the movements, groups, parties and political tendencies joined together in the CNR, proclaim their decision to remain united after the liberation . . .

In order to promote essential reforms:

(a) Economic plan:
—the establishment of a true economic and social democracy, involving the expulsion of the great feudal combines of economics and finance from the direction of the economy;
—a rational organization of the economy assuring the subordination of private interest to the general interest and freed from the direction of employment instituted in the image of the fascist states;
—an increase in national production in accordance with the plan to be issued by the state after consultation with everyone involved in such production . . .

6. *In the social sphere:*
—the right to work and the right to rest, notably by the re-establishment and improvement of the system of contracts of employment;
—a significant readjustment of earnings and the guarantee of a level of earnings and benefits assuring each worker and his family security, dignity and the opportunity to lead a full human life;
—the maintenance of purchasing power through a policy of monetary stability;

—the re-establishment with its traditional freedom of an independent trade unionism, equipped with substantial power in the organization of social and economic life;

—a complete social security plan, assuring all citizens of the means of existence in every eventuality preventing them from earning it by their own labour, with full State representation in the running of the plan;

—security of employment, regulation of hiring and dismissing, and the re-appointment of workshop delegates;

—raising of the guaranteed standard of life of the agricultural workers by a policy of agricultural prices based on, but improving upon, the experience of the *Office du Blé* [Wheat Control Office], by social legislation giving agricultural employees the same rights as industrial employees, by a system of insurance against agricultural calamities, by the establishment of a fair rate for tenant farming or share cropping [*metayage*, paying rent in kind], through facilitating the acquisition of property by young peasant families and a scheme for providing farm equipment;

—retirement pensions sufficient to enable ageing workers to finish their days in dignity;

—compensation for the war wounded and grants and pensions for the victims of fascist terror;

—an extension of political, social and economic rights to native and colonial populations;

—positive opportunities for French children to benefit from education and have access to the most advanced culture, whatever the financial situation of their parents, so that the highest positions may be truly open to everyone with the necessary abilities and a true élite of merit, not birth, be established, and constantly renewed by recruitment from the people.

Thus will a new Republic be founded which will sweep away the régime of vile reaction established by Vichy and which will confer on the institutions of democracy and on the people the power which they were denied by the organs of corruption and treachery which existed prior to the capitulation. Thus will be made possible a democracy which unites continuity of government action with effective control exercised by the representatives of the people.

The unity of the representatives of the Resistance for action now and in the future, in the higher interest of the Motherland, must serve for all French people as a pledge of confidence and an incentive. It must prompt them to eradicate all sectional sentiment, all spirit of division which might inhibit their action and would benefit only the enemy.

Forward, then, in the union of all French people grouped round the CFLN and its President, General de Gaulle. Forward into battle. Forward to the victory through which France will live again.

THE NATIONAL COUNCIL OF THE RESISTANCE comprising:

The Movement for National Liberation (*Combat, Franc-Tireur, Libération, France au Combat, Défense de la France, Lorraine, Résistance*);
The National Front
The Civil and Military Organization (OCH)
Liberation of the Northern Zone;
The People of Resistance;
The People of Liberation;
The General Confederation of Workers;
The French Confederation of Christian Workers;

The following parties and political tendencies:
Communist Party;
Socialist Party;
Radical-Republican and Radical-Socialist Party;
Popular Democratic Party;
Democratic Alliance;
Republican Federation.

(H. Michel and B. Mirkine Guetzevitch, *Les idées politiques et sociales de la résistance*, Paris, Presses Universitaires de France, 1954, pp. 215–18, trans. Arthur Marwick)

II.15   Poster by Committee of Action for the Union of the Italian People (Oct. 1942)

AWAY WITH THE POWER OF MUSSOLINI, WHICH HAS THE MAJOR RESPONSIBILITY FOR THE BOMBING OF OUR CITIES

Italians!

Liguria, Lombardy and Piedmont have been invaded by air and bombarded as never before till the arrival of the bombers of the RAF. Many buildings destroyed, hundreds of children, women and men killed and wounded, the population gripped by the most terrifying panic, such is the balance sheet of this first large bombing raid.

Italians!

Mussolini and his government have the major responsibility for these bomb attacks.

It is the wars and bombing raids willed by Mussolini against the helpless populations of Abyssinia, Spain, Albania, France, England, Greece, Yugoslavia, Poland and Russia; it is the subjugation of Italy to Hitler, planned and willed by Mussolini, and the perpetuation of the war, which has brought upon our cities the bomb attacks of the RAF.

Italians!

Mussolini has brought upon our cities the bombing planes of the RAF and has knowingly left our population without defences.

In Milan and Genoa fighter planes, anti-aircraft batteries and air-raid warning systems are not operational, are not capable of defending the population because they are virtually non-existent. Shelters have been revealed as death traps and not suitable for defence against bomb attacks, the children and the sick were not evacuated, because Mussolini is a criminal, and gave no forethought to the protection of the people against aerial attack.

Lombardians, Ligurians, Piedmontesi!

In every workshop, in every house you must make your own precautions, assisted by the Committee of Action, in organizing assistance for the injured in the bomb attacks, in organizing the evacuation of the children and the sick from the city, in building and making better use of shelters, in organizing an air-raid warning system.

Italians!

Our country finds itself faced with the alternative of making an immediate separate peace, with England, the Soviet Union, and America, or else with being forced to assist the destruction of its own cities and the massacre of its own population by the increasingly powerful forces of the united nations.

Italians!

To save our country from destruction, to save our population from massacre, let us bring about by every means the hounding down of the government of Mussolini, the hounding out of our country of the Germans, immediate separate peace with England, the Soviet Union and America.

> Down with the continuance of Hitler's war!
> Down with the criminal Government of Mussolini!
> Long live separate and immediate peace,
> independence and liberty.

(Committee of Action for the Union of the Italian People, *Il 1943*, Florence, La Nuova Italia Edizione, 1974, trans. Arthur Marwick)

II.16 *L'Unita* report on strike of 100,000 Turin workers (15 March 1943)

STRIKE OF 100,000 TURIN WORKERS. THROUGHOUT THE COUNTRY THEIR EXAMPLE IS BEING FOLLOWED TO WIN BREAD, PEACE AND LIBERTY. LONG LIVE THE STRIKERS OF TURIN.

Since 5 March in the factories of Turin . . . more than 100,000 workers have been on strike. For more than a week, at 10 o'clock every morning, in the workshops the roar of the machines, the screeching of files, the thundering of hammers, is extinguished; the forces of muscle stop, the nervous tension of work on the assembly line lets up; faces marked by dignity and determination rise from the machines and from the benches; arms link together: STRIKE!

A potent mass of men, which fascism thought it had reduced to miserable appendices to the machines and controls, affirms with a unanimous and decisive act its dignity, its strength, its direction.

No law, no decree, no manoeuvre has so far been able to stop this magnificent movement. The attempts of the provincial Secretary of the Fascist Syndicates, Balletti, of the local Secretary and of the Prefect who sent the police into the factory, have not been able to subdue the firm decision of the workers of Turin, have not been able to break the solid bonds which unite workers of every political tendency, of every religious persuasion, in this struggle. The intervention of these party leaders has done nothing more than expose to the masses their function as agents of Hitlerism, as enemies of the people, as traitors of their country.

What are they striking for, what do they want, the strikers of Turin?

They are demanding that the 192 hours' evacuation allowance shall be paid without exception to all workers; a cost of living allowance adequate to the scandalous rise in prices; rations of bread, meat, fats corresponding to the minimum physiological requirements. They are on strike, then, for sacrosanct demands; they are on strike to demonstrate their feelings, and those of their families, over the intolerable weight of privation and sacrifice, of the hunger which the war of Hitler and Mussolini has visited on the ordinary people.

With their firm and courageous action the workers of Turin have demonstrated that the working class, when it is *united*, can stand up against, whatever the situation, the arrogance of those who profit from war and against fascist repression. But the unity of the struggle, the unity and the firmness of the working class must not remain a local phenomenon; this proletarian fire must be extended to all Italian workers to frustrate the starvation plans of the profiteers and the party leaders.

One thing, then, is urgently needed: the intervention in the struggle – by the same method of strike action – of the workers of Milan, of Genoa and of all the industrial centres of the Peninsula. . . .

The strikers of Turin are arousing waves of sympathy and hope in all strata of the Italian population; they have the support of all in the Nation who wish to make an end to the war and to the brigands of the Palazzo Venezia who have sold Italy to Hitler. In this situation the strikers of Turin assume an extraordinary importance: they can become the starting point of the powerful and irresistible struggle for *Bread, Peace and Liberty*.

(reprinted in *Il 1943*, Florence, La Nuova Italia Editione, 1974, trans. Arthur Marwick)

II.17 Statement issued by Field Marshal Rommel (23 Sept. 1943)

The German armed forces have occupied Italian territory. They are not only defending Italian soil, but are seeking to protect the laws of the nation against those people who attempt to disturb the tranquillity and the work of this country.

Whoever attempts to disturb the peace and order of the country, whoever attempts to support communist or anarchist movements against the security of the Italian people, is an enemy of his Motherland. Such people will suffer the penalties established by the severe laws of the military Tribunal.

The German armed forces are clear-sighted and just. Whoever tries to transgress the law and further seeks to support movements of rebellion will incur the full severity of German military law.

Communists and all of you who follow the same opinions, be warned.

The Commanding General of the German Forces
Rommel
Field Marshal

(reprinted in *Il 1943*, Florence, La Nuova Italia Editione, 1974, trans. Arthur Marwick)

II.18   Letter from Supreme Commander of the People's Liberation Partisan Detachments (Tito) to the Command of the Italian Troops of Occupation in Prijepolje (15 Dec. 1941)

The undersigned Headquarters have learned and ascertained that during their campaign of plunder against the peaceful civilian population in the villages of Drenova and Vranjak the units of the Italian Army have perpetrated the following crimes on December 14, 1941:

1. Several farm houses and outhouses have been set on fire and burned.

2. Various movable property, livestock, provisions, etc. have been plundered and looted.

3. Over ten peasants, including women and children, have been slain.

4. Besides, the most brutal crime of all is that in the house of peasant Radak your marauding bands have killed two young women, one of whom was the mother of seven-day-old twins.

In view of the foregoing we are notifying you hereby that these Headquarters have decided to shoot your officer Marini who was taken captive near Nova Varos and 20 of your officers and non-commissioned officers currently held prisoner by us on the territory of Montenegro.

We are warning you that we shall henceforth retaliate in this manner to every case of arson and slaughter of the civilian population at the hands of your soldiers and officers, and thus deter you once and for all from destroying our peaceful population.

We ask you what was the reason for your appalling brutality which is unworthy of true soldiers? Were you given any cause on our part? Did we not set free or exchange your captive officers and soldiers? Can you deny us the right to fight for freedom against your violence? For us you are the enemy, whom we have always treated nonetheless as decent soldiers. Your heinous crimes have exceeded the limit and we are warning you once again that every new misdeed will entail dire consequences for you.

Finally, gentlemen officers of the occupying Italian army, you know but do not wish to know that Hitler, your master, has suffered a major defeat on the Eastern Front, that his armies are falling apart and fleeing in panic. This is the beginning of the end, both Hitler's and the end of your reign of terror and violence as occupiers. You should duly take this into account if you wish to save your skins in this country.

Listen to the broadcast of other radio stations and not only to Rome and Berlin who are lying to you all of the time. Look forth squarely in the face and do not bury your heads in the sand as ostriches. Know then that a great turning point has been reached and that total collapse, yours and your master's, is not far away. We shall fight for the freedom of our people against you and your master Hitler, until final victory which is already near. And in this struggle we are entitled to demand that you behave as true soldiers and not as plunderers, bandits and murderers.

(Nova Varos, about December 15, 1941)

Supreme Headquarters of Partisan Detachments.

(Military Institute of the Yugoslav People's Army, *The National Liberation War and Revolution in Yugoslavia (1941–1945). Selected Documents*, Belgrade, 1982, pp. 171–2)

II.19 Extracts from the Beveridge Report (1942)

In proceeding from this first comprehensive survey of social insurance [carried out by the Beveridge Committee] to the next task – of making recommendations – three guiding principles may be laid down at the outset.

The first principle is that any proposals for the future, while they should use to the full experience gathered in the past, should not be restricted by consideration of sectional interests established in the obtaining of that experience. Now, when the war is abolishing all landmarks of every kind, is the opportunity for using experience in a clear field. A revolutionary moment in the world's history is a time for revolutions, not for patching.

The second principle is that organization of social insurance should be treated as one part only of a comprehensive policy of social progress. Social insurance fully developed may provide income security; it is an attack upon Want. But Want is only one of five giants on the road of reconstruction and in some ways the easiest to attack. The others are Disease, Ignorance, Squalor and Idleness.

The third principle is that social security must be achieved by co-operation between the State and the individual. The State should offer security for service and contribution. The State in organizing security should not stifle incentive, opportunity, responsibility; in establishing a national minimum, it should leave room and encouragement for voluntary action by each individual to provide more than that minimum for himself and his family.

The Plan for Social Security set out in this Report is built upon these principles. It uses experience but is not tied by experience. It is put forward as a limited contribution to a wider social policy, though as something that could be achieved now without waiting for the whole of that policy. It is, first and foremost, a plan of insurance – of giving in return for contributions benefits up to subsistence level, as of right and without means test, so that individuals may build freely upon it. . . .

The main feature of the Plan for Social Security is a scheme of social insurance against interruption and destruction of earning power and for special expenditure arising at birth, marriage or death. The scheme embodies six fundamental principles: flat rate of subsistence benefit; flat rate of contribution; unification of administrative responsibility; adequacy of benefit; comprehensiveness; and classification. . . . Based on them and in combination with national assistance and voluntary insurance as subsidiary methods, the aim of the Plan for Social Security is to make want under any circumstances unnecessary. . . .

The main provisions of the plan may be summarized as follows:

(i) The plan covers all citizens without upper income limit, but has regard to their different ways of life; it is a plan all-embracing in scope of persons and of needs, but is classified in application.

(ii) In relation to social security the population falls into four main classes of working age and two others below and above working age respectively, as follows:

I. Employees, that is, persons whose normal occupation is employment under contract of service.

II. Others gainfully occupied, including employers, traders and independent workers of all kinds.

III. Housewives, that is married women of working age.

IV. Others of working age not gainfully occupied.

V. Below working age.

VI. Retired above working age.

(iii) The sixth of these classes will receive retirement pensions and the fifth will be covered by children's allowances, which will be paid from the National Exchequer in respect of all children when the responsible parent is in receipt of insurance benefit or pension, and in respect of all children except one in other cases. The four other classes will be insured for security appropriate to their circumstances. All classes will be covered for comprehensive medical treatment and rehabilitation and for funeral expenses.

(iv)   Every person in Class I, II or IV will pay a single security contribution by a stamp on a single insurance document each week or combination of weeks. In Class I the employer will also contribute, affixing the insurance stamp and deducting the employee's share from wages or salary. The contribution will differ from one class to another, according to the benefits provided, and will be higher for men than for women, so as to secure benefits for Class III.

(v)   Subject to simple contribution conditions, every person in Class I will receive benefit for unemployment and disability, pension on retirement, medical treatment and funeral expenses. Persons in Class II will receive all these except unemployment benefit and disability benefit during the first thirteen weeks of disability. Persons in Class IV will receive all these except unemployment and disability benefit. As a substitute for unemployment benefit, training benefit will be available to persons in all classes other than Class I, to assist them to find new livelihoods if their present ones fail. Maternity grant, provision for widowhood and separation and qualification for retirement pensions will be secured to all persons in Class III by virtue of their husbands' contributions; in addition to maternity grant, housewives who take paid work will receive maternity benefit for thirteen weeks to enable them to give up working before and after childbirth. . . .

(vii)   Unemployment benefit will continue at the same rate without means test so long as unemployment lasts, but will normally be subject to a condition of attendance at a work or training centre after a certain period. Disability benefit will continue at the same rate without means test, so long as disability lasts or till it is replaced by industrial pension, subject to acceptance of suitable medical treatment or vocational training. . . .

(x)   For the limited number of cases of need not covered by social insurance, national assistance subject to a uniform means test will be available.

(xi)   Medical treatment covering all requirements will be provided for all citizens by a national health service organized under the health departments, and post-medical rehabilitation treatment will be provided for all persons capable of profiting by it.

(xii)   A Ministry of Social Security will be established, responsible for social insurance, national assistance and encouragement and supervision of voluntary insurance and will take over, so far as necessary for these purposes, the present work of other Government Departments and of Local Authorities in these fields.

Under the scheme of social insurance, which forms the main feature of this plan, every citizen of working age will contribute in his appropriate class according to the security that he needs, or as a married woman will have contributions made by the husband. Each will be covered for all his needs by a single weekly contribution on one insurance document. All the principal cash payments – for unemployment, disability and retirement –

will continue so long as the need lasts, without means test, and will be paid from a Social Insurance Fund built up by contributions from the insured persons, from their employers, if any, and from the State. . . .

Social security as used in this Report means assurance of a certain income. The Plan for Social Security set out in the Report is a plan to win freedom from want by maintaining incomes. But sufficiency of income is not sufficient in itself. Freedom from want is only one of the essential freedoms of mankind. Any Plan for Social Security in the narrow sense assumes a concerted social policy in many fields, most of which it would be inappropriate to discuss in this Report. The plan proposed here involves three particular assumptions so closely related to it that brief discussion is essential for understanding of the plan itself. . . .

The first of three assumptions underlying the Plan for Social Security is a general scheme of children's allowances. This means that direct provision for the maintenance of dependent children will be made by payment of allowances to those responsible for the care of those children. . . .

As to the source of children's allowances, the view taken here is that they should be non-contributory, provided wholly out of taxation and not to any extent out of insurance contributions. . . .

The second of the three assumptions [comprehensive health and rehabilitation services] has two sides to it. It covers a national health service for prevention and for cure of disease and disability by medical treatment; it covers rehabilitation and fitting for employment by treatment which will be both medical and post-medical. . . .

The first part of assumption B is that a comprehensive national health service will ensure that for every citizen there is available whatever medical treatment he requires, in whatever form he requires it, domiciliary or institutional, general, specialist or consultant, and will ensure also the provision of dental, ophthalmic and surgical appliances, nursing and midwifery and rehabilitation after accidents. Whether or not payment towards the cost of the health service is included in the social insurance contribution, the service itself should

(i) be organized, not by the Ministry concerned with social insurance, but by Departments responsible for the health of the people and for positive and preventive as well as curative measures;

(ii) be provided where needed without contribution conditions in any individual case.

Restoration of a sick person to health is a duty of the State and the sick person, prior to any other consideration. . . .

Assumption C [maintenance of employment] does not imply complete abolition of unemployment. In industries subject to season influences, irregularities of work are inevitable; in an economic system subject to change and progress, fluctuations in the fortunes of individual employers or of particular industries are inevitable; the possibility of controlling completely the major alternations of good trade and bad trade which are described under the term of the trade cycle has not been established; a country like Britain, which must have exports to pay for its raw materials, cannot be immune from the results of changes of fortune or of economic policy in other countries. The Plan for Social Security provides benefit for a substantial volume of unemployment. In the industries now subject to unemployment insurance, the finance of the Unemployment Fund has been based by the Unemployment Insurance Statutory Committee on the assumption of an average rate of unemployment through good years and bad of about 15 per cent. In framing the Social Security Budget . . . it has been assumed that, in the industries now subject to insurance, the average rate of unemployment will in future be about 10 per cent and that over the whole body of insured employees in Class I unemployment, will average about 8½ per cent. It is right to hope that unemployment can be reduced to below that level, in which case more money will be available in the Social Insurance Fund either for better benefits or for reduction of contributions. But it would not be prudent to assume any lower rate of unemployment in preparing the Security Budget. Assumption C requires not the abolition of all unemployment, but the abolition of mass unemployment and of unemployment prolonged year after year for the same individual. In the beginning of compulsory unemployment insurance in 1913 and 1914, it was found that less than 5 per cent of all the unemployment experienced in the insured industries occurred after men had been unemployed for as long as 15 weeks. Even if it does not prove possible to get back to that level of employment, it should be possible to make unemployment of any individual for more than 26 weeks continuously a rare thing in normal times. . . .

The argument of this section can be summed up briefly. Abolition of want cannot be brought about merely by increasing production, without seeing to correct distribution of the product; but correct distribution does not mean what it has often been taken to mean in the past – distribution between the different agents in production, between land, capital, management and labour. Better distribution of purchasing power is required among wage-earners themselves, as between times of earning and not earning, and between times of heavy family responsibilities and of light or no family responsibilities. Both social insurance and children's allowances are primarily methods of redistributing wealth. Such better distribution cannot fail to add to welfare and, properly designed, it can increase wealth, by maintaining physical vigour. It does not decrease wealth, unless it involves waste in administration or reduces incentives to production. Unemployment and disability are already being paid for unconsciously; it is no addition to the burden on the community to provide for them consciously. Unified social insurance will eliminate a good deal of waste inherent in present methods. Properly designed, controlled and financed, it need have no depressing effect on incentive.

Want could have been abolished in Britain just before the present war. It can be abolished after the war, unless the British people are and remain very much poorer then than they were before, that is to say unless they remain less productive than they and their fathers were. There is no sense in believing, contrary to experience, that they will and must be less productive. The answer to the question whether freedom from want should be regarded as a post-war aim capable of early attainment is an affirmative. . . .

(*Parliamentary Papers, 1942–3*, vol. VI, Cmd. 6404, London, HMSO)

II.20 Orders issued by General Lemelsen, Commander 48th Panzer Corps (June 1941)

(a) 25 June 1941
I have observed that senseless shootings of both POWs and civilians have taken place. A Russian soldier who has been taken prisoner while wearing a uniform after he put up a brave fight, has the right to decent treatment. We want to free the civilian population from the yoke of Bolshevism and we need their labour force. . . . This instruction does not change anything regarding the Führer's order on the ruthless action to be taken against partisans and Bolshevik commissars.

(b) 30 June 1941
In spite of my instructions of 25.6.41 . . . still more shootings of POWs and deserters have been observed, conducted in an irresponsible, senseless and criminal manner. This is murder! The German *Wehrmacht* is waging this war against Bolshevism, not against the united Russian peoples. We want to bring back peace, calm and order to this land which has suffered terribly for many years from the oppression of a Jewish and criminal group. The instruction of the Führer calls for ruthless action against Bolshevism (political commissars) and any kind of partisan! People who have been clearly identified as such should be taken aside and shot only by order of an officer . . . [descriptions] of the scenes of countless bodies of soldiers lying on the roads, having clearly been killed by a shot through the head at point blank range, without their weapons and with their hands raised, will quickly spread in the enemy's army.

(O. Bartov, *The Eastern Front, 1941–45: German Troops and the Barbarisation of Warfare*, London, Macmillan, 1986)

II.21 *Pravda* report on factory moved from the Ukraine to the Urals (18 Sept. 1942)

Among the mountains and the pine forests there is spread out the beautiful capital of the Urals, Svedlorsk. It has many fine buildings, but I want to tell you of the two most remarkable buildings in the area. Winter had already come when Svedlorsk reviewed Comrade Stalin's order to erect two buildings for the plant evacuated from the south. The trains packed with machinery and people were on the way. The war factory had to start production in its new home – and it had to do so in not more than a fortnight. Fourteen days, and not an hour more! It was then that the people of the Urals came to this spot with shovels, bars and pickaxes: students, typists, accountants, shop assistants, housewives, artists, teachers. The earth was like stone, frozen hard by our fierce Siberian frost. Axes and pickaxes could not break the strong soil. In the light of arc-lamps people hacked at the earth all night. They blew up the stones and the frozen earth, and they laid the foundations. . . . Their feet and hands were swollen with frostbite, but they did not leave work. Over the charts and blueprints, laid out on packing cases, the blizzard was raging. Hundreds of trucks kept rolling up with building materials. . . . On the twelfth day, into the new buildings with their glass roofs, the machinery, covered with hoar-frost, began to arrive. Braziers were kept alight to unfreeze the machines. . . . And two days later, the war factory began production.

(quoted in Alexander Werth, *Russia at War 1941–1945*, New York, Dutton, 1964)

II.22 Germans in industrial labour force 1939–44

	Total force (000s)	*No. of women (000s)*
31 July 1939	10,405	2,620
31 May 1940	9,415	2,565
30 Nov. 1940	9,401	2,615
30 Nov. 1941	8,861	2,626
30 Nov. 1942	8,011	2,493
31 July 1943	8,099	2,808
30 Nov. 1943	7,948	2,787
31 March 1944	7,720	2,745
31 July 1944	7,515	2,678

(A. Milward, *The German Economy at War*, London, Athlone Press, 1965, pp. 46–7)

II.23 Günter Grass, extract from *The Tin Drum* (1959)

[Oskar, the narrator, is nineteen, but as a child he made a decision to stop growing when he had reached three feet tall. He plays a tin drum and has a voice that can break glass.]

For three weeks we played every night in the venerable casemates of Metz, long a city of garrisons and once a Roman outpost. We did the same programme for two weeks in Nancy. A few words of French had begun to sprout from Oskar's lips. In Reims we had an opportunity to admire damage created by the previous World War. Sickened by humanity, the stone menagerie of the world-famous cathedral spewed water and more water on the cobblestones round about, which is a way of saying that it rained all day in Reims even at night. But Paris gave us a mild and resplendent September. I spent my nineteenth birthday strolling on the *quais* with Roswitha on my arm. Although Paris was well known to me from Sergeant Fritz Truczinski's postcards, I wasn't a bit disappointed. The first time Roswitha and I – she measured three feet three, three inches more than myself – stood arm in arm at the foot of the Eiffel Tower, looking up, we became aware – this too for the first time – of our grandeur and uniqueness. We exchanged kisses wherever we went, but that's nothing new in Paris.

How wonderful it is to rub shoulders with art and history! Still with Roswitha on my arm, I visited the Dôme des Invalides, thinking of the great Emperor and feeling very close to him, because, though great, he was not tall. Recalling how, at the tomb of Frederick the Great, himself no giant, Napoleon had said: 'If he were still alive, we should not be standing here,' I whispered tenderly into my Roswitha's ear: 'If the Corsican were still alive, we should not be standing here, we should not be kissing each other under the bridges, on the *quais, sur le trottoir de Paris.*'

In collaboration with other groups, we put on colossal programmes at the Salle Pleyel and the Théâtre Sarah Bernhardt. Oskar quickly grew accustomed to the theatrical style of the big city, perfected his repertory, adapted himself to the jaded tastes of the Paris occupation troops: No longer did I waste my vocal prowess on common German beer bottles; here, in the city of light, I shattered graceful, invaluable vases and fruit bowls, immaterial figments of blown glass, taken from French castles. My number was conceived along historical lines. I started in with glassware from the reign of Louis XIV, and continued, like history itself, with the reign of Louis XV. With revolutionary fervour I attacked the crockery of the unfortunate Louis XVI and his headless and heedless Marie Antoinette. Finally, after a sprinkling of Louis-Philippe, I carried my battle to the vitreous fantasies of the Third Republic.

Of course the historical significance of my act was beyond the reach of the field-grey mass in the orchestra and galleries; they applauded my shards as common shards; but now and then there was a staff officer or a newspaperman from the Reich who relished my historical acumen along with the damage. A scholarly character in uniform complimented me on my art when we were introduced to him after a gala performance for the Kommandantur. Oskar was particularly grateful to the correspondent for a leading German newspaper who described himself as an expert on France and discreetly called my attention to a few trifling mistakes, not to say stylistic inconsistencies, in my programme.

(Günter Grass, *The Tin Drum*, trans. Ralph Manheim, London, Secker and Warburg, 1962, pp. 328–30).

II.24 'Vercors' (Jean Bruller), extract from *Le silence de la mer* (1942)

He was standing in front of the library shelves. His fingers followed the bindings, caressing them gently.

'Balzac, Barrès, Baudelaire, Beaumarchais, Boileau, Buffo . . . Chateaubriand, Corneille, Descartes, Fenélon, Flaubert . . . La Fontaine, France, Gautier, Hugo . . . What distinction!' he said with a slight laugh while nodding his head. 'And I am only at the letter H! . . . No Molière, Rabelais, Racine, Pascal, Stendhal, Voltaire, Montaigne, nor all the others!' He continued to glide slowly along the books, and occasionally let slip an imperceptible 'Ha!', when, I suppose, he read an unsuspected name. 'The English,' he continued, 'one thinks immediately of Shakespeare. The Italians: of Dante. Spain: Cervantes. And us, at once: Goethe. After that, one has to think. But if one says: and how about France? Then, what comes rushing out? Molière? Racine? Hugo? Voltaire? Rabelais? Or who else? They rush forward, they are like a crowd at the entrance of a theatre, one does not know who to let enter first.'

He turned round and said seriously: 'But for music, then it is us: Bach, Handel, Beethoven, Wagner, Mozart . . . which name comes first?

'And we are at war', he said slowly, moving his head. He returned to the fireplace and his smiling eyes fixed on the profile of my niece. 'But it is the last one! We will not fight each other any more: we will marry each other!' His eyelids wrinkled, the hollows beneath his cheekbones turned into two long dimples, he revealed his white teeth. He said cheerfully: 'Yes, yes!' A slight nod of the head drove home the repetition. 'When we entered Saintes', he continued after a pause, 'I was happy that the population welcomed us. I was very happy. I thought: This will be simple. And then I saw that it was not that at all, that it was cowardice.' He had become serious. 'I had misunderstood these people. And I was afraid for France. I wondered: Has it *really* come to this?' He shook his head: 'No! No! I then saw her; and now I rejoice in her stern countenance.'

His gaze fell on mine. I looked away. It lingered for a while on various points in the room and then turned again to the unrelentingly expressionless face of my niece.

'I am happy to have found here an elderly man who has dignity, and a young lady who knows how to keep silent. We have to overcome that silence. We have to overcome the silence of all France. I am glad of that.'

Silently, with a grave and persistent expression in which there still lurked the remnant of a smile, he was looking at my niece, at her set, obstinate, delicate profile. My niece felt his gaze, and I saw her blush slightly, as a little frown formed gradually between her eyebrows. Her fingers plucked the needle rather too fast and too hard, risking a break in the thread.

'Yes', went on his slow, droning voice. 'It's better that way. Much better. That makes for a solid union – for unions where both sides gain in greatness. . . . There is a very lovely children's story which I have read, which you have read, which everybody has read. I don't know if it has the same title in both countries. With us it's called *Das Tier und die Schöne*. Beauty and the Beast. . . .

'Poor Beauty! The Beast has her at his mercy – a powerless prisoner – and at every hour of the day imposes on her his heavy and pitiless presence . . . Beauty is proud, dignified – she is made of strong fibre . . . But the Beast prefers that she does not pretend. Oh, he is not very polished! He is clumsy, rough, he seems boorish beside the great delicacy of Beauty! . . . But he has a heart, yes, he has a spirit which aspires to elevate itself. If only Beauty wished it! . . . Beauty took a long time to begin to wish it. However, little by little, she discovered deep in the eyes of the hated gaoler a light – a reflection where one might discern entreaty and care. She was less aware of the heavy power, of the chains of her prison . . . She stopped hating, was touched by his constancy, she held out her hand . . . At once the Beast was transformed, the spell which had held him in this barbarous form was broken: he was now a handsome and noble knight, delicate and cultured, for whom each one of Beauty's kisses added further radiant qualities . . . Their union brought sublime happiness. Their children, who combined and enhanced the gifts of their parents, were the most beautiful ever seen on earth . . .

'Don't you love that story? Me, I shall love it for ever. I read it over and over again. It makes me cry. Above all I like the Beast, because I understand his pain. Once again today, I am moved when I speak of it.'

He stopped speaking, took in a deep breath, and bowed his head: 'I wish you good night.'

('Vercors', *Le silence de la mer*, Paris, Editions de Minuit, 1942; trans. Arthur Marwick)

II.25 Louis Aragon, 'I salute you, my France' and 'Tears are alike'

I SALUTE YOU, MY FRANCE

I write in a land devastated by pest,
One would think a held-over nightmare of Goya,
Where the dogs have no hope save of heavenly feast,
And stooping white skeletons weed the soya.

A land overrun by a merciless gang
Whipping cattle from pastures and pigs from their sties,
A country disputed by claw and fang,
Calamitous days under pitiless skies.

Under the heel of the puppet mutter
Lands cleft in ruts to the heart from their wheels;
Marked for rotated cutting by King Guttersputter. . . .
A white land of fear where the werewolf steals.

I write in a country where men are pastured
In filth and in thirst, in hunger and silence. . . .
Where the son is snatched from the mother and quartered,
As if Herod reigned, with Laval for crown-prince!

I write in this country disfigured by blood,
A midden-mound, now, of wounds and of groans,
An open market that hail and rain flood,
A ruin where death plays at knuckle-bones.

I write in this country where the police
Enter the dwellings at all hours and seasons;
And inquisitors, driving in splinters, won't cease
To scrutinize broken limbs, searching for treasons.

I write in this country of a thousand deaths,
And purple wounds from the pack that harry
Her, swarming upon her with reeking breaths,
While the huntsmen's trumpet sounds the quarry!

I write in this land that the butchers flay,
Leaving nerves and entrails and bones laid bare;
Where the forests are torches burnt away,
And fleeing the wheat on fire, birds in the air. . . .

I write in this night, deep and criminal,
Where I hear the breathing of foreign soldiers. . . .
And the trains strangling in the distant tunnel
From which, if they issue, God alone knows!

I write on a tilting-field of ill-mated
Opponents: one with war-horse and armour;
And the other exposed to the sword, lacerated,
Has solely for armour his right and his valour!

I write in this den, where not simply a prophet,
But a nation, is thrown to the jaws of the beasts,
And is summoned to never forget its defeat
But to give to the bears the flesh due their feasts.

I write on this tragic stage where the actors
Have lost their way, and wander, faint,
In the hollow theatre where the malefactors
Mouth ponderous words for the ignorant. . . .

TEARS ARE ALIKE

In the grey sky were porcelain angels
In the grey sky were stifled cries
I remember those days at Mainz
The Black Rhine and the weeping Loreleis

You would find sometimes at the end of an alley
A Frenchman dead with a knife-blade in the back
You would find sometimes that the peace was cruel
For all the young white wine of the terraces

I drank their transparent Kirschwasser
I drank the vows they whispered with clasped hand
How lovely were the palaces and churches
I was twenty then, I did not understand

What did I know about days of defeat
When your country is a love forbidden
When you need the voice of false prophets
To bring lost hope to life again?

I remember songs that touched the heart
I remember signs chalked in red
Found in the morning scribbled on walls
We never once deciphered what they said

Who can say where memory begins
Who can say where the present ends
Where the past becomes a sentimental ballad
And sorrow a paper yellowed with age?

Like a child surprised among his dreams
The blank looks of the vanquished made you start
Then, at the tramp of guard relieving guard
The Rhenish silence shuddered to its heart.

(H. Josephson and M. Cowley (eds) *Aragon: Poet of Resurgent France*, London, Pilot Press, 1947; translation of the above poems by R. Humphries and M. Cowley)

II.26 Helen Zenna Smith (Evadne Price), extract from *Not So Quiet . . . Stepdaughters of War* (1930)

Booma-boom-booma-boom-boommm!

'God, I hate those bloody guns', mutters Tosh, and this time The BF is silent. We stare ahead. We hate and dread the days following on the guns when they boom without interval. Trainloads of broken human beings: half-mad men pleading to be put out of their misery; torn and bleeding and crazed men pitifully obeying orders like a herd of senseless cattle, dumbly, pitifully straggling in the wrong direction, as senseless as a flock of senseless sheep obeying a senseless leader, herded back into line by the orderly, the kind sheep-dog with a 'Now then, boys, this way. That's the ticket, boys', instead of a bark; men with faces bleeding through their hasty bandages; men with vacant eyes and mouths hanging foolishly apart dropping saliva and slime; men with minds mercifully gone; men only too sane, eyes horror-filled with blood and pain. . . .

My last letter home opens before me, photograph clear, sent in response to innumerable complaints concerning the brevity of my crossed-out field postcards: *'It is such fun out here, and of course I'm loving every minute of it; it's so splendid to be really in it. . . .'*

The only kind of letter home they expect, the only kind they want, the only kind they will have. Tell them that you hate it, tell them that you fear it, that you are as terror-stricken as you were when they left you alone in the dark in that big, quiet house on Wimbledon Common, you who had been accustomed to the cheery trams and rumbling motor-buses of Shepherd's Bush – tell them that all the ideals and beliefs you ever had have crashed about your gun-deafened ears – that you don't believe in God or them or the infallibility of England or anything but bloody war and wounds and foul smells and smutty stories and smoke and bombs and lice and filth and noise, noise, noise – that you live in a world of cold sick fear, a dirty world of darkness and despair – that you want to crawl ignominiously home away from these painful writhing things that once were men, these shattered, tortured faces that dumbly demand what it's all about in Christ's name – that you want to find somewhere where life is quiet and beautiful and lovely as it was before the world turned khaki and blood-coloured – that you want to creep into a refuge where there is love instead of hate. . . .

Tell them these things; and they will reply on pale mauve deckle-edged paper calling you a silly hysterical little girl – 'You always were inclined to exaggerate, darling' – and enclose a patent carbolized body belt; 'the very latest thing for active service, dear, in case you encounter a stray "bitey"' (that's what you used to call a louse yourself, hundreds of years ago; refined, weren't you?), an iron tonic, some more aspirin tablets. 'Stick it, darling; go on doing your bit, because England is proud of her brave daughters, so very proud. . . .'

England is proud of her brave daughters.

Almost as proud as Father and Mother.

'It's so splendid to be really in it. . . .'

The only kind of letter they want. Father can take it to his club and swank: 'I've got two girls out in France now, and a son in training. He'll be ordered out any minute, he says. Ah! One of my girls pretty well in the firing line; not allowed to say, of course – Censor and all that – address Somewhere in France' – swelling himself – 'doing her bit, you know, doing her bit. Just on twenty-one. Plucky? Yes, but loves it. An Englishwoman to her finger-tips – wouldn't keep out of it – proud to do her bit for the old flag' – blowing his nose emotionally – 'proud to do her bit, God bless her. . . .'

And Mother, head of more committees than anyone else on Wimbledon Common, fiercely competing with Mrs Evans-Mawnington in recruiting. Mrs Evans-Mawnington and Mother like the angles at the base of an isosceles triangle: maddeningly equal to one another. Mrs Evans-Mawnington has a son; so has Mother. The angles are equal. Mrs Evans-Mawnington is head of the same number of committees as Mother. The angles are equal again. But Mrs Evans-Mawnington has no daughters, which is where Mother scores. Her angle is two daughters up on Mrs Evans-Mawnington's angle – oh! decidedly two daughters up. She expects soon to out-committee Mrs Evans-Mawnington on the strength of her two daughters. She will make Mrs Evans-Mawnington's angle so small Euclid himself would never recognize it. 'So brave of you, Mrs Smith, to have given your children, so noble. . . .' Mother triumphantly smirking across the room at the disgruntled Mrs Evans-Mawnington, who has no daughters: 'We must all do our bit, mustn't we? Abnormal times. I had a letter today from my Nellie, so cheery, so full of spirit, not at all the kind of life she's been accustomed to – such a sheltered life she's always had – it's a trifle rough out there, but she wouldn't come home for anything.' – Wiping away a tear. – 'When I think of her wee fair head walking along with the wee dark head of my little Trix – she's in a hospital in France – both of them doing their bit . . . we must all do our bit. . . . I am wearing myself to a shadow, but they shall never say Mother didn't do her bit, too; if they are in it, Mother shall be in it too. . . .'

Mrs Evans-Mawnington scowling, furious-mouthed, jealous . . . Mother smug, saccharine-sweet . . . shelves of mangled bodies . . . filthy smells of gangrenous wounds . . . shell-ragged, shell-shocked men . . . men shrieking like wild beasts inside the ambulance until they drown the sound of the engine . . . *'Nellie loves to be really in it'* – no God to pray to because you know there isn't a God – how shall I carry on? . . . *'Proud to do her bit for the old flag.'* Oh, Christ! Oh, Christ! . . . I'm only twenty-one and nobody cares because I've been pitchforked into hell, nobody cares because I'm going mad, mad, mad; nobody cares because I'm afraid I've no guts, I'm white-livered. . . . *'We must all do our bit.'* . . . They've made me a heroine, one of England's Splendid Women, and I'm shaking with fright, I can't hold the wheel . . . one of England's splendid heroines . . . how easy to drive the bus clean over the hill into the valley below . . . an accident. . . . 'She died for King and Country.' . . . Mother in deep mourning, head of another committee, enrolling recruits at top speed . . . one daughter dead on active service equal to how many daughters alive Somewhere in France? . . . Shrieks of torn bodies . . . old men safe in England snubbing slackers. 'By Gad! If I were a few years younger, by Gad!' . . . Flappers presenting white feathers to men who don't want to be maimed or killed . . . ever-knitting women safe from the blood and the mud, women who can still pray to their smug God, the God who is on our side, the God who hates the enemy because He is on our side . . . women who don't have to stare into the black night and hum a revue tune – 'If you were the only girl in the world' – to drown the wild-beast noises of men gone mad with pain . . . one of England's heroines . . . a failure, a failure . . . a coward, a weak, suburban coward . . . screams of men growing louder and louder, maddened men, louder, louder, louder, shrieking down the song and the engine. . . .

The whistle blows.
'Out of it, *mes petites harlots,*' says Tosh.
We scramble from our flea-bags.

(Helen Zenna Smith (Evadne Price), *Not So Quiet . . . Stepdaughters of War,* 1930; reprinted by Virago Press, 1988, pp. 29–35)

II.27 Security Service (SD) reports from the *Reich* on the public reaction to films (1941)

(a) Audience response to the political instructional film Der Ewige Jude (The Wandering Jew)

Following an extensive publicity campaign in the press and on radio, the documentary film *The Wandering Jew* has been *awaited with great interest by the public,* according to reports from all parts of the *Reich.* Numerous reports indicate that audiences are saying over and over again that the film's visual documentation, with its broad panorama of Jewish life and affairs, has completely lived up to these high expectations and that the film is more instructive, convincing and impressive than many an anti-Jewish tract. There has been unanimous acknowledgment of the high standards achieved in collating the available material into a single unit. Particularly favourable comment was made – as reported from Munich, Koblenz, Schwerin, Danzig, Halle, Königsberg, Potsdam and Berlin – on the way the *maps and statistics* catalogued the spread of Jewry (the comparison with rats is mentioned as particularly impressive) and its expanding influence on all areas of life and in all countries of the world. The shots of Jews in America have prompted particular comment. People were surprised by the open revelations of the Jewish influence in and dominance of the USA (Schwerin, Karlsbad). Particularly impressive were thought to be the scenes in which Jews were shown 'in their original state' and 'in European fashion' as men of the world (Leipzig), and in general the *juxtapositions* (Jewish ghetto – parade of German youth at the Party Rally) were thought to make an extraordinarily telling effect. According to a report from Munich, there was immediate relief and enthusiastic applause at the point in the film when the *Führer* appears and in his speech announces that a new war can only bring about the final annihilation of Jewry. Throughout the film the *sequences describing the history of the Rothschild family,* and in particular the information that members of the family had been naturalized in a number of different countries, thus establishing themselves as recognized citizens of the most important countries,' were notably effective and convincing. These sequences and the contrasting of Jewish types from all parts of the world provided devastating proof – as can be deduced from numerous conversations – that for all his apparent adaptation to countries, languages and ways of life, a Jew is always a Jew.

Because of the very intensive publicity for the film and its impressive organization of documentary evidence, the first performances produced remarkably high audience figures. But in some places audience interest has often soon fallen off, because the film has followed too quickly on the feature film *Jud Süss*. Since a large part of the population had already seen *Jud Süss*, it was very often assumed – according to the information to hand – that the documentary film *The Wandering Jew* had nothing really new to say. Reports received from, for example, Innsbruck, Dortmund, Aachen, Karlsruhe, Neustadt/Weinstrasse, Bielefeld, Frankfurt am Main and Munich all agree that it is often only the politically active sections of the population who have seen the documentary film while the typical film audience has largely avoided it, and that in some places there has been a word-of-mouth campaign against the film and its starkly realistic portrait of the Jews. The repulsive nature of the material and in particular the ritual slaughter scenes are repeatedly cited in conversation as the main reason for not seeing the film. The film is repeatedly described as an exceptional 'strain on the nerves' (Neustadt/Weinstrasse). This is why attendance figures fell very sharply in places, particularly in North West, West and South Germany and in the Eastern region [i.e. Austria]. According to reports from West Germany and from Breslau, people have often been observed leaving the cinema in disgust in the middle of a performance. Statements like 'We've seen *Jud Süss* and we've had enough of Jewish filth' have been heard. There have been isolated cases of women and even young men fainting during the ritual slaughter scenes. People have frequently claimed that *Jud Süss* had shown such a convincing picture of Jewry that this new and even more blatant evidence, following immediately after it in this documentary film, served no further purpose. On the other hand, numerous statements have been reported, particularly from the politically active sections of the population, expressing considerable appreciation of the film as a remarkably impressive document.

(b) Audience response to the film Ohm Krüger *(Uncle Krüger)*

The reports from the various areas of the *Reich* all confirm that the general response to this film among all sections of the population has far exceeded the exceptionally high expectations aroused by a strong press campaign. The film is considered the *outstanding achievement of the current year in the cinema*, and particular mention is made of its superlative blending of political message, artistic construction and first-class performances. As a *popular success* it is in fact *exceptional*, as confirmed not only by the fact that every performance is sold out but also by the extensive word-of-mouth publicity and frequent discussion about the film (Hamburg, Koblenz, Berlin, Cologne, Leipzig, Munich, Münster, Frankfurt am Main, etc.). Audiences are for the most part moved to silence while watching the film and are obviously deeply affected by it, and very unusually for a film this is still the case even after the performance. The fact that the film was completed in wartime is considered as distinctive evidence of the capacity of the German film industry.

There is no doubt that *in terms of propaganda the film completely fulfils its function as far as the general public is concerned.* The anti-British war mood has clearly significantly increased and consolidated, since in spite of considerable factual modifications the film is taken by large sections of the audience as a kind of historical document about a period of British colonial history. Younger viewers in particular seem to have received from the film their first clear picture of the defeat of the Boers (Oppeln). This impression is confirmed by a reportedly increased demand for literature about the Boers and their struggle for freedom. The film's description of British brutality has undoubtedly made a very strong impression, and the feeling is that psychologically the story has been constructed with a remarkable sense of the present mood of the German people towards England. Moreover the film has not been wasted on negative propaganda, but has brought out the moral and national values – though in really heroic fashion – of the Boer people's freedom struggle. The crowd scenes of the shooting of the Boer women are on all sides considered to be a particularly impressive highlight of the film. In the realism of this scene the film is thought to have reached the limits of what is tolerable.

In the main most audiences are so completely absorbed by the story that the outstanding achievements of both direction and performances are only later appreciated. The characterization of Ohm Krüger is unanimously regarded as a really masterly piece of acting. On numerous occasions audiences from all sections of the population have expressed the view that the film provides the first convincing demonstration that it is cinematic artistry of the highest order which heightens a film's effectiveness as propaganda.

Critical opinions are in comparison numerically insignificant, and according to reports from various parts of the *Reich* they tend to raise the same fundamental questions. In the first place individual scenes are in some cases considered 'too heavily loaded' or too repugnant – for instance, the English missionaries' distribution of arms and prayer-books. The danger of such propaganda exaggerations is to reduce the plausibility of historical episodes in a film. According to the reports to hand, a number of spectators, particularly those with a knowledge of history but also the wider public, have raised the question of whether the in parts very strong propagandist and tendentious approach of the film was necessary at all, since in straightforward historical terms the suppression of the Boers is known to have been one of the most horrifying chapters of British brutality. The question was whether a greater historical authenticity might not have achieved the same or an even more convincing effect. It was frequently noted that after the performances audiences were reconsidering several of the calculated scenes, regarding them as historically inauthentic and so doubting the historical authenticity of more important parts of the story (Hamburg, Koblenz, Münster, Düsseldorf, Danzig, Berlin, Munich, Kattowitz). Knowledgeable audiences and people with experience of Africa have moreover raised the question of whether it was well-advised to make heroes of the Boers in this way, since along with their good features as a race they also display some very pronounced negative factors, and in terms of character, economics and politics they have by no means always played a positive role. The character of this mixed race is ambivalent, and in view of Greater Germany's colonial mission after the final victory they cannot be put forward as a Germanic ideal.

(from the Federal Archive, Koblenz, 20 Jan. and 12 May 1941; reprinted in Erwin Leiser, *Nazi Cinema*, trans. Gertrud Mander and David Wilson, London, Secker and Warburg, 1974, pp. 157–61)

II.28 Extract from commentary to *Der Ewige Jude* (1940)

Comparable with the Jewish wanderings through history are the mass migrations of an equally restless animal, the rat. This beast followed mankind from his beginnings. Its home is Asia. From there it migrated in vast hordes across Russia and the Balkan states towards Europe. By the middle of the eighteenth century they are already spread across the whole of Europe. In the middle of the nineteenth century, as a result of the growing shipping trade, they also take possession of America and likewise Africa and the Far East.

Wherever rats appear they bring ruin, they ravage human property and food stuffs. In this way they spread disease: plague, leprosy, typhoid, cholera, dysentry, etc. They are cunning, cowardly and cruel and are found mostly in large packs. In the animal world they represent the element of craftiness and underground destruction – no different from the Jews among mankind.

This Jewish race of parasites perpetrates a large part of international crime. Thus in 1932 the part played by the Jews, who represent only a small percentage of the world population, in the entire drug trade of the world was 34 per cent, in robberies it was 47 per cent, in card-sharping and crimes concerning games of chance it was 47 per cent, in international crime organizations it was 82 per cent, and in prostitution 98 per cent.

The professional terminology of international thieves' cant does not originate without reason from Hebrew and Yiddish. These physiognomies refute impressively the liberalistic theories of the equality of all those who bear a human face. Of course, they change their outward appearance when they leave their Polish nests to go out into the rich world. Hair and beard, skull cap and caftan are the distinguishing characteristics of the Eastern Jew for everyone. If he appears without them, then it is only the more keen-eyed among us who recognize his racial origins. It is an intrinsic characteristic of the Jew that he always strives to hide his parentage when he is among non-Jews.

A mass of Polish Jews – now still wearing caftans, and now ready to steal in to Western civilization.

Of course, these ghetto Jews don't know at first how to comport themselves correctly in their fine European suits. These Berlin Jews are a bit better at it. It is true that their fathers and grandfathers still lived in ghettos, but there is no trace of that left now in their external appearance. Here, in the second and third generation, the Aryanization has reached its zenith. In all superficialities they attempt to imitate their hosts. And people lacking in intuition allow themselves to be deceived by this mimicry and regard them as being in truth their equals. Therein lies the dreadful danger. For even these 'civilized' Jews remain foreign bodies in the organism of their hosts, no matter how much their outward appearance may correspond to that of their hosts.

Even those aristocrats with old Jewish names, who, after generations of marriage with the Aryan nobility, belong to the uppermost circles of European so-called society and have completely assumed the manners of their aristocratic surroundings, have remained foreign bodies and are to be assessed as such.

Here we show an excerpt from the film which depicts the history of the House of Rothschild [*The House of Rothschild*, 1934, by Alfred Werker]. American Jews produced it, obviously in order to create a monument to one of the greatest names in Jewish history. They honour their hero in typical Jewish manner and take delight in the way old Meier Amschel Rothschild defrauds the state which made him welcome and feigns poverty in order to avoid paying taxes.

[The German sub-titles read as follows:]
'The tax collector is coming, Papa, he's in the street already.'
'Close the door, hide the silver away, Mama.' 'I already have.'
'We'll say to the tax inspector, We've had no business for 5 days.'
'Are you hungry?' 'Not very.' 'Well, try to put on a hungry face.'
'Mama, hide the roast.'
'Mama, sit down with your sewing. Nathan, take your hands out of your pockets.'
'Who is there, Nathan? Ah, my good friend, the tax inspector.'
'Fetch your ledger out.'
'Of course, I was just looking at it. Times are very bad. That is my good friend, the tax collector. I've never had such a bad month. I've not seen a single guilder for 5 days. Our customers come, yes, but they don't buy anything. My exchange trade is less than nothing. I'll starve to death soon.'
'But there's a lovely smell in here.'
'My neighbour's probably got a roast. Go and shut the window.'
'What do you take me for?'
'I don't understand you, sir.'

'Rothschild, your business is more prosperous than anyone else's. 20,000 guilders tax.'

'20,000 guilders? You may kill me, but I could scarcely raise 1,000.'

'Search the house. Upstairs.'

'Perhaps 2,000 guilders?'

ROTHSCHILD: As a result of the conveyance of gold by mail-coach from one land to another, much gold is lost. In war the enemy gets it; in peace, robbers. There are five of you brothers. Each of you will open a banking-house. One in Paris, the next in Vienna, the third in London, select the most important capitals for yourselves. If money is to be sent to London, no one needs to risk his life. You send a letter to Nathan in London: to pay so and so. As a contra-account there will be loans from London to Frankfurt. Soon there will be many wars and all the states will come to Rothschild's. The money will be safest with you.

COMMENTARY: At this point, it must be noted that transfer of money by cheque was not an invention of the Jews, nor was it cultivated by them for the good of mankind, but simply to serve them as a means of obtaining international influence over and above the heads of their hosts.

ROTHSCHILD: Union is strength. You must always stick together. None of the brothers must suffer failure while another is successful. Our five banking-houses will rule Europe. One firm, one family – the Rothschilds. That will be your strength. When this power comes, think of the ghetto.

COMMENTARY: So Nathan goes to London and becomes an Englishman, Jacob goes to Paris and becomes a Frenchman, Solomon goes to Vienna and becomes an Austrian, Carl goes to Naples and becomes an Italian, but Amschel stays in Frankfurt and remains a German. And yet, of course, they all remain Jews. So that when, during the period of the French Revolution, the Jews were recognized as rightful enfranchised citizens of their respective countries, they suddenly belonged to two nations simultaneously.

And it is not for nothing that they have blood relatives at all the European courts and accordingly confidential knowledge of all events in these courts and their countries. Thus in this industrious century of technical progress, Jewish business blooms as never before. The House of Rothschild is only one example of these machinations of the Jews, to spread the network of their influence over the working man. The same tactics are pursued by the House of Warburg and other Jewish banking families.

At the beginning of the twentieth century they squat everywhere at the junctions of the world's money business. They are an international power. Although only a small percentage of the world's population, with the help of their capital they terrorize the world stock exchanges, world opinion, and world politics.

(translation supplied by the Imperial War Museum)

II.29 Commentary to the film *London (Britain) Can Take It* (1940)

I am speaking from London. It is late afternoon and the people of London are preparing for the night. Everyone is anxious to get home before darkness falls – before our nightly visitors arrive. This is the London rush hour.

Many of the people at whom you are looking now are members of the greatest civilian army ever to be assembled. These men and women who have worked all day in offices or in markets, are now hurrying home to change into the uniform of their particular service.

The dusk is deepening. Listening crews are posted all the way from the coast to London to pick up the drone of the German planes. Soon the nightly battle of London will be on. This has been a quiet day for us; but it won't be a quiet night. We haven't had a quiet night for more than five weeks. They'll be over tonight and they'll destroy a few buildings and kill a few people. Probably some of the people you are watching now.

Now they're going into the public shelters. This is not a pleasant way to spend the night, but the people accept it as their part in the defence of London. These civilians are good soldiers.

Now it's eight o'clock. Jerry's a little bit late tonight. The searchlights are in position. The guns are ready. The People's Army of volunteers is ready. They are the ones who are really fighting this war. The firemen, the air-raid wardens, the ambulance drivers. And there's the wail of the banshee. . . .

The nightly siege of London has begun. The city is dressed for battle. Here they come. Now the searchlights are poking long, white inquisitive fingers into the blackness of the night. These are not Hollywood sound effects. This is the music they play every night in London – the symphony of war.

That was a bomb.

The very young and the very old, with that deep wisdom given only to the very young and the very old, sleep in the shelters. Do you see any signs of fear on these faces?

Now the army of the people swings into action. The bombs have started fires. When a bomber starts a fire he immediately returns, uses it as a target and drops more bombs, hoping to spread the fire. Yet the People's Army ignores the bombs and the spent shrapnel, which rains down consistently. Brokers, clerks, pedlars, merchants by day – they are heroes by night.

The night is long. But sooner or later the dawn will come. The German bombers are creatures of the night. They melt away before the dawn and scurry back to the safety of their own aerodromes.

♦　　♦　　♦

And there's the wail of the banshee again – this time a friendly wail . . . The 'All Clear' signal tells us that the bombers have gone. It's just 6 a.m.

In this last hour of precious sleep, this strange new world finds peace.

London raises her head, shakes the debris of the night from her hair and takes stock of the damage done. London has been hurt during the night. The sign of a great fighter in the ring is: 'Can he get up from the floor after being knocked down?' London does this every morning.

London doesn't look down upon the ruins of its houses, upon those made homeless during the night, upon the remains of churches, hospitals, workers' flats. London looks upwards towards the dawn and faces the new day with calmness and confidence.

The People's Army go to work as they did in that other comfortable world, which came to an end when the invader began to attack the last stronghold of freedom. Not all the services run as they did yesterday, but London manages to get to work on time – one way or another. In the centre of the city the shops are open as usual – in fact many of them are more open than usual.

Dr Paul Joseph Goebbels said recently that the nightly air raids have had a terrific effect upon the morale of the people of London. The good doctor is absolutely right. Today the morale of the people is higher than ever before. They are fused together, not by fear, but by a surging spirit of courage the like of which the world has never known. They know that thousands of them will die. But they would rather stand up and face death than kneel down and face the kind of existence the conqueror would impose on them.

And they know, too, and are comforted by the thought that England is not taking its beating lying down. They are guarding the frontiers of freedom. It is hard to see five centuries of labour destroyed in five seconds. But London is fighting back.

I am a neutral reporter, I have watched the people of London live and die ever since death in its most ghastly garb began to come here as a nightly visitor five weeks ago. I have watched them stand by their homes. I have seen them made homeless. I have seen them move to new homes. And I can assure you that there is no panic, no fear, no despair in London town; there is nothing but determination, confidence and high courage among the people of Churchill's island.

And they know that every night the RAF bombers fly deep into the heart of Germany, bombing munition works, aeroplane factories, canals; cutting the arteries which keep the heart of Germany alive.

It is true that the Nazis will be over again tomorrow night and the night after that and every night. They will drop thousands of bombs and they'll destroy hundreds of buildings and they'll kill thousands of people. But a bomb has its limitations. It can only destroy buildings and kill people. It cannot kill the unconquerable spirit and courage of the people of London.

London can take it!

(Ministry of Information film *London Can Take It*, 1940; commentary reprinted in *Documentary News Letter*, November 1940, pp. 6–7)

II.30   J. B. Priestley, extracts from his radio talks, *Postscripts* (1940)

(a) Talk from 5 June 1940

I wonder how many of you feel as I do about this great Battle and evacuation of Dunkirk. The news of it came as a series of surprises and shocks, followed by equally astonishing new waves of hope. It was all, from beginning to end, unexpected. And yet now that it's over, and we can look back on it, doesn't it seem to you to have an inevitable air about it – as if we had turned a page in the history of Britain and seen a chapter headed 'Dunkirk' – and perhaps seen too a picture of the troops on the beach waiting to embark?

And now that this whole action is completed, we notice that it has a definite shape, and a certain definite character. What strikes me about it is how typically English it is. Nothing, I feel, could be more English than this Battle of Dunkirk, both in its beginning and its end, its folly and its grandeur. It was very English in what was sadly wrong with it; this much has been freely admitted, and we are assured will be freely discussed when the proper moment arrives. We have gone sadly wrong like this before; and here and now we must resolve never, never to do it again. Another such blunder may *not* be forgiven us.

But having admitted this much, let's do ourselves the justice of admitting too that this Dunkirk affair was also very English (and when I say 'English' I really mean British) in the way in which, when apparently all was lost, so much was gloriously retrieved. Bright honour was almost 'plucked from the moon'. What began as a miserable blunder, a catalogue of misfortunes and miscalculations, ended as an epic of gallantry. We have a queer habit – and you can see it running through our history – of conjuring up such transformations. Out of a black gulf of humiliation and despair, rises a sun of blazing glory. This is not the German way. They don't make such mistakes (a grim fact that we should bear in mind) but also – they don't achieve such epics. There is never anything to inspire a man either in their victories or their defeats; boastful when they're winning, quick to whine when threatened with defeat – there is nothing about them that ever catches the world's imagination. That vast machine of theirs can't create a glimmer of that poetry of action which distinguishes war from mass murder. It's a machine – and therefore has no soul. . . .

(b) Talk from 21 July 1940

I hadn't been in his room more than two minutes when this official and I were looking at each other as a cat looks at a dog. We just weren't getting on at all. I ought to have known we wouldn't get on. And we hadn't been together five minutes, this official and I, before I knew that he knew what I thought about him, and he knew that I knew what he was thinking about me. He saw me as an impatient, slapdash, dangerous sort of fellow, wanting everything done all at once, bringing out all manner of half-digested notions and bragging, swaggering, insufferably pleased with myself, rather a bounder and an outsider, really. And I saw him as a coldly conceited, ungenerous, sterile kind of chap, never throwing himself wholeheartedly into anything, always wondering how he was going to come out of it, and just as he'd call me a bounder I'd call him 'a stuffed shirt'.

Well, there we were, not getting on at all and taking a greater and greater dislike to each other. But his manners, being better trained than mine, hadn't worn quite so thin. He made those little movements that politely suggest to a caller that it's time to go. He said: 'We might be able to form a small sub-committee; then, perhaps you'd like to send in some kind of report, just a short memo, embodying . . .' And I said: 'No, I don't think so. Good morning,' and went. And he said to himself: 'Well, thank goodness I've got rid of that fellow, barging in here as if he owned the place. He can't begin to understand our difficulties, relations with the Treasury and so on'; and I said to myself: 'Stuffed shirts and Mandarins, oh dear, oh dear, oh dear, oh dear, oh dear.' Two entirely different and opposed types of mind and temperament, you see, the warmly imaginative against the coldly rational, the slapdash against the punctilious, the impatient against the cautious, the creative against the administrative. Clearly we must have both types of mind working now at full pressure and it's absolutely essential that each should have its own sphere of activity. It's in the relation of eager, imaginative, creative minds and cool, punctilious, administrative minds that we've tended to go wrong. That abortive interview I've just described is probably typical of what happens.

Now, there are two ways of looking at this war. The first way, which, on the whole, we are officially encouraged to adopt, is to see this war as a terrible interruption. As soon as we can decently do it, we must return to what is called peace, so let's make all the munitions we can, and be ready to do some hard fighting, and then we can have done with Hitler and his Nazis and go back to where we started from, the day before war was declared. Now this, to my mind, is all wrong. It's wrong because it simply isn't true. A year ago, though we hadn't actually declared war, there wasn't real peace, or the year before, or the year before that. If you go back to the sort of world that produces Hitlers and Mussolinis, then no sooner have you got rid of one lot of Hitlers and Mussolinis than another lot will pop up somewhere, and there'll be more wars.

This brings us to the second, and more truthful, way of looking at this war. That is, to regard this war as one chapter in a tremendous history, the history of a changing world, the breakdown of one vast system and the building up of another and better one. In this view of things Hitler and Mussolini have been thrown up by this breakdown of a world system. It's as if an earthquake cracked the walls and floors of a house and strange nuisances of things, Nazists and Fascists, came running out of the woodwork. We have to get rid of these intolerable nuisances but not so that we can go *back* to anything. There's nothing that really worked that we can go back to. But so that we can go forward, without all the shouting and stamping and bullying and murder, and really plan and build up a nobler world in which ordinary, decent folk can not only find justice and security but also beauty and delight. And this isn't a 'pipe dream' because many of our difficulties have arrived not because man's capacity is feebler than it used to be, but just because it's actually so much greater. The modern man, thanks to his inventiveness, has suddenly been given a hundred arms and seven-league boots. But we can't go forward and build up this new world order, and this is our real war aim, unless we begin to think differently, and my own personal view, for what it's worth, is that we must stop thinking in terms of property and power and begin thinking in terms of community and creation.

Now, I'll explain just what I mean. First, take the change from power to creation. Now, power – whether on a large or small scale – really boils down to the ignoble pleasure of bossing and ordering other people about because you have the whip-hand of them. All these Nazi and Fascist leaders are power worshippers, they're almost drunk on it. I suspect it's simply a bad substitute for the joy of creation, which everybody understands, whether you're creating a vast educational system or a magnificent work of art, or bringing into existence a vegetable garden or a thundering good dinner. People are never so innocently happy as when they're creating something. So, we want a world that offers people not the dubious pleasures of power, but the maximum opportunities for creation. And even already, in the middle of this war, I can see that world shaping itself.

And now we'll take the change from property to community. Property is that old-fashioned way of thinking of a country as a thing, and a collection of things on that thing, all owned by certain people and constituting property; instead of thinking of a country as the home of a living society, and considering the welfare of that society, the community itself as the first test. And I'll give you an instance of how this change should be working. Near where I live is a house with a large garden, that's not being used at all because the owner of it has gone to America. Now, according to the property view, this is all right, and we, who haven't gone to America, must fight to protect this absentee owner's property. But on the community view, this is all wrong. There are hundreds of working men not far from here who urgently need ground for allotments so that they can produce a bit more food. Also, we may soon need more houses for billeting. Therefore, I say, that house and garden ought to be used whether the owner, who's gone to America, likes it or not. That's merely one instance, and you can easily find dozens of others.

Now, the war, because it demands a huge collective effort, is compelling us to change not only our ordinary, social and economic habits, but also our habits of thought. We're actually changing over from the property view to the sense of community, which simply means that we realize we're all in the same boat. But, and this is the point, that boat can serve not only as our defence against Nazi aggression, but as an ark in which we can all finally land in a better world. And when I say We, I don't mean only the British and their allied peoples, but all people everywhere, including all the Germans who haven't sold themselves body and soul to the evil Nazi idea. I tell you, there is stirring in us now, a desire which could soon become a controlled but passionate determination to remodel and recreate this life of ours, to make it the glorious beginning of a new world order, so that we might soon be so fully and happily engrossed in our great task that if Hitler and his gang suddenly disappeared we'd hardly notice that they'd gone. We're even now the hope of free men everywhere but soon we could be the hope and lovely dawn of the whole wide world.

(J. B. Priestley, *Postcripts*, London, Heinemann, 1940; reprinted in J. B. Priestley, *All England Listened: The Wartime Broadcasts of J. B. Priestley*, New York, Chilmark Press, 1968, pp. 3–5 and 51–8)

II.31   Richard Dimbleby, war report (19 April 1945)

19 April 1945. I picked my way over corpse after corpse in the gloom, until I heard one voice raised above the gentle undulating moaning. I found a girl, she was a living skeleton, impossible to gauge her age for she had practically no hair left, and her face was only a yellow parchment sheet with two holes in it for eyes. She was stretching out her stick of an arm and gasping something, it was 'English, English, medicine, medicine', and she was trying to cry but she hadn't enough strength. And beyond her down the passage and in the hut there were the convulsive movements of dying people too weak to raise themselves from the floor.

In the shade of some trees lay a great collection of bodies. I walked about them trying to count, there were perhaps 150 of them flung down on each other, all naked, all so thin that their yellow skin glistened like stretched rubber on their bones. Some of the poor starved creatures whose bodies were there looked so utterly unreal and inhuman that I could have imagined that they had never lived at all. They were like polished skeletons, the skeletons that medical students like to play practical jokes with.

At one end of the pile a cluster of men and women were gathered round a fire; they were using rags and old shoes taken from the bodies to keep it alight, and they were heating soup over it. And close by was the enclosure where 500 children between the ages of five and twelve had been kept. They were not so hungry as the rest, for the women had sacrificed themselves to keep them alive. Babies were born at Belsen, some of them shrunken, wizened little things that could not live, because their mothers could not feed them.

One woman, distraught to the point of madness, flung herself at a British soldier who was on guard at the camp on the night that it was reached by the 11th Armoured Division; she begged him to give her some milk for the tiny baby she held in her arms. She laid the mite on the ground and threw herself at the sentry's feet and kissed his boots. And when, in his distress, he asked her to get up, she put the baby in his arms and ran off crying that she would find milk for it because there was no milk in her breast. And when the soldier opened the bundle of rags to look at the child, he found that it had been dead for days.

There had been no privacy of any kind. Women stood naked at the side of the track, washing in cupfuls of water taken from British Army water trucks. Others squatted while they searched themselves for lice, and examined each other's hair. Sufferers from dysentery leaned against the huts, straining helplessly, and all around and about them was this awful drifting tide of exhausted people, neither caring nor watching. Just a few held out their withered hands to us as we passed by, and blessed the doctor whom they knew had become the camp commander in place of the brutal Kramer.

I have never seen British soldiers so moved to cold fury as the men who opened the Belsen camp this week, and those of the police and the RAMC who are now on duty there, trying to save the prisoners who are not too far gone in starvation.

(*War Report: D-Day to VE-Day*, compiled and edited by Desmond Hawkins, Ariel Books (BBC), 1985, pp. 318–19)

II.32   Joseph Goebbels, 'total war' speech from *Deutsche Wochenschau* (27 Feb. 1943)

COMMENTATOR: The mighty demonstration in the Berlin Sportspalace, Reichsminister Goebbels speaks. He declares: 'In this winter, the storm over our ancient continent has broken out with the full force which surpasses all human and historical imagination. The *Wehrmacht* with its allies form the only possible protective wall. [*Applause*] Not a single person in Germany today thinks of hollow compromise. The whole nation thinks only of a hard war. The danger before which we stand is gigantic. Gigantic, therefore, must be the efforts with which we meet it. [*Shouts of 'Sieg Heil'*] When my audience spontaneously declared its support for the demands I made on 30 January, the English press claimed that this was a piece of theatrical propaganda. I have therefore invited to this meeting a cross-section of the German people . . .'

GOEBBELS: The English claim that the German people are resisting Government measures for total war.

CROWD: Lies! Lies!

GOEBBELS: It doesn't want total war, say the English, but capitulation.

CROWD: *Sieg Heil! Sieg Heil!*

GOEBBELS: Do you want total war?

CROWD: Yes! [*Enthusiastic applause*]

GOEBBELS: Do you want it more total, more radical, than we could ever have imagined?

CROWD: Yes! Yes! [*Loud applause*]

GOEBBELS: Are you ready to stand with the *Führer* as the phalanx of the homeland behind the fighting *Wehrmacht*? Are you ready to continue the struggle unshaken and with savage determination, through all the vicissitudes of fate until victory is in our hands?

CROWD: Yes!

GOEBBELS: I ask you: Are you determined to follow the *Führer* through thick and thin in the struggle for victory and to accept even the harshest personal sacrifices?

CROWD: Yes! *Sieg Heil!* [*A chant of 'The Führer commands, we follow'*]

GOEBBELS: You have shown our enemies what they need to know, so that they will no longer indulge in illusions. The mightiest ally in the world – the people themselves – have shown that they stand behind us in our determined fight for victory, regardless of the costs.

CROWD: Yes! Yes! [*Loud applause*]

GOEBBELS: Therefore let the slogan be from now on: 'People arise, and storm break loose!' [*Extended applause*]

CROWD: *Deutschland, Deutschland über alles, über alles in der Welt . . .*

(David Welch, 'Goebbels, Götterdämmerung and the Deutsche Wochenschauen', in K. R. M. Short and S. Dolezel (eds) *Hitler's Fall*, London, Croom Helm, 1988, pp. 86–7).

II.33   Top secret *aide-mémoire* on Greece (21 Feb. 1947)

HIS MAJESTY'S GOVERNMENT TAKE THE VIEW THAT IT IS MOST URGENT THAT THE UNITED STATES GOVERNMENT SHOULD BE ABLE TO DECIDE WHAT ECONOMIC HELP THEY WILL GIVE TO GREECE AND WHAT FORM IT WILL TAKE.

His Majesty's Government are giving most earnest and anxious consideration to the important problem that on strategic and political grounds Greece and Turkey should not be allowed to fall under Soviet influence.

2. It will be remembered that at the Paris Peace Conference Mr Byrnes expressed full realization of the great importance of this question and proposed that the United States Government should give active help in sustaining the economic and military position in those two countries, the United States Government in particular taking care of the economic side.

3. On various occasions subsequent to the meeting referred to above the United States Government have exchanged views with His Majesty's

Government, indicating the acute interest of the United States Government in the future of Greece, and from these exchanges His Majesty's Government have understood that the United States Government does not exclude the possibility of helping Greece on the military side as well as the economic.

4. The State Department will recollect the conversation between Mr Byrnes and the Minister of Defence which took place on the 15th October, 1946, subsequent to which the whole question of British military and economic help for Greece has been carefully examined by His Majesty's Government. On the economic side, the reports received by His Majesty's Government from their representatives in Greece show that the Greek economic situation is on the point of collapse, owing to the virtual exhaustion of Greece's foreign exchange reserves and the low level of industrial activity resulting from political instability. In this connection His Majesty's Embassy attach to this *Aide-Mémoire* Appendix 'A' [not printed] which is a report dated the 5th February, from His Majesty's Representative in Athens, on the acute economic and financial situation in Greece.

5. The United States Government are as well aware as His Majesty's Government that unless Greece can obtain help from outside there is certain to be widespread starvation and consequent political disturbances during the present year. The Experts Committee of the United Nations have estimated Greek relief needs in 1947 at £21 million. This figure is based on the maintenance of the present subnormal standard of industrial activity and will, in the view of His Majesty's Government, be wholly inadequate to achieve our political objective of maintaining stability. His Majesty's Government estimate the actual needs of Greece, excluding the foreign exchange cost of the armed forces, at a minimum of £40 million in 1947. However, the serious economic plight of Greece as outlined above is already well known to the United States Government from the reports of their representatives in Greece and is no doubt being supplemented at the present time by preliminary reports from the Porter Mission.

6. In view of the position outlined in the above paragraph, His Majesty's Government take the view that it is most urgent that the United States Government should be able to decide what economic help they will give to Greece and what form it will take.

7. In the event of the United States Government being able to offer economic aid to Greece, it would no doubt consider the despatch of a United States economic mission. If this should be done, the future of the British Economic Mission in Greece would have to be considered.

8. On the military side, Greek needs have been very carefully considered by the British military authorities during the last few months, and the position has been investigated personally by the Chief of the Imperial General Staff during his recent visit to Greece. His Majesty's Government have agreed to pay the foreign exchange cost of the Greek armed forces,

both in regard to maintenance and initial equipment, until the 31st March next. This is likely to cost HMG during 1946 and the first 3 months of 1947 approximately £18 million for maintenance, together with £11 million for initial equipment. This, in view of HMG's financial difficulties, can be regarded as a very generous measure of assistance to Greek reconstruction. Hitherto the Greek armed forces have been built up on an establishment which allows for an army of 100,000 men, the total foreign exchange cost of which is estimated at about £16 million a year. In order to meet the present emergency caused by the bandits, the British service authorities consider that the Greek armed forces should now be reorganized to enable them to make an all-out assault on the bandits in the Spring. The reasons why this reorganization has become necessary are set out in papers which are now in the possession of the British Joint Staff Mission in Washington, who also have full details of the present organization of the Greek armed forces and of the reorganization proposed by the British military authorities. These details are available for study by the State Department and the United States Chiefs of Staff. The Joint Staff Mission are also in a position to provide the United States Government with a list of the equipment required by the Greek armed forces which cannot be supplied from British sources.

9. His Majesty's Government suggest that, if the United States Government agree, the various military questions involved should be taken over for urgent consideration by the combined Chiefs of Staff.

10. In view of the extreme urgency of taking some immediate action to enable the reorganization proposals to be undertaken, His Majesty's Government have agreed to make available additional equipment to the value of £2 million free of charge to the Greek Government. This, supplemented by American supplies of equipment which is not available to HMG, will enable the Greek armed forces to be put in a position to undertake operations in the Spring against the bandits, provided that means can be found to meet the rest of the foreign exchange cost of such operations. On the assumption that operations will last six months, the foreign exchange cost of this reorganization, together with the foreign exchange cost of the operations themselves, will over this period amount to £20 million. (The foreign exchange cost after the end of the operations will be smaller but will remain considerable.)

11. His Majesty's Government had hoped that part of the foreign exchange cost of the Greek armed forces after 31st March, 1947 could be met out of the money due to Greece by His Majesty's Government for the supply of currency and local services to the British forces in Greece. But £5 million out of the amount so due was recently placed at the disposal of the Greek Government for the purchase of food and is therefore no longer available to cover part of the cost of the armed forces.

12. Thus the total amount of assistance for civilian and military needs which Greece requires during 1947 appears to be between £60 million and

£70 million. His Majesty's Government have already strained their resources to the utmost to help Greece and have granted, or undertaken to grant, assistance up to 31st March, 1947 to the amount of £40 million. The United States Government will readily understand that His Majesty's Government, in view of their own situation, find it impossible to grant further financial assistance to Greece. Since, however, the United States Government have indicated the very great importance which they attach to helping Greece, His Majesty's Government trust that the United States Government may find it possible to afford financial assistance to Greece on a scale sufficient to meet her minimum needs, both civil and military.

13. His Majesty's Ambassador is instructed to express the earnest hope of His Majesty's Government that, if a joint policy of effective and practical support for Greece is to be maintained, the United States Government will agree to bear, as from the 1st April, 1947, the financial burden, of which the major part has hitherto been borne by His Majesty's Government. In view of the extreme urgency, both on economic and military grounds, that the Greek Government should know what financial help is going to be available in the present year, His Majesty's Government express the hope that the United States Government will indicate their position at the earliest possible moment.

(Department of State, *Foreign Relations of the United States, Diplomatic Papers: 1947*, Washington, 1971, V, pp. 32–5; reprinted in Joseph M. Siracusa (ed.) *The American Diplomatic Revolution*, Milton Keynes, Open University Press, 1978)

II.34   Top secret *aide-mémoire* on Turkey (21 Feb. 1947)

HIS MAJESTY'S GOVERNMENT WISH NOW TO SUGGEST THAT THE STRATEGIC AND MILITARY POSITION OF TURKEY SHOULD BE CONSIDERED BY THE COMBINED CHIEFS OF STAFF

In the course of his conversations with the Minister of Defence on October 15, 1946, Mr Byrnes emphasized that the United States Government was as interested in developments in Turkey as in Greece, and stated that the United States Government was prepared to do everything possible to help Turkey economically, expressing the hope that His Majesty's Government on their side would be able to provide the military equipment required to bring the Turkish forces into a sufficient state of readiness.

2. His Majesty's Government subsequently undertook a fresh study of the Turkish military and economic situation, the latter being carried out jointly by the British and American Commercial Counsellors in Turkey, in accordance with arrangements made with the United States Government.

3. On the military side, the Chiefs of Staff have examined the strategic importance of Turkey, the state of the Turkish Armed Forces, and the assistance necessary to bring these forces into a reasonable state of

preparedness. The conclusions of the British Chiefs of Staff, which are available at the British Joint Staff Mission in Washington, are briefly as follows:

(a) that it is of the greatest importance that Turkish independence should be maintained;

(b) that the Turkish Armed Forces as they exist at present would not be able to offer effective resistance to aggression by a first-class power;

(c) that in their present state of efficiency the mere provision of modern weapons would do little to increase the Turkish Armed Forces' power of resistance. The first requirement is to strengthen Service requirement in Turkey with a view to advising the Turks how best to improve the organization and raise the general standard of training of all three Services;

(d) that when this has been done it would be possible to estimate more clearly what amount of material assistance would be required. As at present advised, the Chiefs of Staff consider that the Turkish Army will require a very large measure of re-equipment and they do not consider that this task could be undertaken by the United Kingdom owing to shortage of manpower and productive capacity. Consequently the task would have to be undertaken by the United States. His Majesty's Government could probably look after the needs of the Navy and Air Force, provided satisfactory financial arrangements can be made.

4. The economic situation has been exhaustively discussed locally between the British and American Commercial Counsellors, and His Majesty's Government understand that a very full report was sent to Washington by the United States Commercial Counsellor on December 23, 1946. His Majesty's Government have no reason to dissent from the main conclusions of the American representative's report, and the following appear to be the salient features of the Turkish economic situation:

5. Turkey can finance her current foreign exchange requirements out of the proceeds of her exports; she can also maintain her existing industry without further foreign financial assistance. On the other hand, she would not be able to finance any extensive programme of industrial development, such as the Turkish Government have in mind, or meet any substantial foreign exchange demands for armaments without either drawing on her gold resources or borrowing from abroad. As regards foreign exchange, current income and liabilities roughly cancel out over a period of twelve months. On the other hand, the last available Central Bank statement shows gold reserves of approximately pounds sterling 59 million. It is understood that the Finance Minister insists that he must hold at least half of this amount as cover for the note issue if confidence in the currency is to be maintained. The balance could reasonably be used either for a programme of economic and industrial development, transport, ports, agricultural, coal-mining etc., or for the purchase of arma-

ments. There is clearly not enough for both. If, therefore, Turkey is to be able to carry out any plan of extensive military reorganization and also a plan of economic development, which in itself would be desirable in order to increase the military preparedness of the country, Turkey must look for financial assistance from abroad. In their existing financial situation His Majesty's Government could not, as the United States Government will readily appreciate, contemplate themselves making any further credits available to Turkey. Consequently, Turkey would have to look either to the United States Government or to one of its lending agencies, such as the Import-Export Bank, or to the International Bank or the International Monetary Fund.

6. In view of the great interest shown by the United States Government in the situation in Turkey, His Majesty's Government wish now to suggest that the strategic and military position of Turkey should be considered by the Combined Chiefs of Staff in the light of the conclusions reached by the British Chiefs of Staff in their recent studies, with a view to making recommendations to the United States Government and His Majesty's Government regarding the measures which should be taken to bring the Turkish Armed Forces up to a reasonable state of preparedness. For their part, His Majesty's Government would be ready, if the Combined Chiefs of Staff agree that this would be useful, to send to Turkey additional Military, Naval and Air Advisers amounting to some 60 officers, for whom the Turkish Government asked some months ago.[1] On the economic side, His Majesty's Government would be glad to know whether the United States Government have any suggestions to make as to how a programme of military reorganization that may be recommended by the Combined Chiefs of Staff should be financed.

(Department of State, *Foreign Relations of the United States, Diplomatic Papers: 1947*, Washington, 1971, V, pp. 35–7; reprinted in Joseph M. Siracusa (ed.) *The American Diplomatic Revolution*, Milton Keynes, Open University Press, 1978)

II.35 'Memorandum by the Under Secretary of State for Economic Affairs on the impending European crisis' (27 May 1947)

1. It is now obvious that we grossly underestimated the destruction to the European economy by the war. We understood the physical destruction, but we failed to take fully into account the effects of economic dislocation on production – nationalization of industries, drastic land reform, severance of long-standing commercial ties, disappearance of private commercial firms through death or loss of capital, etc., etc.

[1] The British Embassy corrected this sentence in an *aide-mémoire* of March 6, which stated: 'While His Majesty's Government in the United Kingdom are prepared to provide sixty British officers in all, the reference in the *aide-mémoire* [of February 21] should have been to only thirty additional officers as thirty are already there.'

2. Europe is steadily deteriorating. The political position reflects the economic. One political crisis after another merely denotes the existence of grave economic distress. Millions of people in the cities are slowly starving. More consumer's goods and restored confidence in the local currency are absolutely essential if the peasant is again to supply food in normal quantities to the cities. (French grain acreage running 20–25% under prewar, collection of production very unsatisfactory – much of the grain is fed to cattle. The modern system of division of labour has almost broken down in Europe.)

3. Europe's current annual balance of payments deficit:

UK	$2¼ billions
France	1¾ billions
Italy	½ billion
US–UK Zone Germany	½ billion
	$5 billions

not to mention the smaller countries.

The above represents an absolute minimum standard of living. If it should be lowered, there will be revolution.

Only until the end of this year can England and France meet the above deficits out of their fast dwindling reserves of gold and dollars. Italy can't go that long.

4. Some of the principal items in these deficits:

From the US: Coal, 30 million tons	$ 600 million
From the US: Bread grains, 12 million tons	1,400 million
From the US: Shipping services at very high rates on imports and exports	xxxxx million

Before the war, Europe was self-sufficient in coal and imported very little bread grains from the United States.

Europe must again become self-sufficient in coal (the US must take over management of Ruhr coal production) and her agricultural production must be restored to normal levels. (Note: no inefficient or forced production through exorbitant tariffs, subsidies, etc., is here contemplated.)

Europe must again be equipped to perform her own shipping services. The United States should sell surplus ships to France, Italy and other maritime nations to restore their merchant marine to at least prewar levels. (To do it, we will have to lick the shipping lobby, fattening as it is off the US Treasury.)

5. Without further prompt and substantial aid from the United States, economic, social and political disintegration will overwhelm Europe.

Aside from the awful implications which this would have for the future peace and security of the world, the immediate effects on our domestic economy would be disastrous: markets for our surplus production gone, unemployment, depression, a heavily unbalanced budget on the background of a mountainous war debt.

These things must not happen?

6. Mr Baruch[1] asks for the appointment of a Commission to study and report on our national assets and liabilities in order to determine our ability to assist Europe.

This is wholly unnecessary. The facts are well known. Our resources and our productive capacity are ample to provide all the help necessary.

The problem is to organize our fiscal policy and our own consumption so that sufficient surpluses of the necessary goods are made available out of our enormous production, and so that these surpluses are paid for out of taxation and not by addition to debt.

This problem can be met only if the American people are taken into the complete confidence of the Administration and told all the facts and only if a sound and workable plan is presented.

7. It will be necessary for the President and the Secretary of State to make a strong spiritual appeal to the American people to sacrifice a little themselves, to draw in their own belts just a little in order to save Europe from starvation and chaos (*not* from the Russians) and, at the same time, to preserve for ourselves and our children the glorious heritage of a free America.

8. Europe must have from us, as a grant, 6 or 7 billion dollars worth of goods a year for three years. With this help, the operations of the International Bank and Fund should enable European reconstruction to get under way at a rapid pace. Our grant could take the form principally of coal, food, cotton, tobacco, shipping services and similar things – all now produced in the United States in surplus, except cotton. The probabilities are that cotton will be surplus in another one or two years. Food shipments should be stepped up despite the enormous total (15 million tons) of bread grains exported from the United States during the present crop year. We are wasting and over-consuming food in the United States to such an extent that a reasonable measure of conservation would make at least another million tons available for export with no harm whatsoever to the health and efficiency of the American people.

9. This three-year grant to Europe should be based on a European plan which the principal European nations, headed by the UK, France and Italy, should work out. Such a plan should be based on a European economic federation on the order of the Belgium-Netherlands-Luxembourg Customs Union. Europe cannot recover from this war and again become independent if her economy continues to be divided into many small watertight compartments as it is today.

10. Obviously, the above is only the broad outline of a problem which will require much study and preparation before any move can be made.

---

[1] Bernard M. Baruch had served as Chairman of the War Industries Board in 1918, as an adviser to the Director of War Mobilization, 1943–1945, and as US Representative on the UN Atomic Energy Commission in 1946.

Canada, Argentina, Brazil, Australia, New Zealand, Union of South Africa could all help with their surplus food and raw materials, but we must avoid getting into another UNNRA. *The United States must run this show.*

(Department of State, *Foreign Relations of the United States, Diplomatic Papers: 1947*, Washington, 1971, V, pp. 230–2; reprinted in Joseph M. Siracusa (ed.) *The American Diplomatic Revolution*, Milton Keynes, Open University Press, 1978)

II.36   Secretary of State George C. Marshall, 'The Marshall Plan' (5 June 1947)

I need not tell you gentlemen that the world situation is very serious. That must be apparent to all intelligent people. I think one difficulty is that the problem is one of such enormous complexity that the very mass of facts presented to the public by press and radio make it exceedingly difficult for the man in the street to reach a clear appraisement of the situation. Furthermore, the people of this country are distant from the troubled areas of the earth and it is hard for them to comprehend the plight and consequent reactions of the long-suffering peoples, and the effect of those reactions on their governments in connection with our efforts to promote peace in the world.

In considering the requirements for the rehabilitation of Europe, the physical loss of life, the visible destruction of cities, factories, mines, and railroads was correctly estimated, but it has become obvious during recent months that this visible destruction was probably less serious than the dislocation of the entire fabric of European economy. For the past 10 years conditions have been highly abnormal. The feverish preparation for war and the more feverish maintenance of the war effort engulfed all aspects of national economies. Machinery has fallen into disrepair or is entirely obsolete. Under the arbitrary and destructive Nazi rule, virtually every possible enterprise was geared into the German war machine. Long-standing commercial ties, private institutions, banks, insurance companies, and shipping companies disappeared, through loss of capital, absorption through nationalization, or by simple destruction. In many countries, confidence in the local currency has been severely shaken. The breakdown of the business structure of Europe during the war was complete. Recovery has been seriously retarded by the fact that two years after the close of hostilities a peace settlement with Germany and Austria has not been agreed upon. But even given a more prompt solution of these difficult problems, the rehabilitation of the economic structure of Europe quite evidently will require a much longer time and greater effort than had been foreseen.

There is a phase of this matter which is both interesting and serious. The farmer has always produced the foodstuffs to exchange with the city dweller for the other necessities of life. This division of labour is the basis of modern civilization. At the present time it is threatened with break-down. The town and city industries are not producing adequate goods to exchange with the food-producing farmer. Raw materials and fuel are in short supply. Machinery is lacking or worn out. The farmer or the peasant cannot find the goods for sale which he desires to purchase. So the sale of his farm produce for money which he cannot use seems to him an unprofitable transaction. He, therefore, has withdrawn many fields from crop cultivation and is using them for grazing. He feeds more grain to stock and finds for himself and his family an ample supply of food, however short he may be on clothing and the other ordinary gadgets of civilization. Meanwhile people in the cities are short of food and fuel. So the governments are forced to use their foreign money and credits to procure these necessities abroad. This process exhausts funds which are urgently needed for reconstruction. Thus a very serious situation is rapidly developing which bodes no good for the world. The modern system of the division of labour upon which the exchange of products is based is in danger of breaking down.

The truth of the matter is that Europe's requirements for the next three or four years of foreign food and other essential products – principally from America – are so much greater than her present ability to pay that she must have substantial additional help or face economic, social, and political deterioration of a very grave character.

The remedy lies in breaking the vicious circle and restoring the confidence of the European people in the economic future of their own countries and of Europe as a whole. The manufacturer and the farmer throughout wide areas must be able and willing to exchange their products for currencies the continuing value of which is not open to question.

Aside from the demoralizing effect on the world at large and the possibilities of disturbances arising as a result of the desperation of the people concerned, the consequences to the economy of the United States should be apparent to all. It is logical that the United States should do whatever it is able to do to assist in the return of normal economic health in the world, without which there can be no political stability and no assured peace. Our policy is directed not against any country or doctrine but against hunger, poverty, desperation, and chaos. Its purpose should be the revival of a working economy in the world so as to permit the emergence of political and social conditions in which free institutions can exist. Such assistance, I am convinced, must not be on a piecemeal basis as various crises develop. Any assistance that this Government may render in the future should provide a cure rather than a mere palliative. Any government that is willing to assist in the task of recovery will find full co-operation, I am sure, on the part of the United States Government. Any government which manoeuvres to block the recovery of other countries cannot expect help from us. Furthermore, governments, political parties, or groups which seek to perpetuate human misery in order to profit therefrom politically or otherwise will encounter the opposition of the United States.

It is already evident that, before the United States Government can proceed much further in its efforts to alleviate the situation and help start the European world on its way to recovery, there must be some agreement among the countries of Europe as to the requirements of the situation and the part those countries themselves will take in order to give proper effect to whatever action might be undertaken by this Government. It would be neither fitting nor efficacious for this Government to undertake to draw up unilaterally a programme designed to place Europe on its feet economically. This is the business of the Europeans. The initiative, I think, must come from Europe. The role of this country should consist of friendly aid in the drafting of a European programme and of later support of such a programme so far as it may be practical for us to do so. The programme should be a joint one, agreed to by a number, if not all, European nations.

An essential part of any successful action on the part of the United States is an understanding on the part of the people of America of the character of the problem and the remedies to be applied. Political passion and prejudice should have no part. With foresight, and a willingness on the part of our people to face up to the vast responsibility which history has clearly placed upon our country, the difficulties I have outlined can and will be overcome.

(Speech given at Harvard University, 5 June 1947, Department of State, *Bulletin*, XVI, pp. 1159–60; reprinted in Joseph M. Siracusa (ed.) *The American Diplomatic Revolution*, Milton Keynes, Open University Press, 1978)

II.37 Andrei Zhdanov, 'Report on the international situation, at the Founding Conference of the Communist Information Bureau in Poland' (Sept. 1947)

The end of the Second World War brought with it big changes in the world situation. The military defeat of the bloc of fascist states, the character of the war as a war of liberation from fascism, and the decisive role played by the Soviet Union in the vanquishing of the fascist aggressors sharply altered the alignment of forces between the two systems – the socialist and the capitalist – in favour of socialism.

What is the essential nature of these changes?

The principal outcome of World War II was the military defeat of Germany and Japan – the two most militaristic and aggressive of the capitalist countries. The reactionary imperialist elements all over the world, notably in Britain, America and France, had reposed great hopes in Germany and Japan, and chiefly in Hitler Germany: firstly as in a force most capable of inflicting a blow on the Soviet Union in order to, if not having it destroyed altogether, weaken it at least and undermine its influence; secondly, as in a force capable of smashing the revolutionary labour and democratic movement in Germany herself and in all countries singled out for Nazi aggression, and thereby strengthening capitalism generally. This was the chief reason for the pre-war policy of 'appeasement' and encouragement of fascist aggression, the so-called Munich policy consistently pursued by the imperialist ruling circles of Britain, France, and the United States.

But the hopes reposed by the British, French and American imperialists in the Hitlerites were not realized. The Hitlerites proved to be weaker, and the Soviet Union and the freedom-loving nations stronger than the Munichists had anticipated. As a result of World War II the major forces of bellicose international fascist reaction had been smashed and put out of commission for a long time to come.

This was accompanied by another serious loss to the world capitalist system generally. Whereas the principal result of World War I had been that the united imperialist front was breached and that Russia dropped out of the world capitalist system, and whereas, as a consequence of the triumph of the socialist system in the USSR, capitalism ceased to be an integral, world-wide economic system, World War II and the defeat of fascism, the weakening of the world position of capitalism and the enhanced strength of the anti-fascist movement resulted in a number of countries in Central and Southeastern Europe dropping out of the imperialist system. In these countries new, popular, democratic regimes arose. . . .

The war immensely enhanced the international significance and prestige of the USSR. The USSR was the leading force and the guiding spirit in the military defeat of Germany and Japan. The progressive democratic forces of the whole world rallied around the Soviet Union. The socialist state successfully stood the strenuous test of the war and emerged victorious from the mortal struggle with a most powerful enemy. Instead of being enfeebled, the USSR became stronger. . . .

World War II aggravated the crisis of the colonial system, as expressed in the rise of a powerful movement for national liberation in the colonies and dependencies. This has placed the rear of the capitalist system in jeopardy. The peoples of the colonies no longer wish to live in the old way. The ruling classes of the metropolitan countries can no longer govern the colonies on the old lines. Attempts to crush the national liberation movement by military force now increasingly encounter armed resistance on the part of the colonial peoples and lead to protracted colonial wars (Holland–Indonesia, France–Vietnam). . . .

But America's aspirations to world supremacy encounter an obstacle in the USSR, the stronghold of anti-imperialist and anti-fascist policy, and its growing international influence, in the new democracies, which have escaped from the control of Britain and American imperialism, and in the workers of all countries, including America itself, who do not want a new war for the supremacy of their oppressors. Accordingly, the new expansionist and reactionary policy of the United States envisages a struggle against the USSR, against the labour movements in all countries, including the United States, and against the emancipationist, anti-imperialist forces in all countries.

Alarmed by the achievements of socialism in the USSR, by the achievements of the new democracies, and by the post-war growth of the labour and democratic movement in all countries, the American reactionaries are disposed to take upon themselves the mission of 'saviours' of the capitalist system from Communism.

The frank expansionist programme of the United States is therefore highly reminiscent of the reckless programme, which failed so ignominiously, of the fascist aggressors, who, as we know, also made a bid for world supremacy.

Just as the Hitlerites, when they were making their preparations for piratical aggression, adopted the camouflage of anti-Communism in order to make it possible to oppress and enslave all peoples and primarily and chiefly their own people, America's present-day ruling circles mask their expansionist policy, and even their offensive against the vital interests of their weaker imperialist rival, Great Britain, by fictitious considerations of defence against Communism. The feverish piling up of armaments, the construction of new military bases and the creation of bridgeheads for the American armed forces in all parts of the world is justified on the false and pharisaical grounds of 'defence' against an imaginary threat of war on the part of the USSR. . . .

Soviet foreign policy proceeds from the fact of the co-existence for a long period of the two systems – capitalism and socialism. From this it follows that co-operation between the USSR and countries with other systems is possible, provided that the principle of reciprocity is observed and that obligations once assumed are honoured. Everyone knows that the USSR has always honoured the obligations it has assumed. The Soviet Union has demonstrated its will and desire for co-operation. . . .

In their ideological struggle against the USSR, the American imperialists, who have no great insight into political questions, demonstrate their ignorance by laying primary stress on the allegation that the Soviet Union is undemocratic and totalitarian, while the United States and Great Britain and the whole capitalist world are democratic. On this platform of ideological struggle – on this defence of bourgeois pseudo-democracy and condemnation of Communism as totalitarian – are united all the enemies of the working class without exception, from the capitalist magnates to the Right socialist leaders, who seize with the greatest eagerness on any slanderous imputations against the USSR suggested to them by their imperialist masters. The pith and substance of this fraudulent propaganda is the claim that the earmark of true democracy is the existence of a plurality of parties and of an organized opposition minority.

On these grounds the British Labourites, who spare no effort in their fight against Communism, would like to discover antagonistic classes and a corresponding struggle of parties in the USSR. Political ignoramuses that they are, they cannot understand that capitalists and landlords, antagonistic classes, and hence a plurality of parties, have long ceased to exist in the USSR. They would like to have in the USSR the bourgeois parties which are so dear to their hearts, including pseudo-socialistic parties, as an agency of imperialism. But to their bitter regret these parties of the exploiting bourgeoisie have been doomed by history to disappear from the scene. . . .

One of the lines taken by the ideological campaign that goes hand in hand with the plans for the enslavement of Europe is an attack on the principle of national sovereignty, an appeal for the renouncement of the sovereign rights of nations, to which is opposed the idea of a world government. The purpose of this campaign is to mask the unbridled expansion of American imperialism which is ruthlessly violating the sovereign rights of nations, to represent the United States as a champion of universal laws, and those who resist American penetration as believers in obsolete and selfish nationalism. The idea of a world government has been taken up by bourgeois intellectual cranks and pacifists, and is being exploited not only as a means of pressure, with the purpose of ideologically disarming the nations that defend their independence against the encroachments of American imperialism, but also as a slogan specially directed against the Soviet Union, which indefatigably and consistently upholds the principle of real equality and protection of the sovereign rights of all nations, big and small. Under present conditions imperialist countries like the USA, Great Britain and the states closely associated with them become dangerous enemies of national independence and the self-determination of nations, while the Soviet Union and the new democracies are a reliable bulwark against encroachments on the equality and self-determination of nations. . . .

The Truman doctrine, which provides for the rendering of American assistance to all reactionary regimes which actively oppose the democratic peoples, bears a frankly aggressive character. . . .

The vague and deliberately guarded formulations of the Marshall Plan amount in essence to a scheme to create a block of states bound by obligations to the United States, and to grant American credits to European countries as a recompense for their renunciation of economic, and then of political, independence. Moreover, the cornerstone of the Marshall Plan is the restoration of the industrial areas of Western Germany controlled by the American monopolies. . . .

The dissolution of the Comintern, which conformed to the demands of the development of the labour movement in the new historical situation, played a positive role. The dissolution of the Comintern once and for all disposed of the slanderous allegation of the enemies of Communism and the labour movement that Moscow was interfering in the internal affairs of other states, and that the Communist Parties in the various countries were acting not in the interests of their nations, but on orders from outside. . . .

But the present position of the Communist Parties has its short-comings. Some comrades understood the dissolution of the Comintern to imply the elimination of all ties, of all contact, between the fraternal Communist Parties. But experience has shown that such mutual isolation of the Communist Parties is wrong, harmful and, in point of fact, unnatural.

(Robert V. Daniels (ed.), *A Documentary History of Communism*, vol. 2, Hanover and London, University Press of New England on behalf of the University of Vermont, 1984)

II.38   Konrad Adenauer, speech marking the final stage in the setting up of the German Federal Republic (21 Sept. 1949)

I have the honour to pay you a visit in company with some of the members of my Cabinet, thereby establishing the first contact between the Government of the Federal Republic of Germany and the three High Commissioners. Now that the German Federal Assembly has convened, and the Federal president been elected, and now that I have been chosen Federal Chancellor and the members of the Federal Cabinet have been appointed, a new chapter of German history of the postwar years begins. The disaster of the Second World War has left in its wake a Germany almost totally destroyed. Our cities were in ruins. Economic life was largely smashed. All vestiges of a government had ceased. The very souls of men had suffered such injuries that it seemed doubtful whether a recovery would ever be possible. During the four years following the disaster of 1945, legislative and executive power was largely vested in the occupation powers. It was only step by step that executive and legislative functions were redelegated to German authorities on various levels, and with a limited power to make decisions. It is fitting and proper to acknowledge gratefully that the German population was saved during these trying years from starvation by Allied help in supplying food which at the time could not be purchased with the proceeds of German exports. It was this help which made possible the start of reconstruction. Now that the governmental and legislative elements of the German Federal Republic are being built up, a large part of the responsibility and the authority to make decisions will pass into German hands. We do not, of course, possess as yet complete freedom; since there are considerable restrictions contained in the occupation statute. We will do our part to bring about an atmosphere in which the Allied powers will see their way clear to apply the occupation statute in a liberal and generous manner; only in this way will the German people be able to attain full freedom. We hope that the

Allied powers will, by making a corresponding use of the revision clause in the occupation statute, hasten the further political development of our country.

It is the unshakable wish of the new Federal Government first and foremost to tackle the great social problems. The Government is convinced that a sound political entity can only develop when each individual is assured a maximum of economic opportunity to earn a livelihood. Not until we succeed in converting the flotsam millions of refugees into settled inhabitants by providing them with housing and adequate opportunities for work will we be able to enjoy inner stability in Germany. Disorder and crises in this part of Europe, however, constitute a serious threat to the security of the entire continent. For this reason, the social programme of the Federal Government should at the same time act to ensure a peaceful development in Europe. We will, of course, do everything in our power to master these problems with the forces at our command. Nevertheless, I feel I am justified in believing even now that the problem of expellees is not only a national, but an international one. To solve it, the help of the rest of the world is needed. The Federal Government would, therefore, welcome it greatly if the members of the High Commission would urge their governments to devote in future more attention to this problem.

If we want to establish peace in Europe, we can in the view of the Federal Government achieve this only by working along entirely new methods. We see opportunities to do so in the efforts for a European federation which has just borne its first fruits [at] Strasbourg. We do believe, however, that such a federation will only have vitality if built on close economic co-operation among the nations. The organization created by the Marshall Plan represents a good start in this direction. Germany is fully ready to co-operate responsibly in this regard. We see another opening for creating a positive and viable European federation in the hope that the control of the Ruhr region would cease to be a unilateral arrangement and that it would gradually grow into an organism which would embrace the basic industries of other European countries as well. We are certain that the narrow nationalistic conception of the states as it prevailed in the nineteenth and early twentieth centuries may now be said to be overcome. This conception gave birth to nationalism, with its attendant splintering of life in Europe. If we now turn back to the sources of our European civilization, born of Christianity, then we cannot fail to succeed in restoring the unity of European life in all fields of endeavour. This is the sole effective assurance for maintaining peace.

(Beate Ruhm von Oppen, *Documents on Germany Under Occupation 1945–1954*, London, Oxford University Press, 1955, pp. 417–19)

II.39 Allied High Commission, 'Law No. 5 for Safeguarding the Freedom of the Press, Radio and Other Information Media' (21 Sept. 1949)

ARTICLE I

The German press, radio and other information media shall be free as is provided by the Basic Law. The Allied High Commission reserves the right to cancel or annul any measure, governmental, political, administrative or financial, which threatens such freedom.

ARTICLE II

1. An enterprise or a person engaged therein or utilizing the facilities thereof shall not act in a manner affecting or likely to affect prejudicially the prestige or security of the Allied Forces.

2. Where in the opinion of the Allied High Commission an enterprise or a person has violated the provisions of paragraph 1 of this Article, the Allied High Commission may prohibit the enterprise from continuing its activities or the person from engaging in an enterprise or utilizing the facilities thereof, for a definite or an indefinite period of time. The Allied High Commission may impose a like prohibition on an enterprise or person where in its opinion there is sufficient evidence that such person or enterprise is about to violate the provisions of this Law.

3. Where any enterprise is so prohibited for more than three months or any person for more than one month, the enterprise or person affected shall have the right to appeal to an agency to be established for the purpose. Such agency shall, after hearing the appellant or his representative and any witnesses whom the appellant of the agency desires to call, either confirm, extend, reduce or modify the terms of the order appealed from.

ARTICLE III

1. No new radio broadcasting, television or wired radio transmission installation shall be set up and there shall be no transfer of control of any installation of this nature without the authorization of the Allied High Commission. German radio operations shall be conducted in accordance with frequency and power allocations made by the Allied High Commission.

2. International relays, foreign language broadcasting and negotiations with foreign countries on matters of broadcasting shall be subject to prior authorization by the Allied High Commission.

ARTICLE IV

Any broadcasting stations and any publications shall, when required by the Allied High Commission, broadcast or publish any information deemed necessary by the Commission to further the purposes of the Occupation Statute.

ARTICLE V

A copy of every publication or production of any enterprise shall, on publication or production in the federal territory, be filed as the Allied High Commission may direct.

ARTICLE VI

The Allied High Commission may prohibit the distribution, display or possession in the federal territory of any publication or production of any enterprise which in its opinion is likely to prejudice the prestige or security of the Allied Forces. It may also prohibit the bringing into the federal territory of such publications or productions.

ARTICLE VII

The Allied High Commission may confiscate any publication or production distributed or produced contrary to the provisions of this Law.

[Articles VIII–XIII, including a list of legislation to be repealed, omitted.]

(*High Commission Gazette*, 23 September 1949, p. 7; reprinted in Beate Ruhm von Oppen, *Documents on Germany Under Occupation 1945–1954*, London, Oxford University Press, 1955, pp. 416–17)

II.40 German Economic Commission of the Soviet High Commission, 'Announcement of the impending establishment of the German Democratic Republic' (6 Oct. 1949)

The Main Administration for Information of the German Economic Commission makes the following announcement.

The Constitution of the German Democratic Republic, discussed by the widest circles throughout the entire German population, adopted by the German People's Council, confirmed by the Third German People's Congress, will be the basis of the impending establishment of state and government. When the German People's Council has passed a resolution next Friday to reconstitute itself as the Provisional People's Chamber, this truly historic decision will introduce a new phase in German post-war development: Germany leaves a status of occupation and enters the status of sovereignty.

Does this annul the Potsdam Agreement? No: it is now being fulfilled – because it was precisely the intention of the Potsdam Agreement to give back its independence to a democratic Germany. Thus on Friday the democratic Germany will take the first step towards the restoration of its sovereignty, independence, and freedom, while the undemocratic Germany at Bonn, the rump Germany of the war-mongers and the dividers (*Spalter*), of the Hitlerian armaments magnates and large estate owners, continues in the hopeless perspective of enduring occupation and economic dependence.

The members of the German People's Council, who were elected by secret ballot by over 2,000 delegates of the Third German People's Congress, have behind them the millions of affirmative votes of this year's elections for the People's Congress, and are thus backed by the broad majority of the population. When they assemble as the Provisional People's Chamber, the German people will know that their cause is in good hands. All further steps in the creation of state and government will follow automatically from the formation of the Provisional People's Chamber.

Under Article 92 of the Constitution the Minister President will be nominated by the strongest group (*Fraktion*) in the People's Chamber. He will form the government. Under this Article all parliamentary groups are to be represented in the government by Ministers or Under Secretaries of State in proportion to their strength.

Under Article 101 the President of the Republic will be elected by the People's Chamber and by the *Länder* Chamber in joint session. Article 93 lays it down that he will swear in the members of the government when they take up their offices.

The *Länder* Chamber is the representative body of the German *Länder*. Under Article 71 every *Land* will send to the *Länder* Chamber one delegate for every 500,000 inhabitants. These delegates will be elected by the *Landtage* in proportion to the strength of the group, according to Article 72.

The order of events in the process of the formation of government and state during this week and next will therefore be: formation of the People's Chamber and the *Länder* Chamber, election of the President of the State by both Chambers jointly, nomination of the Minister President and formation of the Cabinet, declaration of government policy and debate, and finally the vote of confidence.

The experience of everyday life proves to us that only active self-help can deliver us from calamity. The German people, too, have experienced this. They are about to free themselves from the national emergency by national self-help; they are on the path to independence, to freedom, and to peace.

(*Tägliche Rundschau*, 7 October 1949; reprinted in Beate Ruhm von Oppen, *Documents on Germany Under Occupation 1945–1954*, London, Oxford University Press, 1955, pp. 420–1)

II.41 Central Committee of the Socialist Unity Party, 'Resolution on the fight against formalism in art and literature and for a progressive German culture' (17 March 1951)

When the glorious Soviet Army shattered Hitler fascism and liberated the German people, it created the precondition for the fundamental democratic transformation which made possible the great achievements in all fields of the economic, political, and cultural life of the German Democratic Republic. The decree of 31 March 1949 on the preservation and development of German science and culture, the further improvement in the situation of the intelligentsia and the increase in its role in production and in public life, and the decree of 16 March 1950 for the development of a progressive democratic culture of the German people and for the further development of the working and living conditions of the intelligentsia created the conditions for the development of a truly democratic culture in Germany.

The main task in the field of cultural policy was formulated in the resolution of the Third Party Congress of the Socialist Unity Party of Germany as follows: 'The present situation and the tasks of the SED.'

In the field of cultural policy, too, the fight for peace, for the democratic unity of Germany, and for the consolidation of our anti-fascist democratic order is the core of all our work. Cultural policy teaches men to be true democrats, citizens to act independently and responsibly, highly skilled expert personnel to put all their abilities at the service of peace, progress, and democracy.

Education to this end can only be given in an implacable fight against the cannibalist teachings of the imperialist war-mongers. Every attempt to represent these hostile ideologies in an objectivist manner means the dissemination of, and therefore the strengthening of, these ideologies. It is therefore a decisive task of cultural policy to bring about a fundamental change in all fields of cultural life and thus to put an end once and for all to lukewarmness and conciliationism.

The accomplishment of the great tasks of the Five Year Plan demands increased efforts to raise still further the cultural level of the urban and rural population and to establish close relations between science, art, literature, and the working people.

The fight against remilitarization, for the reunification of Germany on a democratic basis, and for the conclusion of a peace treaty with Germany in the year 1951 are the most important tasks of the whole German people. These tasks can only be fulfilled in a resolute fight against American war-mongering imperialism which has reached a stage of open and brutal provocation of war.

[. . .]

SITUATION AND TASKS IN WESTERN GERMANY

In contrast with the cultural successes achieved in the German Democratic Republic, cultural life in Western Germany has reached a catastrophically low point owing to the pernicious influence of American monopoly capitalism. The hostility to culture of Americanism is shown by such things as the restrictions placed on the freedom of artistic creation, by the persecution of progressive scientists and artists, and by the boycott and pogrom propaganda against them.

Although the majority of cultural workers in the West of our country are against remilitarization, many artists can only eke out an existence by using their art in the service of the enemies of Germany. Thus painters took part in a poster competition for the popularization of the Marshall Plan.

The task of the progressive cultural workers in Western Germany consists in supporting the Plebiscite against remilitarization and for the conclusion of a Peace Treaty with Germany in 1951 with all their strength and resisting remilitarization; making the creation of a united, democratic, peace-loving, and independent Germany not only the criterion for their personal conduct but also for the content of their artistic work. The chief thing is that all peace-loving and patriotic intellectuals of Western Germany should become aware of their all-German responsibility, should intensify the struggle against American cultural barbarism and work for the preservation of the national cultural heritage and the development of a democratic culture that serves the people.

WEAKNESSES AND DEFECTS IN CULTURAL WORK

Despite all successes, development in the cultural field has not kept pace with the great achievements in the economic and political field.

Comrade Johannes R. Becher said at our Third Party Congress:

It would be nonsensical and injurious to deny or to cloak by any accusations the fact that we cultural workers have so far, with our artistic achievements, remained far behind the demands of the hour, the demands of the epoch. Apart from a few exceptions, what can we put beside the achievements of the activist movement?

The main cause for the lagging of the arts behind the tasks of the epoch lies in the rule of formalism in art and in lack of clarity concerning the ways and means of cultural creativity in the German Democratic Republic.

Many of the best representatives of modern German art are faced in their work by the great discrepancy between a new content and the useless means of formalist art. In order to express a new content it is necessary to overcome formalism.

Formalism means the disintegration and destruction of art itself. The formalists deny the fact that the decisive importance lies in the content, the idea, the thought of a work. They hold that the significance of a work of art lies not in its content but in its form. Everywhere where the question of form achieves an independent importance, art loses its humanist and democratic character.

When form in art is not determined by the content of the work of art we get abstraction. A form that is in contradiction to objective reality cannot convey knowledge of objective reality. If art does not convey knowledge of reality, it does not fulfil its high mission, since, according to Karl Marx, art is the practical artistic method at all stages in the development of humanity of assimilating the world in an act of cognition.

To deny the fundamental importance of the content of a work of art is not only a sign of backwardness to which a true artist must never reconcile himself, but leads to the destruction of artistic form – and that means disintegration and destruction of art itself.

The most important characteristic of formalism consists in the endeavour to break completely with the classical cultural heritage under the pretext or with the erroneous intention of developing something 'completely new'. This leads to the deracination of national culture and to the destruction of national consciousness, and promotes cosmopolitanism, thus giving direct support to the war policy of American imperialism.

In order to prepare the peoples of the American satellite states for their task of pulling the chestnuts of American imperialism out of the fire in a third world war and in order to paralyse the resistance of the peoples in the camp of democracy and peace, those who look after the interests of the imperialists make all efforts to destroy the national dignity and the national consciousness of the peoples.

A decisive ideological weapon used by imperialism for attaining this criminal aim is cosmopolitanism. In art it is formalism in all its variations which in the first place fulfils the task of undermining and destroying the national consciousness of the peoples. It is therefore one of the most important tasks of the German people to preserve their national cultural heritage. The task of our artists and writers must therefore be to develop a new German democratic culture on the basis of the cultural heritage.

A further characteristic of formalism is the turning away from the human and from the popular elements in art, and the desertion of the principle that art must serve the people.

THE ROLE OF FORMALIST ART

Capitalist production is inimical to certain branches of intellectual production such as art and poetry (Karl Marx, *Theories of Surplus Value*). In imperialist epochs capitalism destroys true art.

By the economic and political power they wield, the imperialist rulers prevent art from conveying a knowledge of reality and abuse it for the preservation of their power in order to prevent the working people and the oppressed from fighting for freedom and independence, and to impede humanity in the fight for peace.

All artistic schools and concepts which divorce art from life and lead to abstraction are, seen objectively, a help for imperialism. Because formalist art does not convey knowledge of reality, divorces art from the people, and leads to abstraction, it, too, gives aid to imperialism. The isolation of art and the artist from the people, the glorification of the 'mystical', the 'mysterious', and the 'supernatural' are symptoms of decay in the art of the imperialist epoch of capitalism. Other such symptoms are the glorification of a belief in brute force, reaction, vulgarity, murder, brutality, and pornography.

[. . .]

THE FIGHT FOR REALISM IN ART AND LITERATURE

In order to eliminate the reign of formalism in art it is necessary to develop a realistic art.

'In my opinion realism means, apart from faithfulness of detail, the faithful rendering of typical characters in typical circumstances' (Engels to Margaret Harkness, April 1888).

In order to develop a realistic art, we take our orientation from the example of the great socialist Soviet Union, which has created the most progressive culture in the world.

Comrade Zhdanov said in 1934:

Comrade Stalin has called our writers the engineers of the human soul. What does that mean? What obligation does that name put upon them?

It means, firstly, to know life, to be able to depict it not scholastically, not as though it were something dead, not as 'objective reality', but as reality in its revolutionary development.

A truthful and historically concrete artistic rendering must be combined with the task of educating and ideologically remodelling the working man in the spirit of socialism. This is the method which we call the method of socialist realism in literature and in literary criticism.

What lessons does this teach us in our cultural activities in the German Democratic Republic? In order to develop a realist art 'which . . . expresses the new social conditions in the German Democratic Republic' (Resolution passed by the Third Party Congress of the SED), our artists must depict life correctly, i.e. in its progressive development. This requires knowledge of the development of life as it is. The typical circumstances of our time in which typical characters are to be depicted truthfully are the new social conditions in the German Democratic Republic, that is, the struggle for the solution of the vital problems of our people.

In accordance with these conditions, a truthful and historically concrete artistic rendering must be connected with the task of educating men and women in the spirit of the struggle for a united democratic, peace-loving, and independent Germany, for the fulfilment of the Five Year Plan, for the fight for peace.

Realistic art transmits knowledge of reality and awakens strivings in people which are calculated to find their embodiment in progressive, creative activity tending to the solution of the vital problems of our people.

[. . .]

CRITICISM AND SELF-CRITICISM IN ART

The continuation of intensive discussion of all fields of art and literature is of great importance for the overcoming of backwardness in art. This debate and open discussion of all mistakes and shortcomings will be of the greatest help to our artists and writers themselves. Open discussion combined with objective criticism is an important precondition for the further development of art. Whoever is afraid of criticism of his work will make no progress and will not overcome his weaknesses.

[. . .]

THE NEXT TASKS IN ART AND LITERATURE

To achieve progress in the field of art the Central Committee of the Socialist Unity Party of Germany thinks the following measures should be taken:

(a) The Central Committee of the Socialist Unity Party of Germany thinks the time has come to prepare a State Commission for Art whose main task will be the direction of the work of theatres, of state institutions for music, dancing, and singing, of institutes of art and art academies and training colleges. The State Commission for the Arts will also give general methodological instruction in the development of amateur art and will support the work of the social organizations in this field.

(b) For the further improvement of artistic work in the German Democratic Republic it is necessary to establish the closest connexion between literature and art and the tasks of the day, especially the tasks set by the Five Year Plan. The Five Year Plan does not only contain many themes that require artistic expression, but its fulfilment also demands outstanding artistic achievements in the realization of its individual projects.

A study of the way in which the great classics gave expression to the problems of their time is the greatest help for an artistically successful expression of the themes of our day. To treat present-day subjects using the lessons learnt from such study is the most important contribution that artists can make towards the fulfilment of the Five Year Plan. . . .

(c) We recommend the SED comrades in the Ministry for Popular Education of the German Democratic Republic to see to it that measures for the better training of young artists are introduced quickly. Attention must here be paid to overcoming the under-estimation or merely formal implementation of instruction in social sciences at the art schools. Curricula for specialized training as well as for training in social science which are as yet partly unsystematized must be drawn up anew. It is necessary for students to be introduced to the classical heritage and for the works of the classics to be made the subject of special study. A study of the works of Marx, Engels, Lenin and Stalin on dialectical and historical materialism and on art and literature is the decisive precondition for a correct understanding of the role of art in the development of society.

It is also necessary to overcome a tendency on the part of students to underestimate the importance of serious study in the fields of art and also a certain disdain of craftsmanship in art. In this respect, too, much can be learnt from the old masters, who were supreme craftsmen and who always worked with great care and thoroughness.

The proportion of workers' and peasants' children among art students is to be increased and new, uniform rules of admission are to be worked out, keeping in mind the desirability of admitting the most gifted members of amateur art groups.

(d) Comrades in the 'Cultural League for the Democratic Renewal of Germany' are advised to put the main emphasis in the work of the

Cultural League on bringing about the active participation of artists in Eastern and Western Germany in the struggle for peace, in intensive support for the fight against remilitarization and for the conclusion of a peace treaty with Germany in the year 1951. It is imperative to organize the fight *against* the American cultural barbarism and *for* the creation of a democratic culture based on our cultural heritage.

In order to bring about the unity of cultural workers in Eastern and Western Germany in the struggle for peace and for a united, democratic, peace-loving, and independent Germany, all-German meetings must be organized in greater measure in all fields.

[. . .]

(*g*) It is the task of comrades in the section for composers and musicologists in the Cultural League for the Democratic Renewal of Germany to engage in constant discussion and criticism of formalism in music, so that the Composers' Section will from the very beginning help the development of musical work, especially in opera and symphonic music, to reach new achievements, and to overcome backwardness. . . .

(*h*) For all three sections [writers, artists, and musicians] it is necessary to organize the study by cultural workers of Marxism–Leninism, under the guidance of the Cultural League for the Democratic Renewal of Germany. The study of Marxism–Leninism – knowledge of the evolutionary laws in nature and society – best enables cultural workers correctly to depict life in its progressive development. Since the active participation of artists in political life and democratic reconstruction, e.g. in the work of the Peace Committees, the Committees of the National Front of Democratic Germany, in the social organizations and their close and direct contact with activists, workers and members of the intelligentsia in people's enterprises, Machine Lending Stations, and People's Farms, etc., is the precondition for a succesful expression of current problems, the directorate of the sections must organize on a planned basis the participation of cultural workers in this work. The Sections must form directorates capable of developing methods of collective work, and of ensuring on the one hand that the isolation of some artists from the people is overcome and, on the other, that the artist is freed from an excess of organizational and technical work which deprives him of time for creative activity.

Increased attention to the rising generation must play a decisive part in the further improvement of the work of these Sections. Greater stress than before is to be laid on the training of new and young elements, particularly from among the ranks of the FDJ, and their instruction by the ablest and most experienced artists.

In the study of the culture of the Soviet Union the closest collaboration with the Society for German–Soviet Friendship is necessary; this will make possible the acquisition of the experience of the Soviet Union, through the organization of cultural activities and film shows and assistance in selecting and providing the literature, etc., requisite to a knowledge of cultural achievements.

(*i*) The Central Committee of the Socialist Unity Party of Germany advises SED comrades in the Artists' Trade Union (stage, film, music, variety artists, radio) to develop broadly based discussions on questions of literature and art in order to bring about the full understanding of a work of art, through truthful representation based on high artistic quality. This, however, implies the necessity to increase the consciousness of the artist, because a work of art can only be presented to perfection if the artist comprehends it in its entire significance. Therefore it is essential that the quality of the training work by the Artists' Union should be improved and that in all theatres, when work on a new production begins, an introduction should be given by someone competent to deal with the political and social problems treated in it.

The Central Committee of the Socialist Unity Party of Germany states that all those engaged in artistic work in the German Democratic Republic will have the full support of the Party, so that backwardness in the cultural field can be overcome and literature and art can become a mighty weapon of the German people in the fight for the solution of their vital problems.

(SED *Dokumente*, iii, p. 431; reprinted in Beate Ruhm von Oppen, *Documents on Germany Under Occupation 1945–1954*, London, Oxford University Press, 1955, pp. 554–61)

II.42   Government of the German Democratic Republic, 'Statement regarding the Berlin riots' (17 June 1953)

Measures taken by the Government of the German Democratic Republic to improve the situation of the population have been answered by fascist and other reactionary elements in West Berlin by provocations and serious disturbances in the democratic sector of Berlin. These provocations are intended to impede the unification of Germany.

Yesterday's decision on the question of norms has removed the cause of the cessation of work by the building workers in Berlin.

The unrest which ensued is the work of *agents provocateurs* and fascist agents of foreign Powers and their accomplices from German capitalist monopolies. These forces are dissatisfied with the democratic power in the German Democratic Republic, which is organizing improvements in the situation of the population. The Government appeals to the people:

1. To support measures for the instant restoration of order in the city and to create conditions for normal and peaceful work in the factories.

2. Those guilty of instigating the unrest will be taken to task and severely punished. The workers and all honest citizens are asked to seize *agents provocateurs* and hand them over to the state authorities.

3. It is necessary for the workers and the technical intelligentsia themselves to take measures, in collaboration with the state authorities, to restore normal working conditions.

FURTHER STATEMENT

While the Government of the German Democratic Republic directs its endeavours towards the improvement of the standard of living of the population by new and important measures, paying special attention to the situation of the workers, mercenary elements, i.e. agents of foreign Powers and their accomplices belonging to the circles of German monopoly lords, have tried to foil these Government measures.

It has been established that yesterday's stoppages of work in a number of enterprises, and also provocation and rioting by single groups of fascist agents in the streets of the democratic sector of Berlin, took place under a uniform plan drawn up in Western Berlin for a specific propitious moment.

The excesses ended with the total collapse of the adventure thus instigated, because they met with resistance from large parts of the population and from the state authorities.

Normal work is being resumed everywhere. Order is being maintained in the streets. No excesses by *agents provocateurs* and criminal elements will be tolerated.

The infamous attempts by foreign agents to interfere with the measures of the Government aimed at an improvement in the living conditions of the population have foundered. The attempt to sow confusion in order to put new obstacles in the way of the reunification of Germany has been foiled.

The Government of the German Democratic Republic will take decisive measures to ensure the stern punishment of those guilty of these excesses.

The *agents provocateurs* must not expect clemency.

(*Neues Deutschland*, 18 June 1953; reprinted in Beate Ruhm von Oppen, *Documents on Germany Under Occupation 1945–1954*, London, Oxford University Press, 1955, pp. 590–1)

II.43   An average French town in 1950: leisure activities in Auxerre (pop. 24,000) (1950)

Division of male population by social position (%)

Agriculture	3
Servants	1
Unskilled labourers	6
Factory workers and supervisory staff	36
Owners of small workshops	9
White-collar workers	21
Executives	5
Technicians and liberal professions	11
Small businessmen	5
Directors	3
	100

[. . .]

By their nature, their diversity, and the place they occupy in the different social strata, leisure activities constitute one of the most distinctive elements of the social life of a town.

I THE CINEMA

The cinema definitely takes first place in the leisure of the people of Auxerre. It has become, as in all French towns, the most important and the most widely appreciated entertainment among the different categories of the population.

The cinemas. There are three cinemas in Auxerre, as clearly distinguished by the numbers they hold as by the public which frequents them. The most important is the *Casino* (500 seats) which, as required, also serves as a theatre, or concert or conference hall. It has a change of programme twice a week and in general shows films which have had critical acclaim, that is to say that the films one sees there are relatively selective. It is equipped with fine projection facilities, which means that audiences can be confident about the quality of the show.

The *Select* is a small cinema with 200 seats presenting weekly programmes where the quality of the films is less under control. It is frequented by a less fastidious and much more rowdy public; one section of the Auxerre bourgeoisie never goes there.

The third picture house was built by Monsignor Deschamp in 1932, with the aim of equipping the town with a cinema showing carefully selected films: not deliberately moralizing films, but current commercial films. Monsignor Deschamp wanted above all to avoid having shown on this screen people of rather low moral standards and habituating dubious milieux. The choice of films is not made in Auxerre but in Paris, where the organization 'Familia' determines the programmes and their distribution. This cinema, when all is said and done, does show interesting films; it is patronized, without distinction of class, by the totality of the population of Auxerre. The building is recent, relatively comfortable, and quite well equipped.

As far as the *Select* is concerned, even though it was reconstructed in 1948, that does not seem to have changed its audiences.

Films and the preferences of the public. The directors of the three cinemas are unanimous in declaring that the public favour French films and deplore the fact that there are not enough of them.

Films like *Le père tranquille* (*The Quiet Father*) or *La symphonie pastorale* (*The Pastoral Symphony*) were extremely successful, and had the highest box office takings of 1947. Comic films, whether of Bourvil or Laurel and Hardy, share public preferences with romantic films.

Among American films, those involving straightforward situations and 'fine sentiments', like *The Bells of St Mary's* and *The Keys of the Kingdom*, were greatly enjoyed. In general, American films have to be shown at the time when they are receiving publicity in the film journals, for their titles are very quickly forgotten. Westerns (*Buffalo Bill*) and cloak-and-dagger films (*Cyrano*) have regular audiences among the young.

The melodrama still exercises all its power over the ordinary public and particularly over women: *Les deux gosses* (*The Two Lads*), *Roger-la-Honte* (*Roger in Disgrace*), *Les deux orphelines* (*The Two Orphans*) always bring in the crowds.

The appeal of cartoons is very variable: if the public was disappointed by *Pinocchio*, and if *Fantasia* was a disaster, *Snow White*, by contrast, ran for a month during the war at the *Familia* – and the house was as full on the last day as on the first. . . .

The following table summarizes the preferences of a hundred people questioned:

	All	Men	Women
Documentaries	30	32	27
Romantic	28	22	33
Comic	18	21	16
Crime	12	15	10
No preference	12	10	14

[. . .]

IV   LEISURE IN THE HOME

Radio. There are 5,499 licence holders in Auxerre (about 75 per cent of all households). Eighty-two per cent of the men and 72 per cent of the women listen to the radio. . . .

Reading. Reading indisputably shares first place with the cinema in the leisure activities of Auxerre. The Municipal Library, originally founded at the time of the Revolution, brought together the collections of the two abbeys and of the cathedral. . . .

It is calculated that, since 1921, the number of readers as well as the number of books borrowed has increased; however, the curve has not been steady: there have been, from time to time, declines and increases, particularly during the occupation. In total, the number of readers has increased from 4,000 in 1921 to 5,000 in 1946, and the number of books borrowed from 11,000 in 1922 to 14,000 in 1939 and 26,000 in 1945. . . .

Detective stories are above all read by manual workers, white-collar workers of both sexes and by shop-keepers; biographies and poetry by the liberal professions, executives, and white-collar workers.

A survey among the different bookshops in the town revealed a taste (which is not peculiar to Auxerre) for foreign novels, most particularly translations from the English. In general the books bought are those on which a film has been based, and those which have been widely reviewed in the newspapers.

[. . .]

VI   SPORT

The Auxerre Stadium, built in 1942, specializes above all in athletics. The athletics section had 120 members and has won many successes not only in the regional championships, but also, from time to time, in national and international championships. Its inspiration is M. Norland, technical adviser to the athletics federation.

Football comes next as the second activity, with 100 members. The Auxerre Youth Club, created in 1905 by Monsignor Deschamp, specializes in football; there are five teams. Basketball comes next, with three teams. First-team football matches are supported by 800 to 1,000 spectators, other matches drawing very small crowds.

(Charles Bettelheim and Suzanne Frère, *Une ville française moyenne: Auxerre en 1950. Etude de structure sociale et urbaine*, Paris, Armand Colin, 1950, pp. 117, 197–8, 206, 209, 211, 214; trans. Arthur Marwick)

II.44   Simone de Beauvoir, extracts from *The Second Sex* (1949)

Extract (a)

In Soviet Russia the feminist movement has made the most sweeping advances. It began among female student intellectuals at the end of the nineteenth century, and was even then connected with violent and revolutionary activity. During the Russo-Japanese War women replaced men in many kinds of work and made organized demands for equality. After 1905 they took part in political strikes and mounted the barricades; and in 1917, a few days before the Revolution, they held a mass demonstration in St Petersburg, demanding bread, peace, and the return of their men. They played a great part in the October rising and, later, in the battle against invasion. Faithful to Marxist tradition, Lenin bound the emancipation of women to that of the workers; he gave them political and economic equality.

Article 122 of the Constitution of 1936 states: 'In Soviet Russia woman enjoys the same rights as man in all aspects of economic, official, cultural, public, and political life.' And this has been more precisely stated by the Communist International, which makes the following demands: 'Social equality of man and woman before the law and in practical life. Radical transformation in conjugal rights and the family code. Recognition of maternity as a social function. Making a social charge of the care and education of children and adolescents. The organization of a civilizing struggle against the ideology and the traditions that make woman a slave.' In the economic field woman's conquests have been brilliant. She gets equal wages and participates on a large scale in production; and on account of this she has assumed a considerable social and political importance. There were in 1939 a great many women deputies to the various regional and local soviets, and more than two hundred sat in the

Supreme Soviet of the USSR. Almost ten million are members of unions. Women constitute forty per cent of the workers and employees of the USSR; and many women workers have become Stakhanovites. It is well known that Russian women took a great part in the last war, penetrating even into masculine aspects of production such as metallurgy and mining, rafting of timber, and railway construction. Women also distinguished themselves as aviators and parachute troops, and they formed partisan armies.

This activity of women in public life raised a difficult problem: what should be woman's role in family life? During a whole period means had been sought to free her from domestic bonds. On 16 November 1924, the Comintern in plenary session proclaimed: 'The Revolution is impotent as long as the notion of family and of family relations continues to exist.' The respect thereupon accorded to free unions, the facility of divorce, and the legalizing of abortions assured woman's liberty with relation to the male; laws concerning maternity leave, day nurseries, kindergartens, and the like alleviated the cares of maternity. It is difficult to make out through the haze of passionate and contradictory testimony just what woman's concrete situation really was; but what is sure is that today the requirements of re-peopling the country have led to a different political view of the family: the family now appears as the elementary cell of society, and woman is both worker and housekeeper. Sexual morality is of the strictest; the laws of 1936 and 1941 forbid abortion and almost suppress divorce; adultery is condemned by custom. Strictly subordinated to the State like all workers, strictly bound to the home, but having access to political life and to the dignity conferred by productive labour, the Russian woman is in a singular condition which would repay the close study that circumstances unfortunately prevent me from undertaking.

The United Nations Commission on the Status of Women at a recent session demanded that equality in rights of the two sexes be recognized in all countries, and it passed several motions tending to make this legal statute a concrete reality. It would seem, then, that the game is won. The future can only lead to a more and more profound assimilation of woman into our once masculine society.

Extract (b)

According to French law, obedience is no longer included among the duties of a wife, and each woman citizen has the right to vote; but these civil liberties remain theoretical as long as they are unaccompanied by economic freedom. A woman supported by a man – wife or courtesan – is not emancipated from the male because she has a vote; if custom imposes less constraint upon her than formerly, the negative freedom implied has not profoundly modified her situation; she remains bound in her condition of vassalage. It is through gainful employment that woman has traversed most of the distance that separated her from the male; and nothing else can guarantee her liberty in practice. Once she ceases to be a parasite, the system based on her dependence crumbles; between her and the universe there is no longer any need for a masculine mediator.

The curse that is upon woman as vassal consists, as we have seen, in the fact that she is not permitted to do anything; so she persists in the vain pursuit of her true being through narcissism, love, or religion. When she is productive, active, she regains her transcendence; in her projects she concretely affirms her status as subject; in connection with the aims she pursues, with the money and the rights she takes possession of, she makes trial of and senses her responsibility. Many women are aware of these advantages, even among those in very modest positions. I heard a charwoman declare, while scrubbing the stone floor of an hotel lobby: 'I never asked anybody for anything; I succeeded all by myself.' She was as proud of her self-sufficiency as a Rockefeller. It is not to be supposed, however, that the mere combination of the right to vote and a job constitutes a complete emancipation: working, today, is not liberty. The social structure has not been much modified by the changes in woman's condition; this world, always belonging to men, still retains the form they have given it.

We must not lose sight of those facts which make the question of woman's labour a complex one. An important and thoughtful woman recently made a study of the women in the Renault factories; she states that they would prefer to stay in the home rather than work in the factory. There is no doubt that they get economic independence only as members of a class which is economically oppressed; and, on the other hand, their jobs at the factory do not relieve them of housekeeping burdens. The majority of women do not escape from the traditional feminine world; they get from neither society nor their husbands the assistance they would need to become in concrete fact the equals of the men. Only those women who have a political faith, who take militant action in the unions, who have confidence in their future, can give ethical meaning to thankless daily labour. But lacking leisure, inheriting a traditional submissiveness, women are just beginning to develop a political and social sense. And not getting in exchange for their work the moral and social benefits they might rightfully count on, they submit without enthusiasm to its constraints.

[. . .]

Today it is already less difficult for women to assert themselves; but they have not as yet completely overcome the age-long sex-limitation that has isolated them in their femininity. Lucidity of mind, for instance, is a conquest of which they are justly proud but with which alone they would be a little too quickly satisfied. The fact is that the traditional woman is a bamboozled conscious being and a practitioner of bamboozlement; she attempts to disguise her dependence from herself, which is a way of consenting to it. To expose this dependence is in itself a liberation; a clear-sighted cynicism is a defence against humiliations and shame: it is the preliminary sketch of an assumption. By aspiring to clear-sightedness women writers are doing the cause of women a great service; but – usually without realizing it – they are still too concerned with serving this cause to assume the disinterested attitude towards the universe that opens the widest horizons. When they have removed the veils of illusion and deception, they think they have done enough; but this negative audacity leaves us still faced by an enigma, for the truth itself is ambiguity, abyss, mystery: once stated, it must be thoughtfully reconsidered, re-created. It is all very well not to be duped, but at that point all else begins. Woman exhausts her courage dissipating mirages and she stops in terror at the threshold of reality.

Extract (c)

But is it enough to change laws, institutions, customs, public opinion, and the whole social context, for men and women to become truly equal? 'Women will always be women', say the sceptics. Other seers prophesy that in casting off their femininity they will not succeed in changing themselves into men and they will become monsters. This would be to admit that the woman of today is a creation of nature; it must be repeated once more that in human society nothing is natural and that woman, like much else, is a product elaborated by civilization. The intervention of others in her destiny is fundamental: if this action took a different direction, it would produce a quite different result. Woman is determined not by her hormones or by mysterious instincts, but by the manner in which her body and her relation to the world are modified through the action of others than herself. The abyss that separates the adolescent boy and girl has been deliberately widened between them since earliest childhood; later on, woman could not be other than what she *was made*, and that past was bound to shadow her for life. If we appreciate its influence, we see clearly that her destiny is not predetermined for all eternity.

We must not believe, certainly, that a change in woman's economic condition alone is enough to transform her, though this factor has been and remains the basic factor in her evolution; but until it has brought about the moral, social, cultural, and other consequences that it promises and requires, the new woman cannot appear. At this moment they have been realized nowhere, in Russia no more than in France or the United States; and this explains why the woman of today is torn between the past and the future. She appears most often as a 'true woman' disguised as a man, and she feels herself as ill at ease in her flesh as in her masculine garb. She must shed her old skin and cut her own new clothes. This she could do only through a social evolution. No single educator could fashion a *female human being* today who would be the exact homologue of the *male human being*; if she is brought up like a boy, the young girl feels she is an oddity and thereby she is given a new kind of sex specification. Stendhal understood this when he said: 'The forest must be planted all at once.' But if we imagine, on the contrary, a society in which the equality of the sexes would be concretely realized, this equality would find new expression in each individual.

(Simone de Beauvoir, *The Second Sex*, trans. H. M. Parshley, London, Cape, 1968, pp. 157–9, 689–90, 718–19, 734–5)

II.45 Transcript of commentary to film *Your Job in Germany* (1945)

The problem now is future peace. That is your job in Germany. By your conduct and attitude while on guard inside Germany, you can lay the groundwork of a peace that could last forever, or just the opposite, you could lay the groundwork for a new war to come. And, just as American soldiers had to do this job 26 years ago, so other American soldiers, your sons, might have to do it again another 20-odd years from now. Germany today appears to be beaten. Hitler out. Swastikas gone. Nazi propaganda off the air. Concentration camps empty. You'll see ruins. You'll see flowers. You'll see some pretty scenery. Don't let it fool you. You are in enemy country. Be alert. Suspicious of everyone. Take no chances. You are up against something more than tourist scenery. You are up against German history. It isn't good. This book was written chapter by chapter. Not by one man, not by one *Führer*. It was written by the German people.

Chapter 1. The *Führer* – Bismarck. The title – Blood and Iron. The armies – German. Under the Prussian Bismarck the German empire was built, the German states combined, serving notice to all that their religion was iron, that their God was blood. Bismarck's German empire built itself by war. At the expense of Denmark, Austria and France, it became in 1871 the mightiest military power in all Europe. Enough conquest for a while. Time out to digest it. Europe relaxes. The danger's over. Nice country, Germany. Tender people the Germans. Very sweet music indeed.

Chapter 2. A new *Führer* – Kaiser Wilhelm. New title – 'Deutschland über alles' (Germany over all). And the same tender German people smacked us with their World War I against Serbia, Russia, France, Belgium, Italy, Britain and the United States of America. It took us all to do it but we finally knocked that *Führer* out, defeated the German armies. Second chapter ended.

We marched straight into Germany and said: 'Why, these people are OK. It was just the Kaiser we had to get rid of. You know, this is really some country. When it comes to culture, they lead the world.'

We poured in our sympathy. We pulled out our armies. And they flung chapter 3 in our faces. *Führer* number 3; slogan number 3 – today Germany is ours, tomorrow the whole world. And the tender, repentant, sorry German people carried the torch of their culture to Austria, Czechoslovakia, Poland, France, England, Norway, Holland, Denmark, Belgium, Luxembourg, Russia, Yugoslavia, Greece, and the United States of America. Over the shattered homes, over the broken bodies of millions of people who had let down their guard. We almost lost this one. It took everything we had. Measure the cost in money. There isn't that much money. Measure the cost in lives. You can only guess at the figure. It took burning and scalding, drenching, freezing. It took legs, fingers, arms, and it took them by the millions. It cost hours, days and years that will never return. We threw in our health, our wealth, our past and our future. It took every last ounce of our courage and guts. Now, what happens?

'Ah, hell, this is where we came in.' Yeh, this is where we came in. And chapter 4 will be – it can happen again.

The next war. That is why you occupy Germany. To make that next war impossible. No easy job. In battle you kept your wits about you. Don't relax that caution now. The Nazi party may be gone. But Nazi thinking, Nazi training, and Nazi trickery remains. The German lust for conquest is not dead. It's merely gone undercover. Somewhere in this Germany are the SS guards, the *Schutztruppe*, the Gestapo gangsters. Out of uniform you won't know them. But they'll know you. Somewhere in this Germany are stormtroopers by the thousands. Out of sight, part of the mob, but still watching you and hating you. Somewhere in this Germany there are 2 million ex-Nazi officials. Out of power but still in there and thinking, thinking about next time. Remember that only yesterday, every business, every profession was part of Hitler's system. The doctors, technicians, clockmakers, postmen, farmers, housekeepers, toymakers, barbers, cooks, dock workers. Practically every German was part of the Nazi network. Guard particularly against this group – these are the most dangerous – German youth. Children when the Nazi party came into power, they know no other system than the one that poisoned their minds. They're soaked in it. Trained to win by cheating. Trained to pick on the weak. They've heard no free speech, read no free press. They were brought up on straight propaganda. Products of the worst educational crime in the entire history of the world. Practically everything you believe in, they've been trained to hate and destroy. They believe they were born to be masters, that we are inferiors, designed to be their slaves. They may deny it now but they believe it, and will try to prove it again. Don't argue with them. Don't try to change their point of view. Other Allied representatives will concern themselves with that.

You are not being sent into Germany as educators. You are soldiers on guard. You will observe their local laws, respect their customs and religion, and you will respect their property rights. You will not ridicule them. You will not argue with them. You will not be friendly. You will be aloof, watchful and suspicious. Every German is a potential source of trouble. Therefore, there must be no fraternization with any of the German people. Fraternization means making friends. The German people are not our friends. You will not associate with German men, women or children. You will not associate with them on familiar terms either in public or in private. You will not visit in their homes nor will you ever take them into your confidence. However friendly, however sorry, however sick of the Nazi party they may seem, they cannot come back into the civilized fold just by sticking out their hand and saying, 'I'm sorry'. Sorry? Not sorry they caused the war, they're only sorry they lost it. That is the hand that heiled Adolf Hitler. That is the hand that dropped the bombs on defenceless Rotterdam, Brussels, Belgrade. That is the hand that destroyed the cities, villages, and homes of Russia. That is the hand that held the whip over the Polish, Yugoslav, French and Norwegian slaves. That is the hand that took their food. That is the hand that starved them. That is the hand that murdered, massacred, Greeks, Czechs, Jews. That is the hand that killed and crippled American soldiers, sailors, marines. Don't clasp that hand. It is not the kind of a hand you can clasp in friendship.

'But there are millions of Germans. Some of those guys must be OK.'

Perhaps. But which ones? Just one mistake may cost you your life. Trust none of them. Someday the German people might be cured of their disease, the super race disease, the world conquest disease. But they must prove that they have been cured beyond the shadow of a doubt before they ever again are allowed to take their place among respectable nations. Until that day, we stand guard. We are determined that they shall never again use peaceful industries for warlike purposes. We are determined that our children shall never face this German terror. We are determined that the vicious German cycle of war/phoney peace, war/phoney peace, war/phoney peace, shall once and for all time come to an end. That is your job in Germany.

(US Government film; transcription by Tony Aldgate)

II.46   Transcript of commentary to film *A Defeated People* (1946)

'What's it like in Germany?' 'Must be terrible.' 'Well, they asked for it, they got it.' 'Yes, but you can't let them starve.' 'I don't know about that. I've got a son out there. As far as I can see it would be a good thing if some of them did die.'

Well, a lot of Germany is dead. Our last bombing was directed against their communications, against convoys, trains, road and rail bridges, against goods yards, stations, viaducts. We not only smashed up the towns but smashed up the links between the towns. And at the finish, life in Germany just ran down, like a clock. Place and time meant nothing. Because the people, the links between the people, were smashed too. They were left just wandering, searching, looking for food, looking for their homes, looking for each other.

'Ich suche meine Frau.' 'Ich suche mein Mann.' 'Ich suche Frieda Wintler, geborene Jonuscheit, Königsberg.' 'Ich suche meine Frau, Elfriede Schulz, und Tochter Christa.' 'Achtung Stalingradkämpfer. Wer kennt den Sanitäts Unterofficier Heinz Kuhlmann.'

There are 70 million people in Germany. And about 30 million of them are looking for someone. Or are lost and lie looking without seeing, like the eyes of a dead rabbit. They are still stunned by what hit them. Stunned by the war they started. But in the search for food and the urge to get home, the life force is beginning to stir again. Today, our powers of destruction are terrifying. But the will to live is still stronger. That's why we can't wash our hands of the Germans. Because we can't afford to let that new life flow in any direction it wants.

Our military government – that is your husbands and sons – have to prod the Germans into putting their house in order. Why? We have an interest in Germany that is purely selfish: we cannot live next door to a disease-ridden neighbour. And we must prevent not only starvation and epidemics but also diseases of the mind, new brands of fascism, from springing up. What is more we have to persuade the Germans to do this themselves.

First of all, the material patching up. And where, in the meantime, do they live? Yes, all looks lifeless. But, underneath the rubble, there are people, living. Living in the cellars. The smoke from the cooking stoves drifts up from the ruins to the open third storey where people are living too. Many in the big towns living without light, without coal, without water, without soap. Living in the stench of corpses and sewerage, but still with the will to live.

But the one thing on which all reconstruction depends is coal. Without coal, there can be no power and no transport. In Essen, our coal control has taken over the Krupp family mansion as its headquarters. And from here we organize the output and distribution from the whole Ruhr coalfields. Last summer, what was called 'Operation Coalscuttle' brought 30,000 miners back from the *Wehrmacht*. But today the great problem is moving the coal from the pit-head to the liberated countries, to the German power plants, and to the Allied military dumps. For the Germans themselves, there is no coal. They must go out in the woods and parks to cut wood, to strip the bark off the trees, to collect brushwood, and carry it home in handcarts and prams. We say 'the great problem'. But in Germany today, for military government officers, there is no such thing as a single problem.

For example, the liberated countries won't get this coal unless there is transport to carry it. The transport cannot move any distance unless the tracks and bridges have been repaired. They can't be repaired without steel, and the steel cannot be made without coal.

There are some 17 newspapers published in the British zone. They all carry advertisements asking for the whereabouts of relatives. At Hamburg, there is a British-run postal search station, indexing inquiries coming in at the rate of 50,000 a day. But when someone contacts their relatives, they must get a permit before they can travel by train. Hoards of cyclists and pedestrians and horse-drawn trucks wait to cross the pontoon and bailey bridges built by our engineers, wait to cross after the military government traffic. And all this has to be supervised by our sergeants and our MPs.

In all this we have to safeguard ourselves. First of all, from crime and disorder. So, military government courts are set up with British judges. These courts are public, there is an interpreter, a German defence counsel, and a British prosecutor. Then, the German police force is being remade. The new German policeman has to understand that he is the servant of the public and not its master. Then, we have to safeguard ourselves from disease. The Germans are getting 1,000 to 1,200 calories a day, according to type of work, about half our rations. But we have a survey team in the field staffed by the Red Cross and the RAMC, checking the effect of these rations on the population. Tests are made of blood content, of blood pressure, of height and weight, and reports sent to the control commission for them to judge whether the food is just sufficient to keep Germany at work.

But the greatest headache is education. You will never get Nazi ideas out of the heads of some of the adults, particularly those living away from the devastated areas. What about the children? For them, the desolated landscape provides a dream playground. The derelict weapons of war might have been specially designed to have games with. There are Germans who know this can't go on. That teachers must be found and themselves taught to teach the children that there are other things in life beyond Nazism and war. But, again, the complexity of problems. The schools are in ruins, the teachers too few, the children too many. And as the months go by, the children are growing up, and getting more like their fathers. We just cannot afford to leave them to stew in their own juice.

Today, Berlin has still the aspect of a battle field. The *Reichstag*, the seat of past German governments, has been gutted. The Krupp family, who with the other German industrialists first backed Hitler and then produced the weapons for world domination, have been scattered and arrested. This family armed Germany in the Franco-Prussian War, they made Big Bertha and the first submarine for the Kaiser in World War I, they are just as responsible for killing Allied soldiers as Hitler and Goering. And by killing they grew rich. This time, their war plants have been left a mess of twisted girders. Look.

This time, the *Wehrmacht* are really beaten. From the wire cages all over Germany the master race of men are slubbering along. They are stripped of their insignia, deloused, and numbered. But this mass of humanity has to be sorted out into something like order. Not only their bodies but also their minds. What about the ideas in their heads? They have to be demobilized and got back to work. But let one man or woman, who still believes in the Nazi regime or the destiny of the German people to rule the world, take office and you have the beginnings of another war. So, they are put through a screen. To begin with, selected Germans interrogate them and fill in their demobilization papers. Note this neat little man who looks like a clerk or a grocer. Here is his portrait in *Luftwaffe* uniform. Then all their thumb prints are taken for record and they are stripped and examined for the SS mark tattooed under the left armpit. Then their past history and character is examined by our intelligence officers – German-speaking ex-commandos and parachutists. The majority of Germans get through this close examination and are demobilized. But every so often there appears one who is suspect or who is wanted, whose papers are too good, or whose answers are not good enough. Rejected. Back to the cage.

As night falls in Germany the people must remember the curfew. Those without homes or caught in the street, disappear into the air-raid shelters. Then the air-raid siren wails again, to remind them they lost a war of their own making. To remind them that it is up to them to regain their self-respect as a nation and to learn to live in friendly manner with their neighbours. To remind them that, much as we hate it, we shall stay in Germany until we have real guarantees that the next generation will grow up a sane and Christian people. A Germany of light and life and freedom. A Germany that respects truth and tolerance and justice.

'Now, gentlemen, you will raise your right hands and take the oath with me. I swear by Almighty God . . . that I will at all times . . . apply and administer the law without fear or favour . . . and with justice and equity to all persons . . . of whatever creed, race, colour or political opinion they may be . . . I will obey the laws of Germany . . . to establish equal justice under the law for all persons . . . So help me God.'

(Ministry of Information film; transcription by Tony Aldgate)

II.47   Two commentaries: (a) *Welt im Film*, Issue No. 7 (29 June 1945); (b) *Welt im Film – die Welt Blickt auf Berlin* (June 1948)

(a) Welt im Film, Issue No. 7, 29 June 1945

UPRISING IN PRAGUE

In the last days of the war, Prague, after six years of slavery, rose against its oppressor. This was not the revolt of a faction – it was the uprising of the embittered citizens of a nation. The struggle began in a city still under the control of SS troops. The Czechs captured the radio station, from where, calling repeatedly for assistance on the nations of the free world, they fought in the streets their desperate fight against the overwhelming adversary. The Czechs knew that the SS took no prisoners. They fought with the courage of desperation. They did not yet know that help was already on the way, that the Americans from the west and the Red Army from the east were approaching. The 9th of May dawned. The whole free world was celebrating Germany's surrender – Prague still lay in darkness. German soldiers were flushed out of cellars. As the battle began to turn in the Czechs' favour, some of the SS pulled back from the city and left others to their fate. They were taken prisoner. So were the traitors. On the

10th May, the first Russian armoured spearheads entered the city. The struggle of the freedom fighters was over. Prague was free. Six days later, an enormous crowd gathered at the station. They were greeting their President, Eduard Benes, who was returning home after seven years' exile. Czechoslovakia, which had been among the first nations to lose its freedom, was the last to win it back. Now she will take her place among the nations of Europe, and join, in freedom and peace, in the collective work upon which the world's hope rests – the building of a happier Europe.

STOLEN ARTWORKS DISCOVERED

In a mountain cave near Berchtesgaden, American troops discovered a collection of art treasures. This was where Goering stored his loot, sculptures and paintings stolen from European museums and private collections. Now these treasures will be carefully packed, and will be returned under the direction of the Allies to their rightful owners. This officer is an American art expert, entrusted with the checking of the collection. Here too, in Neuschwanstein, in Ludwig II's castle, Goering had secreted a matchless collection of art treasures. A coffer of jewellery of inestimable value, from a French private owner. A silver tureen, from the collection of the former director of a famous French museum. These are only a few of the 23,000 artworks that the American soldiers found here. The National Socialists took from the people they overran not just their peace, their freedom and their bread – they took from them also that which they loved and were most proud of: the works of their country's great men.

A PRISONER OF WAR COMES HOME

In the barracks square at Plauen, German prisoners of war are summoned for the last time to the administration building. One of them is Private Fritz Riedel. After thorough checking of his reliability, he is to be released from the *Wehrmacht* to work on the land. He is examined by British and German doctors. Everything is in order; the release paper is presented for signature. The German military insignia, now meaningless, are removed from his uniform. He is a free man – free from the duties of soldiering, and free to return to his family. From soldier Riedel to Fritz Riedel, whose important job it now is to help avert the danger of famine this year in Germany – a danger which Germany's irresponsible continuation of the war has brought so near.

AIRFIELDS FREED FROM FOG DANGER

Safe landings for Allied aircraft even in thick fog have now become possible. Through this device, fuel oil is pumped through a special pipe system along the runway. When burning, the oil warms the air and causes the fog to disperse. The oil can be ignited within one second. This development was the invention of British engineers, and enabled Allied bombers to continue their day-and-night attacks without interruption during the last winter of the war. It has a double purpose – the fog is dispersed, and the pilot returning from his mission can see the landing strip outlined in flames and so put down safely. In peacetime, this will make possible a safer air service – faster air traffic, not dependent on the weather, for passengers and freight.

MILITARY GOVERNMENT

Water supplies have received the first interim assistance from the Allied Military Government. From the banks of the Ruhr, water is pumped up to the bomb-damaged city of Essen. The inhabitants come to fetch water and carry it home in buckets. Because the Ruhr chlorine-treatment plants are still not working, as the result of considerable damage, the citizens are warned of the danger of infection. Every pail-full must be boiled before use. Meanwhile, repair of the water system is being carried out by civilian labour; slowly but purposefully, under the direction of the Allies, order is made out of chaos. Water flows once more in the town.

In this classroom, Germans – under the direction of the Military Government – are learning to become responsible citizens again. They learn, for example, the tasks of traffic policemen. Conscious of his responsibility, he carries out his duty. This man is proud to become a useful member of the new Germany.

Hamburg: production of a newsheet in five languages: German, Italian, Dutch, French and Polish. Written by men and women of these different nationalities in the premises of the *Hamburger Anzeiger*, *Victory Herald* is published by the Military Government for the many thousands of people brought by the Nazis to Hamburg as slave labourers who will soon be returning to their homelands. The papers are packed and distributed in the camps where these people are living under the protection of the Allies. After almost six years of darkness, they are learning to see the light of the world again.

INVESTIGATING COMMISSION FOR WAR CRIMES

In London, the conference of the United Nations on proceedings against war criminals opened. Delegates from sixteen countries took part. On the list of war criminals are nearly 3,000 Germans.

In Norway, Quisling fights for his life. Quisling, whose name has become universally known in the vocabulary of the free peoples of the world as an international synonym for 'traitor'. For Quisling, the long-awaited day of reckoning has arrived.

Near Brunswick, two German spies were tried before an Allied military court. In February they were smuggled over the Ruhr in civilian clothes to collect information on the state of readiness of American troops. They were captured within 24 hours. The military court sentenced them as war criminals to death by firing squad. Soldiers of the American 9th Army carried out the sentence.

DRAMA OF AN AIRCRAFT CARRIER

In the endless expanse of the Pacific lies the theatre for one of the greatest actions of this war. An American fleet, including the aircraft carrier *Franklin*, is locked in combat with swarms of Japanese aircraft. The *Franklin* was hit, and caught fire. Powder magazines began to explode. In the tumult of battle the wounded are rescued. A priest comforts the dying on deck. A destroyer comes alongside. It seemed no more could be done to save the *Franklin*. The sailors were exhausted. One after another they were brought to safety from the flames and twisted steel of the deck. A few of the crew stayed at their posts. But the *Franklin* did not sink. The flag is still flying. The listing ship is stabilized, and the bulkheads secured, and slowly, slowly, the *Franklin* and her remaining crew members began the difficult journey homewards. The dead were committed to the sea. In Pearl Harbour, temporary repairs were carried out. Then, at the triumphant entry into the Panama Canal, at a ceremony on the sunny flight deck the medals were presented that had been won for heroism and selfless duty on the burning vessel. The first memory for these men is that of giving of their strength and heroism in the hour of need. The carrier *Franklin* and her crew return home from halfway round the world. The *Franklin* will be repaired, and then the ship that was abandoned as lost will be ready for new feats.

(b) Welt im Film – die Welt blickt auf Berlin, June 1948

It was a quiet Sunday in Berlin. The sun shone for the first time in days, and overhead as usual the planes were droning. Then came Monday, and many began their working week without work. Quiet chimneys dramatized the plight of industry in the western sectors as many factories fell victim to the Soviet-sponsored coal shortage. The Borsig plant in the French sector strove to sustain all West Berlin. To fully exploit its limited resources, allocations were set up which sometimes turned the working day into a working night. The latest word in coiffure now came very late for Berliners, and when electric power gave out altogether, there was always manpower. The Russians, concerned as always with the city's welfare, announced the dismissal of two high German railroad officials. Now, they implied, the Helmstedt-Berlin track would be repaired in no time. Then, a new tactic: only Soviet-written interzonal passes were valid. But Berlin could not be cut off from the rest of the world. All week, big planes brought big names into the city. From Australia came Prime Minister J. B. Chifley; after inspecting the air bridge operation at Gatow, he told Berliners 'Australia stands firmly behind the Western Allies.' After him, Mr Lewis Douglas, US Ambassador to Great Britain, here greeted by General Clay. Another visitor – Mr Arthur Henderson, British

Secretary of State for Air. One thing was certain – these men did not come to Berlin to discuss the weather. Next day, Anthony Eden, Deputy Leader of the Opposition in Parliament, attended a special reception at the British Information Centre. Seen arriving at the meeting are Berlin's acting Mayor, Louis Schroeder; Franz Neumann of the SPD; Kaiser and Landsberg of the CDU; and Brigadier Benson, British Deputy-Commandant for Berlin. [Eden speaks:]

How essential it is, if we are to build peace on firm foundations, that there should be respect for international engagements. [Interpreter] Therefore we of the Opposition in Parliament in Britain strongly endorse the action which the British Government, together with its western allies, is taking in Berlin. [Interpreter] In this you are showing that you are not prepared to be intimidated by methods wholly alien to our conception of democracy. [Interpreter]

Later, LDP leader Schwennicke said: 'Berlin will remain not only the German capital, but the symbol of the new democratic order in a Germany that hungers after peace.' That night, Western Allied planes set a new record: more than 2,000 tons of food and supplies over the air bridge in 24 hours. Each US crew on landing reports to the operations room, nerve centre of all Tempelhof air traffic. Around the clock, these pilots and their British partners bring flour, sugar, potatoes, medicine, coal and oil in one of the most unique air operations of all time. To these men, the impossible has become the routine. Not Soviet sanctions, but the weather is their chief headache. These are the faces of some of the American pilots now helping to feed Berlin [ranks, names and home towns not transcribed] . . . American names, American towns, American effort. And finally it came – the Soviet answer to the Western Allies' note: eight days and fourteen hundred words, just to say 'Nyet'. Meanwhile, Britain, France and the USA continue to build a bigger and better air bridge. A new strip is constructed at Gatow, new bases being prepared in the west, new planes coming from England and America. At Tempelhof too a new strip will soon be ready. Rain or shine, the work went on. American, British, French, German, working together so the Soviet blockade of Berlin serves only to intensify the determination of democratic peoples everywhere.

((a): translation of German commentary by Roger B. N. Smither and Kay G. T. Gladstone, Imperial War Museum; (b): transcript of English language version of film, entitled *Berlin – World Focal Point*)

II.48 Lord Reith, speech in the House of Lords debate on commercial television (May 1952)

[*A vigorous debate broke out in Parliament, the press and the country in general in the wake of the Conservative Government's proposal to create a form of commercial television. The House of Lords was one of the centres of opposition, and it was the scene of a major debate in May 1952. Lord Reith joined in the debate and made a famous outburst.*]

What grounds are there for jeopardizing this heritage and tradition? Not a single one is even suggested in the White Paper. Why sell it down the river? Do we find leadership and decision in this White Paper; or compromise and expediency – a facing-both-ways? A principle absolutely fundamental and cherished is scheduled to be scuttled. It is the principle that matters, and it is neither here nor there that the scuttling may not take place for years. The Government are here on record to scuttle – a betrayal and a surrender; that is what is so shocking and serious; so unnecessary and wrong. Somebody introduced dog-racing into England; we know who, for he is proud of it, and proclaims it *urbi et orbi* in the columns of *Who's Who*. And somebody introduced Christianity and printing and the uses of electricity. And somebody introduced smallpox, bubonic plague and the Black Death. Somebody is minded now to introduce sponsored broadcasting into this country.

(*Hansard*, House of Lords, 22 May 1952, col. 1297; reprinted in Anthony Smith (ed.) *British Broadcasting*, Newton Abbott, David and Charles, 1974, p. 103)